Scarecrow Professional Intelligence Education Series
Series Editor: Jan Goldman

In this post–September 11, 2001 era, there has been rapid growth in the number of professional intelligence training and educational programs across the United States and abroad. Colleges and universities, as well as high schools, are developing programs and courses in homeland security, intelligence analysis, and law enforcement, in support of national security.

The Scarecrow Professional Intelligence Education Series (SPIES) was first designed for individuals studying for careers in intelligence and to help improve the skills of those already in the profession; however, it was also developed to educate the public in how intelligence work is conducted and should be conducted in this important and vital profession.

1. *Communicating with Intelligence: Writing and Briefing in the Intelligence and National Security Communities*, by James S. Major. 2008.
2. *A Spy's Résumé: Confessions of a Maverick Intelligence Professional and Misadventure Capitalist*, by Marc Anthony Viola. 2008.
3. *An Introduction to Intelligence Research and Analysis*, by Jerome Clauser, revised and edited by Jan Goldman. 2008.
4. *Writing Classified and Unclassified Papers for National Security: A Scarecrow Professional Intelligence Educational Series Manual*, by James S. Major. 2009.
5. *Strategic Intelligence: A Handbook for Practitioners, Managers, and Users*, revised edition by Don McDowell. 2009.
6. *Partly Cloudy: Ethics in War, Espionage, Covert Action, and Interrogation*, by David L. Perry. 2009.
7. *Tokyo Rose / An American Patriot: A Dual Biography*, by Frederick P. Close. 2010.
8. *Ethics of Spying: A Reader for the Intelligence Professional*, edited by Jan Goldman. 2006.
9. *Ethics of Spying: A Reader for the Intelligence Professional*, Volume 2, edited by Jan Goldman. 2010.
10. *A Woman's War: The Professional and Personal Journey of the Navy's First African American Female Intelligence Officer*, by Gail Harris with Pam McLaughlin, 2010.

A Woman's War

The Professional and Personal Journey of the Navy's First African American Female Intelligence Officer

GAIL HARRIS
WITH PAM MCLAUGHLIN

JAN GOLDMAN
SERIES EDITOR

Scarecrow Professional Intelligence Education Series, No. 10

THE SCARECROW PRESS, INC.
Lanham • Toronto • Plymouth, UK
2010

Published by Scarecrow Press, Inc.
A wholly owned subsidiary of The Rowman & Littlefield Publishing Group, Inc.
4501 Forbes Boulevard, Suite 200, Lanham, Maryland 20706
http://www.scarecrowpress.com

Estover Road, Plymouth PL6 7PY, United Kingdom

British Library Cataloguing in Publication Information Available

Library of Congress Cataloging-in-Publication Data

Harris, Gail, 1949-
 A woman's war : the professional and personal journey of the Navy's first African American female intelligence officer / Gail Harris with Pam McLaughlin.
   p. cm. — (Scarecrow professional intelligence education series ; no. 10)
 Includes bibliographical references.
 ISBN 978-0-8108-6793-2 (pbk. : alk. paper) — ISBN 978-0-8108-7100-7 (eBook)
 1. Harris, Gail, 1949- 2. Harris, Gail, 1949—-Travel. 3. United States. Navy—Intelligence specialists—Biography. 4. United States. Navy—African Americans—Biography. 5. United States. Navy—Women—Biography. 6. Women intelligence officers—United States—Biography. 7. Intelligence officers—United States—Biography. 8. African America women—Biography. 9. Military intelligence—United States. I. McLaughlin, Pam. II. Title.
 VB231.U54H37 2010
  359.0092—dc22
  [B]
                                                                              2009032126

∞ ™ The paper used in this publication meets the minimum requirements of American National Standard for Information Sciences—Permanence of Paper for Printed Library Materials, ANSI/NISO Z39.48-1992.

Printed in the United States of America

To James and Lena Harris, you not only brought me into this world, you taught me how to master it. I love you more than words can ever say.

Contents

Acknowledgments

To Mark Victor Hansen, thank you for giving me the seed of a new dream. I am forever grateful that you took time out of your busy schedule to chat with and give advise to a stranger who came up to you at the Omaha airport. To the Late Dottie Walters one of the greatest speakers ever, thanks for showing me how to build a runway in order to allow those behind me to take off.

A special thanks to my writing partner, Pam McLaughlin. Working with you was a joy. Thanks also to Dr. Larry Keefauver and Sam Horn for helping me put together my book proposal and to Will Gray and my cousin Ann Glover for reading my manuscript and providing much-needed editorial assistance. A special shout-out to my life-long best friend Captain Catherine Swan, USN (retired) for reading various versions of the manuscript and providing feedback and tweaking my memory of events as needed. To my agent, Lois De La Haba, thank you for believing in the book. Last, but certainly not least, a shout out to my brothers James and Chucky and my sister, Annette. I've enjoyed walking down the path of this thing called life with you!

Editor's Foreword

As this series develops and expands, it is only logical that it will begin to include people that have contributed to the intelligence profession. Consequently, it is ironic that the first person to discuss their career in intelligence for this series is also the first African American female intelligence officer in the U.S. Navy. In this book, Gail Harris is very honest in how she viewed her environment and, just as importantly, how her environment viewed her.

I hope that other professionals in the military or civilian sectors of the intelligence community will come forth and that other books will be included in this series. It is only through the application of theory with experience that future generations of intelligence professionals can both understand and appreciate the past and be better prepared for the future.

Jan Goldman
Washington, DC

Introduction: We're All Battling Some*one* or Some*thing* . . .

Whether anyone wants to admit it, the truth is, all of us battle some*one* or some*thing* trying to keep us from fulfilling our potential. Who or what is it for you? Are you dealing with an office bully or competing for a job you know you are uniquely qualified to do? Maybe you're battling an organizational status quo mentality when you have a vision to achieve so much more. Do you have a dream to be the first in your field but feel you are moving up stream against a current of racism, sexism, or some other "ism"? Perhaps your battle is of a more personal nature—depression, weight gain, or substance abuse.

From an early age, I've fought to overcome racial and sexual prejudice, labored to prove I had the skills and talent to succeed, endured with great determination, and stood my ground against the status quo. I've battled to overcome personal issues to finally achieve a destiny I believe was ordained for me the day I was born.

As you read my personal and professional journey, you'll come to see how I found the strength and intelligence to prevail against seemingly insurmountable odds. I'll share with you the techniques I used to pioneer in an international career as an intelligence analyst and become a war gaming staff member at the Naval War College. More importantly, I'll show you how you can use these same techniques to fight and win the battles you face both on and off the job.

I write to advocate this truth: Conflicts are a fact of life and naïveté *will not* help you to succeed. Realizing that everyone faces prejudice in one form or another, I'll share with you what I've learned on my incredible journey. I'll teach you how to do your homework and learn what is needed for you to succeed in your chosen career. I've developed fourteen intelligence strategies you can use to stand strong and prevail in the face of institutional and interpersonal obstacles so you can achieve your goals and fulfill your destiny, even though you face a *war . . . on any day!*

1

In the Beginning . . . A Dream

Never tell a young person that anything cannot be done. God may have been waiting centuries for someone ignorant enough of the impossible to do that very thing.

—*John Andrew Holmes*[1]

Whatever you can do or dream you can, begin it. Boldness has genius, power, and magic in it.

—*Johann Wolfgang von Goethe* (1749–1832)[2]

DREAM A DREAM: MAKE A WISH, SAY A PRAYER

Ever dreamed an impossible dream, whispered a secret wish, or prayed for a miracle? If you have, then there's a dream deep down inside of you, and don't let anyone tell you it can't come true. God gave you that dream and the strength, courage, and vision to make it happen regardless of the circumstances of your birth or the status of your current surroundings. The road that led to my career in naval intelligence is a living example of this principle. So go ahead—dream a dream, make a wish, and say a prayer.

My dream began at age five as my father and I watched Don Ameche in the movie *Wing and a Prayer*. It was the story of the aircraft carrier the USS *Enterprise* as it moved toward the Battle of Midway in the aftermath of the Pearl Harbor attack. As brave pilots approached this climatic battle, Commander

Harper (Don Ameche) gave them an intelligence briefing detailing the capabilities of the Japanese forces they were up against. I turned to my father and
said, "Daddy, that's what I'm going to do when I grow up." A dream was born
in the heart of this five-year-old African American girl and spoken to a man
who encouraged her to do what others might have labeled as impossible.

My father was a man far ahead of his time. Instead of killing my dream
by listing the odds against pursuing it, he chose to encourage me by relating his own military experiences in a constructive and positive way. Later,
I learned about the obstacles my father had faced as an African American
serving his country in the aftermath of World War II. Blacks were still
discriminated against and allowed to serve only in segregated outfits. He
didn't tell me any of that or the fact that in 1955, there were very few African American male officers in the Navy, let alone any females. He encouraged me to hold onto my dream when he could have very easily burst my
bubble.

I know that hindsight is 20-20, but in my mind there is no doubt that at the
age of five, I had a glimpse of my divine destiny with my parents encouraging
me every step of my journey. To my knowledge, none of the women on either
side of my family had ever served in the armed forces, and all the men had
served in the army. Only God could have inspired such a dream in my young
heart to be one of the first female naval intelligence officers.

NO MERE PASSING FANCY

This dream within me was no mere passing fancy, as those around me would
soon discover. From the time I saw that movie and the dream was birthed
within me, my fascination with anything that had to do with the Navy was
obvious even to the causal observer. Whenever I heard the song "Anchors
Aweigh," I'd jump up and start marching around the house. My favorite movies were those depicting great naval battles, especially those fought in World
War II. I'd draw scenes of naval battles as I had learned about them in school.
I always rooted for the Navy in the annual Army/Navy football classic. My
friends were initially puzzled when they discovered my fanaticism for the Dallas Cowboys until I explained that Roger Staubach, the Naval Academy Heis-
man trophy winner, went on to quarterback for the Cowboys when his naval
career ended. People around me could see I was serious about this dream,
but most would think there were far too many obstacles to overcome for an

African American female to succeed at it; however, I firmly believed the decks were stacked in my favor.

CIRCUMSTANCES OF BIRTH

Some might say that one of my initial obvious obstacles was growing up in a very poor neighborhood in Newark, New Jersey, but I was also born in a country where dreams are for everyone, not just a particular socioeconomic class or ethnic group. I was also given James and Lena Harris as my birth parents, and it was from them that I learned the life skills I would need to press forward and achieve my goals and fulfill my dreams.

My family may have been financially poor, but we were rich in love and steeped in vision to seek more in life than what the circumstances appeared to dictate. It's a heritage passed down to my parents by their parents. My parents were both born in Alabama, but my dad's mother, Mary, moved north to New Jersey during World War II to improve her life. She knew no one in the North, yet she had a vision that there was more to life than what she was experiencing. She dreamed of a better life for her children, so she left my father, his older brother Sam, and sister Bea with her mother, Mama Sarah, a Cherokee Indian, until she found a job as a butcher. She married, bought a house in East Orange, New Jersey, and sent for her children. I'm told I get a lot of my strength and determination from her. What a legacy she left behind for us.

Even though I don't have memories of my grandmother Mary, I did grow up around her children. They all exemplified the strong, positive legacy she left behind. Tommy, a high school and college football star, went on to become a successful corporate executive. Michael has a successful career in the music business, and Sam has a prospering construction business. Aunt Bea, a mom extraordinaire, raised her children with the same strength and determination passed on to her by her mother Mary. Several are successful corporate executives; one is a minister, and her son, David, is a constant source of wisdom for us all.

My mother was the youngest of twelve children born to Dollie and Alto Blue. She was known as the most beautiful "colored girl" in Andalusia, Alabama. As an interesting side note, my cousin Tiffany Porter became the first African American female to win the town beauty pageant. My mother often spoke of how her older brothers and sisters spoiled her rotten, like the time they put their money together so she could go to boarding school.

She met my father in an interesting twist of fate when her Uncle Tommy returned for a visit to Andalusia. Mother said it was love at first sight but was afraid she had fallen in love with her cousin. It turned out they were related by marriage only as her Uncle Tommy was her love's stepfather. That cleared up, they started courting officially when he was seventeen. Most of their courtship was via mail, as my dad was stationed at Guam and later reassigned to Camp Kilmer in New Jersey. They were married soon after, and I was their first born. My brother, James Jr., followed a little over two years later, and my sister Annette came along eight years later when we begged our parents for a sister or brother. I believe the circumstances of my birth were a strong positive in my life, preparing me to become all I was born to be.

DREAM, WORK HARD, BE PREPARED

Dad had a hard time finding a job after the war because many refused to hire blacks, so we lived with his parents for the first two years of my life. The best he was able to do was loading and unloading trucks at a machine shop. One cold winter day, my father looked longingly at the guys working inside on the machines where it was warm and spoke his vision to a coworker: "I still have the GI Bill educational benefits available, so I'm going to go to school to learn to be a machinist."

Others told him that he was crazy and that no one would hire a black man to do anything but manual labor. As I said, my father was a man way ahead of his time. He had a dream and declared that one day the doors would open to blacks, and when they did he would be prepared to do the job he was dreaming of. He began to pursue that dream. Even as he supported his growing family, he entered trade school to prepare for his family's future.

After my father finished trade school, he did get a job as a machinist, and we were able to move into our own apartment. The apartment building was owned by one of my mother's older cousins Mae Ester and her husband Levi, who became surrogate grandparents to my brother and I. Although my father now had a job as a machinist, it didn't pay very much. It was a while before I realized that the reason we couldn't eat dinner on Friday until my father came home was because Friday was pay day. We were out of food and money by Friday.

My dad continued to work hard and pursue his dream. As he gained more experience, he applied for higher-paying jobs. He would see an ad in the paper, call and state his qualifications, be told to come, fill out the paperwork, and the job was his. When he showed up, they'd look at his skin color and say, "Sorry we just filled that position." Never once did I hear my father complain about his fate. He just kept working hard and learning everything he could to be one of the best machinists ever. He told me whenever he felt down he would ride around and look at people who were worse off than we were and count his blessings. He dreamed a dream and then worked hard to fulfill it.

These were some of the first of many lessons my father and mother would teach us as we grew up under their loving guidance and care. We learned that while doors may at first be closed to us because of our ethnic or financial background, we could work hard in school and prepare ourselves for our chosen profession. Then, when the doors did open, we would be ready to rush through them. My father stood on his belief that the doors would eventually open. He encouraged us to dream the dream but also taught us to do what we could to be prepared when those doors did open. Hard work and being prepared to move ahead were powerful tools our parents equipped us with as we stepped into our own destinies.

A HERITAGE OF LOVE

In the midst of family financial difficulties, we had a great time growing up. After work, Dad would take us to the park and play baseball or football with us. I remember one day my father was teaching us how to catch fly balls. I caught one right in the mouth. His sense of humor helped stop my crying when he looked at me and said, "Gail, you're supposed to catch it with your glove, not your mouth." He tried for years to teach me how to throw a ball. I'd look in one direction and throw in another, thus my nickname, "Old Crooked Arm." I learned the value of not giving up and of maintaining a sense of humor.

As you may have guessed, I was a tomboy. All the girls in the neighborhood were tomboys as well, so I had plenty of company. We'd play baseball and football, roller skate, and ride our bikes in the big parking lot across the street. I was never good at any of those sports, but I was the fastest runner on my block, male or female. I would get challenged often and found that although I was unbeatable at short distances, I'd come in last in any kind of distance running. Years later I took a sophisticated test that determined I had the body and muscles of a sprinter, which explained my difficulty with distance running.

Mom had a hard time getting me to wear a dress, but I did enjoy playing with "girl toys," like dolls and miniature cooking sets. On Christmas Eve, mother would bake a cake for Santa, and I would make a miniature version of her cake, complete with icing. I was awed when I got up Christmas morning to find Santa had taken a big slice from my mom's cake and a small slice from mine as well. Life was good.

Music was also a very important part of our family life. Both my mom and dad had great singing voices. We'd learn the words to a song, Mom would teach us harmony, and we'd form our own family choir. To this day I have a terrible singing voice, but thanks to my Mother I can at least harmonize pretty well. My dad made sure we listened to all types of music from classical to jazz. People are often surprised at the diversity of my music collection. I have everything from Frank Sinatra to Luther Vandross, Aretha Franklin to Doris Day, and Aaron Copeland to George Duke. This love of music would eventually prove very valuable to me as I moved out into the real world.

One big advantage of living in Newark was the close proximity to New York City. When I was growing up, a Broadway play ticket was the same price as a movie ticket. When I was sixteen, my parents would let me travel to New York by myself during daytime hours. I would save up my money, buy a bus ticket, and ride to New York City to see an afternoon Broadway show. I was only able to afford two or three shows a year, but as far as I was concerned life didn't get much better.

TWO THINGS TO DO ABOUT A PROBLEM

We spent our summers with my mom's side of the family in Andalusia, Alabama—a world of difference from our life in New Jersey. Once as we were driving through Tennessee, a carload of white men drove us off the road, yelled the "N" word at us, laughed, and then drove away. My father got out of the car and stood there with a stick in his hand daring them to come back. At the time, I was too young to fully grasp the danger of the situation or understand the era we were living in—the law in that part of the country would not have come to our aid had they come back and faced my father.

As we drove through the South, even if my parents had had the money, no hotel or motel would have let us have a room. We experienced water fountains with "black" and "white" signs over them and segregated rest rooms at gas stations. During this time, my parents taught us valuable lessons and instilled solid values in us that would benefit us all through life's challenges. Not once did my parents complain or make hateful comments about other ethnic groups. My father just dug down within himself and worked harder to better himself and his family. One of his core beliefs was that everyone experienced discrimination of one sort or another in life. The key to overcoming it was to not let it get you down or wallow around in self-pity. He said there were two things you could do about any problem in life: *something or nothing.*

When I grew up and started to experience the trials and tribulations of life, Dad further reinforced these same principles in my life. He had no patience with me if I started to whine and complain about being dumped on because I was a woman in a male-dominated workplace. He'd say, "If you can't take the pressure of the politics and the stress involved in achieving more in life, get a job as a janitor!"

A SPIRITUAL FOUNDATION

My summers in Alabama were like paradise to me. My mom would stay with her mother, but my brother and I would stay with relatives who had kids our age. Compared to our life in Newark, we had total freedom. In Newark, we couldn't play outside in our poor, crime-filled neighborhood unless one of our parents had time to sit on the front porch and watch us. In Alabama, we could roam all over town without parental supervision since Andalusia was a small town where everyone knew everyone else. Essentially, we had much of the town looking out for us no matter where we played. One of the hottest days one summer, I made my cousin Dot take me down to the post office and get some recruiting brochures on the Navy. She never let me forget it either. No matter where I was, the dream was still a very real part of my life.

Mother and her side of the family gave me my spiritual foundation. Every Sunday, we would attend the Methodist Church service and Sunday school. I didn't appreciate it at the time, but Mom was adamant that we all attend until we were twenty-one. Then we could make up our own minds about our faith. When I grew up, I found that I had absorbed far more than I realized at the time. There were times in my life I don't believe I would have survived without this spiritual grounding mother gave us. During the early part of my life, I believed in God but somehow was under the mistaken belief that He only got involved with humans when He had to do something huge, like parting the Red Sea or carving the Ten Commandments in stone for Moses. I would eventually come to know the need for a more personal relationship with the God of my mother.

SCHOOL DAYS, SCHOOL DAYS

My elementary school was just a few blocks from our house. Although we were poor, our neighborhood was made up primarily of hard working, honest people. All of my friends lived with both of their parents, and there was very little alcohol or drug abuse around in our neighborhood.

We had two neighborhood winos and that was about it. They were always happy and never bothered anyone except to ask for money now and then to buy more wine. One of the wino's name was Smithy. One day my brother and I came home from school to find my mother very agitated because one of the winos, Smithy, had come to the door asking for a handout. Shaking her head in disgust and disapproval, mother, notorious for getting people's names wrong, told us, "Spitty had the nerve to ring our doorbell and ask for money to buy some more wine!"

My happy childhood came to an end as I graduated from elementary school and was promoted to the seventh grade. The junior high school I had to go to was in one of the worse neighborhoods in Newark. The school itself had a terrible reputation, with kids running many of the classrooms. I was a good student, which had been a mark of honor in elementary school, but in junior high I found myself ostracized instead. I was so unhappy that I seriously considered quitting school in the seventh grade. The kids went out of their way to make my life miserable each and every day.

Two things saved me during this trying time in my life. One was the love and support of my family. Father went on the night shift at work so he could take me to and from school every day. I had the security of knowing that whatever happened to me in the world, I could always go home where I was loved unconditionally. Second, I had my dream motivating me to get the education I needed to fulfill it. My second year there, the school formed a separate class made up of good students and life got a little easier.

At the time though, I wondered why I had to go through such a negative experience. It didn't seem fair to me to be treated that way when I was working so hard to better myself; however, I can see now that my junior high experience taught me how to function in a daily environment where most of the people I was associating with not only disliked me but many even hated me. I've heard it said that the "hottest fire makes the strongest steel." I believe God was giving me the coping and survival skills I would need to endure what was to come if I was to move on and fulfill my dream.

At that time, junior high school was seventh and eighth grades and high school consisted of ninth through twelfth grades. I did indeed endure through junior high only to find that the high school I was slated to attend had an even worse reputation than my junior high school. Only 12 percent of their graduates went on to college. With my family's financial situation, a private school was out of the question. To achieve my goal and fulfill my dream, I definitely needed to go to college. Keeping in mind my father's saying that there are two things you could do about a problem, "something or nothing," I decided to do something about it. I signed up to take a test to try and get into a high school for the artistically talented. Music had been a big part of my upbringing, and as a result I had studied violin and learned a great deal about the technical aspects of music. The key for me was that this school had a safe and positive learning environment, and more than 50 percent of their graduates went on to college. I passed the test and was accepted.

As it turned out, I only attended this high school for half a year because my Father was finally able to get a better job. He was the first African American hired by a machine shop in Somerville, New Jersey. He did so well they made him a foreman shortly after he started working there. The increased pay allowed him to buy a house in a good neighborhood in Plainfield. My parents had achieved their objective of having a stable living environment for their family.

The remainder of high school was relatively uneventful in comparison to junior high. Academically, I did well, but I did bring one negative mindset with me from my Newark school years. I had become very introverted and kept pretty much to myself at school. My parents worried about my lack of social interaction and were always trying to push me out of the house to socialize. The parents of the other kids liked me, so they would make their kids invite me to their social functions. I was probably the only teenager in the neighborhood that didn't have a curfew. Neither fact really helped make me very popular with my peers.

What this whole experience did was nurture my already strong, independent spirit. I came to believe it was more important what my parents thought of me than what my peers thought or said. I learned to make decisions independent of the opinion of others. This would benefit me after I entered the Navy. Many times during my career, I've found myself at a roadblock caused by the negative opinion a person, group, or organization had about me. Dealing with the issues of junior high and high school had already taught me to examine criticism, see if it had any merit, correct what needed to be corrected, and shrug off what was just an opinion. I found much of what was said was not a truth in my life unless I allowed it to be. I am forever thankful for the strength of character I witnessed in my parents.

NEXT STOP, COLLEGE

So in high school, instead of interacting with my peers, I focused on my dream and made sure I took the college prep courses I would need to keep moving forward toward fulfilling it. I was the first in my immediate family to even go to college, so I had to figure out for myself the steps I needed to take to achieve my goal. My grades were good, but I needed to know when to take the SATs and how to apply for scholarships. Somehow the folks from the United Negro College Fund heard about me and sent me a college preparation questionnaire to fill out. A few weeks after I returned the form, they sent me a suggested list of schools for me to apply to. Their help was invaluable, and I was accepted at all five colleges I applied to. I ended up choosing Drew University, a small Methodist university in Madison, New Jersey.

The primary appeal for me was their junior year abroad program. You could spend the fall semester in Great Britain studying the British parliamentary system and the spring semester in Belgium studying the European Economic Community. One of the instructors was a Nobel Prize–winning economist. I also liked the fact that Drew University was only a couple of hours drive from home, so I could go to the safety and security of my family whenever I wanted or needed to. I had developed very few social skills in junior high or high school and really didn't anticipate a major change in my social life as I entered college, so I liked the close proximity of the school to my home.

As it turned out, it was the involvement in the travel abroad program that tremendously changed my life and widened my horizons. I did manage to make a few friends during my first and second years in college, but none of these friends were participating in the travel abroad program. I realized I had to learn how to socially interact with others without the safety net of having my parents living nearby or it would be a very long and lonely year abroad. I was fortunate that my roommate's fiancé was part of the overseas program, and he aided me in my attempts to intermingle. By the end of the year, I had lost much of my shyness and acquired what would become a lifelong love of travel.

DEALING WITH ANTIWAR, ANTIMILITARY, ANTIWHITES

During these years, my dream to enter the Navy lay dormant in my mind. Service in the military was very unpopular due to the turmoil surrounding the Vietnam War. I still wanted to enlist in the Navy but decided it wasn't something I wanted to share with others. My campus didn't have many antiwar demonstrations, but I refused to participate in the few they had stating I could understand why people opposed the war but not the hostility directed at military personnel. These were the days of the military draft, and it seemed to me that a lot of the protesters had misdirected their concern, blaming the soldiers instead of focusing their energies on ending the conflict and bringing these brave warriors home. Father had taught me to respect the rights of the protesters to state their views. I knew that this was the United States, and everyone was entitled to their opinion.

That same principle applied to the demonstrations held by the black students on campus. I questioned their political sincerity as I witnessed the leaders screaming hatred of the white race on one hand but dating white women on the other. I told them I felt their actions were phony, opportunist, and trouble making. I have no problem with interethnic dating, having myself dated men from all races and ethnic backgrounds, but I feel a true political activist talks the talk and walks the walk. One of the things these activists advocated was a separate dormitory for the black students. I refused to stay in it feeling the idea was beyond stupid. On the one hand, we had a civil rights group working hard to bring down the walls of segregation, while this activist group not only advocated it but demanded it.

The heritage my father had given me helped me peacefully coexist even with the more radical of my fellow students. As a matter of fact, my conservative views caused me no problems at all, even as a member of the black student organization. I openly disagreed with a lot of their views but always respected another's right to voice their opinion. One of the more radical black students who shared my interest in music and the theater told me I wasn't hassled because I hung around with people who shared my interests regardless of whether their political views and ethnic background differed from mine. My attitude has always been, "I may disagree with what you say, but I will defend your right to say it with my life."

NEVER GIVE UP ON YOUR DREAMS

As graduation approached, I was uncertain of my next step. I had received a scholarship to attend a two-year graduate program at the University of Denver's School of International Studies. I was encouraged to accept it by both my academic advisors and my family, saying I should grab any educational opportunity that came my way. I took their advice, but my heart wasn't really in it. I was tired of studying history, I was ready to go out and start making it.

One of my academic advisors was Dr. Josef Korbel, Madeleine Albright's father. He called me into his office and asked me why such an outstanding student wasn't working to her full intellectual potential. I shared with him that I felt guilty not wanting the university to feel they had wasted a valuable scholarship on me, but in my heart I was ready to move ahead toward fulfilling my dream. After agonizing the whole summer between my first and second year of graduate school, I decided to drop out and apply to the Navy.

The big lesson I learned in all of this was *never give up on your dreams.* I was miserable at graduate school because I wasn't pursuing that dream. The minute I began to move toward my goal, obstacles fell by the wayside and things started happening in my favor.

A WING AND A PRAYER

At the time I applied to the Navy, they were only accepting one out of every five female applicants. Not counting the Nurse Corp, the Navy only had 400 women officers and 4,000 enlisted women on active duty. Legal restrictions limited female career opportunities to administrative fields only. I told the Navy recruiter I wanted to be an intelligence officer. She said it wasn't possible at the time but maybe things would change in the future. I was determined to follow my dream, and I applied even though it looked like my dream job was not available.

The movie I had seen long ago proved to be prophetic, as I literally joined the Navy on a "Wing and a Prayer." My faith was rewarded, and by the time

I graduated from Officer Candidate School, the Navy had opened up their intelligence training to women. There was one opening available for my class. I was chosen over the others mainly because I had participated in that one year of graduate school taking the international studies course. I was the fourth woman and the first African American female to attend the twenty-week program at Lowry Air Force Base in Denver, Colorado. At the time, the Navy's school was located at the same facility as the air force intelligence training.

On my first day of class, one of the instructors went around the class and asked each one of the students what type of assignment they would like to pursue after graduation. I was the only woman in my class and said I wanted to go to an aviation squadron like many of my male classmates. The instructor smugly explained the military legal restrictions to me and then said to my face, "You don't belong in the Navy, let alone in a squadron!" He then sarcastically predicted I would end up at a desk in Washington, DC.

Past history had taught me to handle comments and attitudes like this with humor rather than anger or logical arguments. As I contemplated a rebuttal, I remembered a myth I had heard concerning the sexual capabilities of African American men. I looked back at the instructor who was senior to me in both rank and position, smiled sweetly, and replied, "You can say whatever you want but everyone *knows* black people are superior sexually." The instructor gasped in shocked horror and my classmates laughed hysterically, but from that moment onward I experienced great teaching and professionalism from my instructors. I worked hard, didn't ask for any special favors, and found my fellow classmates very supportive.

I still had to face the legal issues concerning women joining aviation squadrons. I refused to give up on my dream, so I continually sought ways to overcome the system. As it turned out, I had an air force roommate who told me that the air force sent their women intelligence graduates to aviation squadrons. In fact, many women served overseas in outfits that were fighting the war in Vietnam. So, I marched back into class armed with this information and asked why I couldn't be sent to one of the Navy's land-based aviation squadrons. From what I had learned, the federal law wouldn't restrict me since these aircraft didn't operate from aircraft carriers. The instructors were carefully noncommittal, but I was persistent. Whenever the topic of job assignments came up, I held my ground, worked hard in class, and eventually got exactly what I wanted. The intelligence community decided to make me their *test case for women* and allowed me to join an operational squadron. Needless to say, I was ecstatic.

COINCIDENCES

As I saw my dream coming to fruition, I reflected on several "coincidences" that marked my journey. My father had been born in Enterprise, Alabama. Coincidentally that was the name of the aircraft carrier from the movie that had inspired me years before, "Wing and a Prayer." My mother's parents, brothers, and sisters were all been born in Midway, Alabama—coincidentally the name of the famous battle depicted in that same movie. I decided to watch the movie again for the first time in many years. I noticed that all throughout the movie they kept flashing a chalk board with the names of the pilots in the squadrons sent into battle. At least three times "Ensign Harris" was one of the names listed on that blackboard. Just a coincidence? The Navy would not open most of its career fields to African Americans until the early 1970s.

The door would not officially open to women until the mid-1990s. It was not until the law changed in 1994 that significant numbers of women were allowed to go to sea. In 1973, most of the Navy's aviation squadrons operated aboard aircraft carriers, so it seemed my dream was impossible, yet I became the first woman assigned to an operational aviation squadron as an intelligence officer. I continued to pursue my dream and, at the time of my retirement in December 2001, I was the highest-ranking African American female in the Navy. God had given me that dream and then gave me the strength, courage, and vision to make it happen no matter what obstacle came my way.

Takeaway: Your dream is waiting for you to come true.

Key principles I learned in the area of fulfilling your dreams:

1. I had to dream my dream but then work hard to fulfill it.
2. I had to dream the dream but also do what I could to be prepared when those doors opened. Hard work and being prepared to move ahead are powerful tools.
3. I learned the value of not giving up and maintaining a sense of humor.

4. The key to overcoming is to not let a situation or a circumstance get me down; I couldn't afford to wallow around in self-pity. There are two things I could do about any problem in life: *something or nothing.*

5. I learned to make decisions independent of the opinion of others.

NOTES

1. www.famous-quotes.com/author.php?aid=3523-

2. http://www.famous-quotations.com/asp/search.asp?keyword=Goethe&Submit=Find

2

First Assignment—
A Magnificent Obsession

You don't become enormously successful without encountering some really interesting problems.

—*Mark Victor Hansen*[1]

Most people never run far enough on their first wind to find out they've got a second. Give your dreams all you've got and you'll be amazed at the energy that comes out of you.

—*William James*[2]

Lloyd Douglas's 1950s bestselling novel *The Magnificent Obsession* tells of a wealthy, young playboy who kills a man while driving under the influence of alcohol. In a freak occurrence a few days later, he causes an accident that leaves the man's widow blind. These life-changing accidents transformed the playboy's life, prompting him to return to medical school with a very specific goal in mind: to spend the rest of his life performing good deeds. Along the way, he was able to use his medical skills needed to operate and restore the woman's sight. He succeeded because he wanted it with all of his heart and soul. My dream to become an intelligence officer was for me a "magnificent obsession." My obsession gave me the strength and fortitude to endure my first year in the Navy.

THE WORST OF TIMES
The most accurate description of life as the first woman assigned to an operational squadron is that "it was the best of times and the worst of times."[3] Due

to the complex nature of antisubmarine warfare, all new naval intelligence officers, before becoming senior intelligence officers, were required to spend a year learning the ropes as an assistant under a junior officer who was either a pilot or a navigator. While extremely excited about embarking on this assignment, I soon discovered that although the squadron's senior officers wanted the bragging rights of having the first female intelligence officer, they didn't expect me to actually *do* anything. As a result of this mindset, I was destined to remain as an assistant for more than two years.

I naïvely began my first assignment thinking hard work was all that was needed to achieve promotion. I was shocked to discover that hard work was only one of the components needed to succeed in the real world. As is true for most people, when I was in the midst of this experience I didn't see the value of the process. I thought my stalemated position was awful; too much of my time was spent drowning myself in self-pity. Although I wouldn't want to go through it again, hindsight reveals it was the best thing that could have happened to me. The lessons I learned going through this ordeal were invaluable to me as I strove to fulfill my dream. I saw the value of doing my best but also discovered persistence and perseverance were essential when circumstances made achieving that dream seem hopelessly out of reach.

Over the course of my career, I encountered many more such situations where people thought my job assignments were simply equal opportunity statements. A perception that left me feeling frustrated and unfulfilled. The insight I gained from this first assignment taught me to stay prayed up, remain focused on the task at hand, and do everything in my power to be the best intelligence officer I could be. The end result of enduring through the "worst of times" on this first assignment was to be requested by name for what was considered the most prestigious assignment available for a junior intelligence officer for my next job.

THE BEST OF TIMES

When the instructors at the Naval Intelligence Training School informed me that I would be the test case for female intelligence officers in operational squadrons, they impressed upon me the importance of my success. The intelligence community needed me as a successful example so other patrol aviation squadrons would be more apt to accept females. To achieve this, I needed to not only excel at the job, but I also had to "fit in."

Apparently one of the main reasons I was chosen for this assignment was they felt my sense of humor would be an effective asset in getting the guys to accept me. As I was briefed on how to achieve acceptance, they explained the hierarchy of the aviation community. The flight crews were at the top of the heap, and those without flight status were the ground-pounders and were generally treated as second-class citizens. I was also made aware of how hard it was for even male intelligence officers to gain acceptance in a flight squadron. To achieve flight crew acceptance and respect, they warned, I had to be exceptionally good at my job and fit in with their established culture.

I took their advice to heart and began learning everything I could about my assigned squadron. I discovered they were the first patrol squadron to get the P-3C, which was the latest version of a land-based, long-range, antisubmarine warfare (ASW) aircraft. This particular aircraft also had a secondary role in maritime surveillance. Since I was entering the field of military intelligence during the period in history known as the Cold War, I needed to be aware of the potential threats that existed against the United States Navy.

Norman Polmar and Jurrien Noot report that, "In 1970–1971 the Soviet Union overtook the United States in total numbers of nuclear propelled submarines built and under construction."[4] Of particular concern to the Navy were the ballistic missile submarines (SSBNs) that carried nuclear-tipped missiles targeted at locations within the continental United States. I learned that the role of the P-3C aircraft was to locate and track the movements of these submarines so we could sink them before they launched their missiles if the Cold War went hot.

My research revealed that the Soviets also had a large number of attack submarines that posed a threat to our maritime trade. In that year, the United States had a total of 145 submarines, and the Soviets had 356.[5] Of course, our submarine force was superior to theirs in capability, but because of the sheer number of Soviet submarines, the threat they posed could not be dismissed. The P-3C also worked closely with the Carrier Battle Groups and in maritime surveillance monitoring Soviet surface ships and merchant ships suspected of such suspicious activity as arms shipments to countries hostile to U.S. interests. I realized I had walked into a high-stakes environment.

I did my homework. I felt that I was ready for my first test as a new squadron intelligence officer, my critical first briefing to the squadron. Once a week squadrons have what is known as an All Officers Meeting (AOM), where the squadron air intelligence officer (AI) gives a current events brief. Traditionally these presentations were laced with off-color jokes and slides. Knowing the importance of first impressions, my instructors and fellow classmates had put their heads together trying to give me some opening jokes that would fit this historic occasion. They came up with two.

"Hi, my name is Ensign Gail Harris, and in case you haven't noticed, I'm a girl." This bought a few nervous chuckles, but the second, which is so off-color I will not repeat it here, brought the house down. Nearly thirty years later, that joke was still being told around the fleet. The immediate result was some of the guys started thinking I might be okay after all. I was later told that some of the initial resentment and skepticism toward me had been due to the commanding officer instructing everyone to take down their nude centerfolds and watch their language because a woman was coming on board.

Remembering to pull on the sense of humor my instructors felt was essential to my survival, I found a way to deal with the language thing without upsetting the apple cart. Anyone who knows anything about sailors knows that the expression "cursing like a sailor" is based on a strong element of truth, so if someone slipped and did say a "bad word" in my presence, I'd smile sweetly and say, "Oh, that's alright, I don't speak French." I took a more direct approach with the centerfold issue by hanging a *Playgirl* centerfold of a naked guy on skis in my office and invited the commanding officer down to look at it. He laughed and told me to take it down. The guys quietly put their pictures back up but in their lockers, and that issue was also effectively dealt with. Phase one completed.

My initiation into this squadron taught me the value of handling the gender issue with humor. When an enlisted man refused to salute me, I'd give them a big smile, go against tradition, and salute them first adding a hearty "Good morning." Generally this caused them to blush and return my salute. When accused of taking a job from a man, I would smile and agree saying, "You know, you're right, but I come from a poor family and no one wanted to marry me." Usually they'd react with laughter, and the gender crisis was over.

WOMAN ON THE DECK

Life as the first woman officer in this environment posed many other unique challenges. For instance, my squadron was located in a huge blimp hangar that now housed four squadrons but boasted of only one ladies' room, which was of course located on the other side of the building from our offices. Most of the time I would head for the closest men's room, push the door open, and scream, "Woman on the deck." If I didn't hear, "No wait, don't come in!" I'd take my chances and go in. Every once in a while I'd take the long hike over to the woman's room and grab a nap on the couch, announcing as I returned to work how I just had to lie down and rest after that long, long walk. They never put in an additional ladies' room during my time there, but four years later one of the bathrooms did sport a flip sign that read men on one side and women on the other.

My initial briefing cracked the door open with both the flight crew and ground-pounders. I followed that up by requesting permission to attend the flight crew introductory course. This served both objectives given to me when I entered into this test assignment. It showed I wanted to fit in and really learn all I could about the P-3 Orion and its mission. This extremely difficult course required learning the function and purpose of every button, lever, and piece of equipment on the aircraft. The flight crews went on actual training flights to reinforce their book learning, but since I was not allowed to go, they allowed me to spend extra time evenings and on weekends in the flight simulators.

Though I flunked every weekly quiz, the instructors knew I was putting in long hours of study and provided the emotional support and encouragement I needed to persevere and ultimately pass the final written exam. After that, the flight crews started inviting me to go flying with them and even allowed me to work the radios. Typically we'd check in with the flight controllers as we entered an area and give our call sign. The guys would be disappointed if the flight controllers didn't react to the sound of a female voice coming from a military airplane. We found it was important that I identify us as a Navy aircraft before giving the call sign so they'd believe we were legitimate.

As much as I loved to fly with the guys, the "ladies' room" thing was still an issue since the aircraft restroom generally consisted of a canister tube thing and a "potty" used only as a place to pile stuff. Not only was it extremely inconvenient to use, but if you did use it you had to buy the crew a case of beer. I figured out how to use the tube thing, but it involved a great deal of physical contortion. The guys took great pleasure in threatening to open the door and take a picture of me or start rocking the aircraft back and forth if they knew I was in there. Resourceful as ever, my plan was not to drink anything before or during the flight. Problem was a P-3 can fly for twelve or thirteen hours, so it got really interesting at times.

If we flew into a foreign country, upon landing the customs people came onboard and wouldn't let us off the plane until they had done their inspections. After one particularly long flight, I started jumping up and down screaming during their inspection, so one of them took pity on me and escorted me to the nearest ladies' room. I can safely say that over the course of my three-year assignment there I learned where every ladies' room was located on every Navy base in the western Pacific.

JOIN THE NAVY AND SEE THE WORLD

One of the greatest adventures a young person can have is to join the Navy. When I was growing up, the Navy's slogan was "Join the Navy and See the World." During the first three years with this squadron, I certainly saw much of the western Pacific. Typically, an aircraft squadron spends one year at their home base training and then deploys to an overseas location for six months. My squadron was going to split its assets between Guam and Adak, Alaska, which was actually one of the islands west of continental Alaska—deployment locations that were obviously as different as night and day.

Adak is also known as the "Birth Place of the Winds" and labeled by many of the guys in the squadron as the worst place on earth. Rumor had it that anyone who went there became severely depressed because there was absolutely nothing to do between flights but drink. Hurricane force winds and blizzards were the norm, and the sun, they complained, never shined. Normally each squad member would spend three months in Guam and three in Adak. Because my boss had it in for me, I spent the majority of my six months in Adak while he hung out in Guam. Nonetheless, I was excited that I would finally be allowed to use all of the training I had received.

He had taken an instant dislike to me. I was puzzled but I worked hard to try to show him I could do a good job. To my face, he always told me I was doing okay. I thought I was making progress with him until the day the Assistant Department Head called me in the office to go over my first performance report. He asked me if I had a personality conflict with my immediate supervisor. He said my boss had provided the first draft to him and had marked me as low as possible in all performance areas. He continued saying that the marks didn't fit with his interpretation of my performance. He thought I was doing a good job. I was devastated but held up my head, telling him I didn't understand the animosity but would continue to do my best to win my boss over. This was a battle I was never able to win. Over the coming months, people kept warning me that my boss was telling everyone who would listen that I was worthless and incompetent. I gritted my teeth and put up with it. Because I would spend the majority of my time in Adak while he was in Guam, I felt everyone would be able to see what I could or could not do without his negative vibes hanging over me and I could prove him wrong. I just figured it was part of the price I paid for being a pioneer. Over the years, I've learned that personal biases and prejudices can cause you to view a person or group through a much distorted filter. If you don't watch yourself, it can develop into a very unhealthy obsession. Nonetheless, I was excited that I would finally be allowed to use all of the training I had received.

I can remember standing around the runway waiting to leave for Adak in anticipation of the first major test of my newfound capabilities. As I watched, I got my first look at some F-14s as they were doing their flight proficiency practice take offs and landings. Awestruck, I watched as one landed and both crew members turned and pointed in my direction. Even though I thought surely they couldn't be looking at me, I decided to wave and see what would happen. Amazingly, even dressed in a shapeless, baggy man's flight suit, with a ball cap jammed on top of my head, they had figured out I was a woman and wildly waved back at me. Sailors!

WELCOME TO ADAK

When we finally took off for Adak, the guys let me sit up in the cockpit; I had an incredible panoramic view of the Aleutian chain. When we landed, the squadron that we were relieving met us with big grins and beer. To say they were happy to see us is an extreme understatement. The weather that day was typical for Adak—overcast, cold, windy, and snowing. Since I knew I was going to be here for some time, I decided I wasn't going to buy in to all the negative stuff I had heard and make the most of my time there. In spite of my resolution, I was going to need all of the determination I could muster to deal with the grueling work schedule I was about to take on.

While training at Moffett Field, I had put in some long hours, and the majority of my duties involved briefing the flight crews before each flight. Most of these flights were Monday through Friday and generally not around the clock. When we deployed to Adak, the situation was totally different. We were at the height of the Cold War and defending the United States was now a twenty-four hours a day, seven days a week job. Flights could be on any day as well as at any and all hours of the day or night.

The Soviet Union had a large Navy and one of the largest submarine forces in the world. Our job was to track them when they operated in international waters. Twenty-four hour shifts were not unusual for me and my two enlisted specialists, so we slept when we could between flight briefings. It took a couple of weeks for my body to adjust to this challenging schedule.

Another trial was discovering and then giving the flight crews exactly what they needed to do their jobs. Apparently intelligence officers had the reputation of not sharing vital information because it was "classified" and consequently were considered by a lot of the flight crews as being arrogant, clueless, and basically useless. I had done my homework and felt prepared professionally but decided to connect with a group of junior officers who were part of these actual flight crews to find out exactly what type of information they were looking for from us. The guys seem to appreciate the fact that I took the time to find out what they really needed to do their jobs. Seemed like a no-brainer to me.

Once I knew what information they were looking for, the next challenge was to assimilate that information. As the intelligence officer, I needed to efficiently divide up the duties between myself and my two enlisted assistants. To effectively do the flight briefing I had to read through the intelligence traffic reports looking for anything of possible significance, go over the Sound Surveillance System (SOSUS) reports to see if there were any Soviet submarine contacts reported, and make sure to include the latest information on any submarine location in the flight crew packet of information. If there were any reports of Soviet surface ships operating in the scheduled fly areas, I'd obtain pictures for the flight crews and include information on the weapons capability of each ship. They also needed to be aware of anything on board that could be used against their aircraft and be informed of any other air traffic scheduled to be in their area as well as the current locations of any U.S. military ships. Obviously this information changed frequently.

To clarify, I'll share some intelligence geek stuff with you. To assist in the ASW process, the Navy had developed a system called Sound Surveillance System (SOSUS). SOSUS consists of a bunch of hydrophones mounted on the ocean floor connected by undersea cables to shore locations. Essentially they were listening devices. All things in the ocean emit sounds. Based on the sound frequencies you can identify what the source of the sound is. P-3Cs also carried sound detection equipment called sonobuoys. You'd drop them in the water and monitor the sounds listening for something that sounds like a submarine. This is a very complex process. Just because you hear a submarine doesn't mean you know its exact location. Once you got an initial detection of a submarine, you had to go through a very complex process to determine the

exact location. The guys operating the systems on the aircraft and the SOSUS
stations were masters at this. I was always in awe of the process.

The Soviets had learned the value of having a large submarine force from
observing the effectiveness of the German submarine force in both World War
I and World War II against nations like the United States and Great Britain
that have a heavy dependence on maritime trade. Something like 90 percent
of imports into the United States come by way of sea. The war against German
U-boats during the World War II was known as the Battle of the Atlantic. It was
the longest and hardest-fought battle of the conflict. As Terry Hughes and John
Costello say in their book *The Battle of the Atlantic*, "the battle began with the
sinking of the passenger liner *Athenia* and was remorselessly sustained by U-
boats for the next five years and eight months—the entire duration of the war.
Twice, the crippling losses of merchant shipping brought Britain to the brink
of starvation and Hitler to the threshold of victory. Defeat in the longest, most
bitterly fought campaign of the war finally cost the Germans 784 U-boats and
28,000 crewmen. Victory cost the Allies 2,603 merchant ships, 175 naval vessels,
and 40,000 lives, including 26,000 civilians."[6]

When the flight returned, I would debrief the flight crew and write a detailed account of everything significant that happened during that trip. My
enlisted assistants would take the film from the aircraft cameras over to the
photo lab and pore over the films searching for anything of significance. If
they found something, they had to do a detailed analysis of each ship, annotate the photos, and provide a detailed intelligence report within a very short
window of time. We had to get these reports right back out to the next set of
flight crews. My two guys were fabulous workers and got a lot of commenda-
tions for their work while we were in Adak.

In spite of the long hours, I had what ended up being an unexpected career
advantage. Since my boss, who was never happy with my work, was in Guam,
the senior officers in Adak had an open view of my performance, so I would
stand or fall truly on my own merits. In Adak, I learned some valuable lessons.
In tough situations:

- Hold your head up high; be confident in yourself.
- Give your personal best regardless of how others assess you; be excellent.
- Look for opportunities to have fun; maintain a good sense of humor.
- Help others do their jobs; empowering others to succeed opens doors for
  future personal success.

FUN, EVEN IN ADAK

Once I adjusted to my work schedule, I decided I was going to have fun even while deployed in Adak. I began to scope out my fellow laborers and noticed there was a group that always seemed to be having the time of their lives. It was a varied group consisting primarily of doctors and nurses stationed at the hospital and teachers assigned to a school run by the Department of Defense, but it also included some helicopter pilots and a few guys assigned on the island patrol boats.

Until my deathbed, I'll remember my first interaction with this lively bunch. I got off of work at about one or two in the morning—which was early for me—and these characters were sitting in the base club celebrating somebody's birthday or something. They invited me to join them and, just as I sat down, one of the guys challenged another to take off his clothes and run around the table three times. I looked incredulously at one of the nurses, Catherine Swan, who would become a life-long friend, and she looked back with a, "Oh yes they are!" expression on her face, and sure enough they did! I was in shock but eventually saw the humor in it and laughed hysterically.

In spite of that weird introduction, I found they were normally very conservative and of high moral character, with most of their exploits more inclined toward practical jokes. For instance, one of the department heads that was known to be extremely difficult to get along with was scheduled to arrive in Adak after his three months in Guam. Some of the junior officers came up with a diabolical plan to welcome him. His name was Bill but behind his back we junior officers nicknamed him, "The Turkey." There was this big rock just below the Bachelor Officer Quarters (BOQ) that was extremely visible as you approach the building, so they painted, "Welcome Bill, gobble, gobble."

Most of the time, the behavior was more good-natured than mean-spirited. One exception involved the few women on base, and we decided it had to be dealt with. As I've said, there were not many women on Adak, so you would think the guys would have been appreciative of the ones they encountered. One night a few of the guys started going on and on about how ugly some of the women were. So we came up with a plan to deal with it without putting them on report and possibly damaging their careers over it. We decided to give them a taste of their own medicine.

A group of us girls sat at a table right in the middle of the Officers Club Bar, and every guy who walked by was given a grade of B+ or above based on how handsome they were. We'd hand out their grade and then start hooting and hollering and pounding on the table. Needless to say, we only had to do that for one night, and never during that deployment did we have any further problems with the guys putting down any of the women.

The immediate result was that the boorish behavior stopped, but my reputation for dealing with guys in the workplace actually became professionally damaging as I moved up in rank. When people repeated these stories, they'd tell them out of context and wouldn't explain the motivation behind these actions. I have no regrets, though, and probably wouldn't change anything about my early tactics because they worked for the times we were in.

ANOTHER TOUGH YEAR

I truly thought things were going great. I was having fun, was fitting in, and felt I had accomplished what my instructors had required of me. I had learned a great deal from those I had been working with and believed I had done a good job in spite of the circumstances surrounding my first assignment. I was totally shocked and deeply disappointed when the deployment ended and the senior officers decided I was to remain an assistant for another year instead of moving up to the number one position. At the end of that year, our P-3C squadron received not only a new commanding officer but new department heads as well. This new regime apparently felt that although I had done a good job on my first deployment, I still wasn't qualified to be the number one person. I was completely devastated to say the very least.

I also found out that everyone had known what was going to happen except me. My new boss turned out to be a guy I thought was my friend but who told me I should be happy that I had oversight personnel who actually liked me. He also informed me that I had almost been moved to the administrative department, so I should consider myself lucky and stop complaining. Happy was not exactly the term I was thinking of to describe how I was feeling right at that moment.

The naval intelligence community found out what was going on and informed the new commanding officer that they were going to file charges against him for racial and sexual discrimination. The commanding officer was understandably upset and called me into his office and proceeded to scream and yell at me. I needed some expert advice, so I called and talked the situation over with my Father.

Dad listened to me complain and then made one profound statement, "If you want to make the Navy a career you'd better call off the discrimination charges." He explained that it really didn't matter whether I was right or wrong because the bottom line was the Navy would consider me a troublemaker and no one would want me in their command. I told the intelligence community I would tough it out but appreciated the fact that they went to bat for me.

The naval intelligence community support gave me the strength to go on, but I'm embarrassed to admit that, at first, I sat around whining and complaining to all my friends. I'm surprised I have any friends left from that time in my life; I was really miserable and extremely difficult to be around. I finally decided it really didn't matter what anyone said or thought about me, I would become one of the best intelligence officers ever recorded in history. It turned out to be one of the toughest years of my life but also one of the most valuable as far as my career was concerned.

BIG BROTHER IS WATCHING

Since my own squadron didn't give me any work to do, I had a lot of time on my hands. My new resolve caused me to look outside my own four walls and discover ways to improve myself. I started spending time over at the COMPATWINGPAC offices (Commander Antisubmarine Patrol Wings Pacific) just across the way from my squadron. I was still available in the unlikely event my squadron needed me, but I began to learn a great deal from the wing. I discovered they did the in-depth analysis, carried out the briefing and debriefing of all of the flights, ran all of the operations throughout the Pacific, and even had a small intelligence detachment headed by a Lieutenant Commander who took me under his wing.

I started helping out in whatever way they needed, which led to me learning how to operate all of their computers and gaining a more in-depth concept of the ASW problem. I also kept flying with the flight crews. They let me work all of the equipment, and I even got to fly the aircraft once. Granted it was on autopilot and the regular pilots were hovering over me, but I flew the plane.

I didn't realize it at the time, but all of this brought me under the direct scrutiny of the senior members of the Pacific Patrol staff. I found out later I was developing a very good professional reputation as I found productive ways to use my time in spite of the low professional opinion the senior officers in my squadron had of me. The people that would ultimately determine my future were very impressed with how I kept working, learning, and giving my all despite the negative aspects of my situation. The flight crews and maintenance guys continued to be supportive, giving me the emotional stamina to go on.

It was also during this period that I received the best complement I've ever been given. It came at the end of a particularly humiliating day. I had retreated to my office to have a good cry when one of the senior chiefs in the squadron knocked on my door. Any sailor will tell you that it's the chiefs and the admirals who actually run the Navy. Apparently all the squadron chiefs had been discussing my work, and he wanted me to know that they thought I was the best junior officer in the squadron. That single moment in time gave me the strength to continue on. I knew that if the chiefs said it, it must be true.

I persevered and finally received some good news on the professional front. The commander slated to be the squadron commanding officer during my last deployment called me into his office and asked me how I liked being in the squadron. "It sucked!" He laughed and asked me why, to which I replied, "Because I'm not the intelligence officer."

"Under me you will be," he promised, and he kept his word. My perseverance had paid off. As we prepared for what would be my last deployment, I was on cloud nine. I was finally going to get a chance to do the job I'd been preparing for since I started this journey. I was really going to be the person in charge of intelligence under a commanding officer that thought I could do it.

ANOTHER KIND OF BATTLE

Seems, however, I had one more hurdle to get over before I could embark on this long-awaited assignment. I began to have some serious medical problems starting with extreme tiredness, mood swings, and depression. My apartment was on the second floor, and when I got there I was so tired I had to lie down. I also had itchy skin often so intense that the only relief I could get was by sitting in a tub of cool water. I started having heart palpitations and nearly fainted at work one day. I started loosing weight even though I had not changed my eating habits. I seemed to be hungry all the time. I'd eat a hearty breakfast, big lunch, and full dinner yet continued to lose weight. My first thought was God had answered my prayers and I could finally eat whatever I wanted and not gain weight. Then my hair started falling out, causing my hairdresser to ask if I had a thyroid problem. I didn't even know what a thyroid was much less what it did.

What I did know was something was wrong, so as I encountered each symptom, I went to the doctor, who insisted it was all stress related and wanted to put me on Valium. I refused. I didn't know what was wrong with me, but I instinctively knew I didn't need a nerve medicine to fix it. Finally, I was able to connect with a doctor that paid attention to and considered all my symptoms. After he examined me, he had me put my finger on my wrist and take my own pulse, carefully counting every beat of my heart. I told him I thought it was around 130. He nodded, looking a little upset by the fact, so I asked what normal was supposed to be and he said between 60 and 80. It turns out I had Graves' disease, which directly affects the thyroid gland. I learned that the thyroid controls the body's metabolism, and Graves' disease causes your body's metabolic rate to run too fast. If not caught in time a person can die of heart failure. Apparently, because my case had not been diagnosed earlier, I was a very sick woman.

I had to have surgery to remove 90 percent of my thyroid gland, thereby missing the first month of my "dream" deployment. Again, though I thought I'd been dealt a bad blow, it turned out to be the best thing that could have happened. First off, my hospital stay turned out to be a hoot. I had the surgery done in the hospital where my girlfriends worked, so I only had to stay the day before, the day of, and the day after the surgery. Then my friends, Cathy and Donna, whom I had originally met in Adak, came and got me out and we hit the restaurants. I admit I got some weird looks as I walked in with a huge bandage around my neck and a Frankenstein walk. I couldn't turn my head to the left or right because of the surgery, but I had no trouble swallowing food.

When I was finally given medical clearance to join my squadron, I was flown over to Japan on a military transport. Surprisingly, my squadron's senior officers were all there to meet the plane. As I looked around at my fellow passengers trying to figure out whom they had come to meet, they walked up to and enthusiastically welcomed me! It seemed even with my two enlisted assistants there to help, it took three guys to fill in for me. My medical leave caused them to realize how much work was involved in providing the level of intelligence support I had been supplying. I was viewed with a new professional respect.

It turned out to be a great deployment involving lots of hard work and a few more challenges but resulted in a follow-on assignment to one of the most prestigious jobs available for a junior intelligence officer. Hard work, perseverance, and professional excellence won out. I was requested by name for this esteemed assignment. Now I was ready for the next chapter of my career; however, at the time, I didn't realize I was still a work in progress with many more lessons to learn.

Takeaway: Nobody said it would be easy.

Key principles I learned from my first assignment:

1. I saw the value of doing my best but also discovered persistence and perseverance were essential when circumstances made achieving that dream seem hopelessly out of reach.
2. In tough situations, I learned to
   hold my head up high and be confident in myself,
   give my personal best regardless of how others assessed me and be excellent,
   look for opportunities to have fun and maintain a good sense of humor,
   help others do their jobs—empowering others to succeed opens doors for future personal success.
3. I learned to keep working, learning, and giving my all despite the negative aspects of my situation.
4. Hard work, perseverance, and professional excellence won out.

NOTES

1. http://inspirationandmotivation.com/mark-victor-hansen-quotes.html.

2. http://en.proverbia.net/william-james-quotes.

3. Charles Dickens, *A Tale of Two Cities*. (New York/London: Macmillan and Co., 1896), 1.

4. Norman Polmar and Jurrien Noot, *Submarines of the Russian and Soviet Navies, 1718–1990*. (Annapolis, MD: United States Naval Institute Press, 1991), 198.

5. Norman Polmar and Jurrien Noot, *Submarines of the Russian and Soviet Navies, 1718–1990*. (Annapolis, MD: United States Naval Institute Press, 1991), 199.

6. Terry Hughes and John Costello, *The Battle of the Atlantic*. (New York: The Dial Press/James Wade, 1977), front cover flap.

Persistence—The Key to Success

Our greatest glory is not in never falling, but in rising every time we fall.

—*Confucius*[1]

There has never been a successful or creatively gifted person who hasn't known failure, frustration, or tough times. . . . The hallmark of success is the ability to ride out these moments and prevail. . . . Often, those who overcome the fiercest difficulties are the men and women who ultimately achieve the greatest triumphs and inspire us the most.

—*Dennis Kimbro*[2]

I was looking forward to beginning my new assignment. I had expected to be able to live in the Bachelor Officer Quarters (BOQ) located near my new command, but they informed me there was no room there. They ended up putting me up in a BOQ room on the Navy base in Atsugi, Japan, which turned out to be about five miles or so from my new job located on another small Navy base in Kamiseya, Japan. It was not a really positive start to my new assignment.

As I stood outside waiting for one of my new coworkers to drive me to my new job, I began to feel alarmingly out of my element. My car had been shipped from the States to the Japanese port of Yokohama, and I needed to figure out how to go get it. How was I going to find my way when I couldn't read the street signs or the letters on a map? On top of that, the Japanese drove on the left side of the road instead of the right. I was beginning to see an uncomfortable pattern emerging. I'd been told if I wanted to be able to read Japanese, I would have to memorize 500 or so of the Japanese characters. As I got to this point in my thinking, I was in a really bad mood. Oh, the challenges of having a moody, creative nature.

I knew I had to get my mental act together before I got to my new office. When I was in the States and I got in one of these moods, I would call my dad and he would help me work it through and get my head on straight. I couldn't call him, but I began to ask myself what would Dad say to me? "Gail, after spending three years with an organization that didn't want you, you should be walking on air. This command asked for you. They really went out of their way to get you. Isn't this one of the most prestigious assignments a junior intelligence officer could receive? Quit complaining, make sure your uniform is perfect and your shoes are shined."

By the time my ride arrived, I had managed to start getting my act together. I spent the next couple of days getting all the administrative stuff done, which in the military can be a pretty tedious process. I had to get indoctrinated into all of the various security clearances I would need for my new job, arrange to be paid, take my medical records to the hospital, pick up my car from the sea port, and find a more permanent place to stay. My new coworkers were very friendly and helpful, and one even took me to pick up my car to make sure I didn't get lost. My spirits started to improve.

ORIENTATION: WELCOME TO THE 7TH FLEET
After all of the check-in stuff was taken care of, my new bosses sent me to orientation. It started simple enough with a brief history of the command given by my new department head. He explained that Fleet Ocean Surveillance Information Facility Western Pacific (FOSIF Westpac) was actually part of the 7th Fleet staff and that the navy had divided the world up into geographic regions with commands assigned to each area. As they say on their website, "Established in 1943, United States 7th Fleet is the largest of the Navy's forward deployed fleets. At any given time, there are 60–70 ships, 200–300 aircraft, and about 40,000 Navy and marine corps personnel."[3]

He proudly explained that the 7th Fleet was responsible for protecting U.S. interests in the western Pacific and Indian Oceans. The fleet had three primary missions: defend U.S. citizens, territory, and maritime interests in the region; deter aggression; and if deterrence failed, conduct combat operations.

I was excited to learn that the fleet headquarters was located aboard a ship that operated out of Yokosuka, Japan.

As my supervisor continued my orientation, I learned that my new organization was considered the intelligence arm ashore of the 7th Fleet. He emphasized that the purpose of our command FOSIF Westpac was to augment the 7th Fleet ship board intelligence staff and assist them in the intelligence evaluation process. Our mission was to provide near real-time coverage of the location and intentions of the Soviet military. The Soviet Union's Pacific Fleet was their largest fleet, and we were still in the midst of the Cold War, so a crisis or war could erupt at any time. Both the United States and the Soviets maintained a large arsenal of nuclear weapons that could be launched at a moment's notice. The nukes could be dropped by aircraft or launched from submarines, naval surface ships, or land-based sites. Our job as Intelligence Watch officers was to ensure we gave the decision makers plenty of advance warning if anything changed in the balance of power.

My new supervisor also wanted to ensure that I knew that while Commander Joey Hegerman, FOSIF Westpac's officer in charge, was my boss and would be writing my performance reports, the command came directly under the 7th Fleet senior intelligence officer. I guess that was his way of preparing me to not be surprised if the 7th Fleet intelligence officer or any of his staff called me at work requesting information on current events. That sure never happened to me in my job as squadron intelligence officer. I had figured I was too far down the food chain for those folks to notice me or even know my name.

OSIS

My organization was part of a new worldwide network set up by naval intelligence to provide operational intelligence (OPINTEL) to the fleet. The Navy's other forward deployed fleet at the time was 6th Fleet, which operated in the Mediterranean. They were supported by FOSIF Rota located in Spain. Pacific Fleet headquarters, Atlantic Fleet headquarters, and Naval Forces in Europe had similar shore-based intelligence organizations called Fleet Ocean Surveillance Information Centers (FOSICs) that provided similar support to their respective fleet staff. Collectively these organizations were known as OSIS (Ocean Surveillance Information System) nodes.

There was also an OSIS command in Suitland, Maryland, the Naval Ocean Surveillance Information Center (NOSIC), which supported senior Navy staff in the Washington, DC, area. They were responsible for the in-depth analysis and long-term threat assessments as well as keeping track of merchant shipping worldwide. The OSIS nodes that supported the fleets focused more on near-term analysis of Soviet military operations. The Soviet Union was the focus, but we were to monitor any potential threat to security. That meant we also had to keep track of the military activities of the Chinese, North Koreans, and countries surrounding the Indian Ocean and report any potential threats. Since the 7th Fleet's home port was in a foreign country, which made it a potentially vulnerable target for terrorists wanting to do harm to U.S. assets, we also continually monitored known terrorist group activities.

WHAT IN THE WORLD IS SIGINT?

Colocated with my new command was an organization called a Cryptologic Support Group (CSG). They were part of the Naval Security Group, which was the naval component of the National Security Agency (NSA). My supervisor went on to explain that CSG's role was to interpret and analyze signals intelligence (SIGINT). As I continued to listen, I pasted what I hoped was a calm expression on my face because as soon as he mentioned SIGINT, I knew I was in trouble. What the heck was SIGINT? I didn't want to ask the question because the way he was blasting through my orientation, it was apparent he assumed I knew exactly what he was talking about. All I could think about at the moment was, I finally get a job where they want me, but I won't be able to do it because of my total lack of knowledge on anything he had been talking about.

I realized I would have a tremendous learning curve and started to panic since I was not familiar with most of the intelligence sources my new department head continued to talk about during my orientation. As a squadron intelligence officer, my only focus had been on the capabilities of the Soviet military forces. The only intelligence collection system I had needed to understand was the SOSUS network. Every day in addition to the SOSUS reports on submarine locations, I had received a newspaper-like report that told me where the Soviet navy ships and aircraft were operating in the Pacific. It didn't occur to me to wonder how they knew this, I just used what I needed and went on with my work.

I wasn't brain-dead on the subject but cautious because of the "need to know" military intelligence code I had learned about the hard way. You only had access to the intelligence information you needed to do your job. Rules regarding the handling and dissemination of intelligence information were pretty strict. We were told if you violated them you were going to jail. I learned the hard way they weren't kidding. During my last couple of months in my squadron before my transfer, I had conducted an inventory of the classified material I was responsible for and discovered there were several pieces unaccounted for. The command initiated a formal investigation that could have led to a court martial and jail time for me if the issue had not been resolved. As you can see, I had a valid reason for not asking too many questions; however, my attitude was about to be changed and in a big way.

NSA: NEVER SAY ANYTHING

I shook off my growing discomfort and focused my attention back on my orientation. Officially, the CSG answered only to the NSA, but in reality they worked with the FOSIF. As my new department head continued his spiel, I realized I didn't know much about the NSA either. The standard joke was the initials stood for Never Say Anything and their motto was, "In God we trust, all others we monitor."

As my boss continued to talk, I kept nodding my head like I knew what he was talking about but wondered why I hadn't learned any of this as part of my initial intelligence training three years earlier. The intelligence school training was superb, but the focus had been on teaching us what we would need to perform successfully as squadron intelligence officers. There had been very little information on the intelligence collection systems themselves. Now I was fighting the urge to get up and run from the conference room screaming, "Somebody help me!"

FOSIF

FOSIF Westpac, like the other OSIS nodes, was divided into two groups of people. The first group consisted of the management and analysts who worked Monday through Friday, six in the morning to late afternoon or early evening shift. The analysts were specialists and usually focused on one area, such as a potential adversary's submarines, aircraft, or surface ships. Many had worked those areas for years and would prove very helpful to me in the months to come. This group was referred to as the day workers.

The second group was the Intelligence Watch. Typically, most new workers started out on this watch, which operated twenty-four hours a day, seven days a week. We were set up in four teams of four or five people each plus at least one member of the CSG and were headed up by a navy lieutenant. Each team stood an eight-hour watch.

On the first two days of your rotation, you came in to work from seven in the morning to three in the afternoon. Because of the intensity of the work environment, you were expected to actually arrive at work an hour before your scheduled watch, and you generally didn't leave until an hour after your shift was over. On the second day, you started your watch at seven, left work at three, and had to be back at eleven the evening of the same day to stand a watch from eleven at night to seven the next morning. This was called a *double back*. You then left work, went home, and came back at eleven that evening to work until seven the next morning. After that second all-night watch, you went home and had to come back to work at three in the afternoon that same day and work from three until eleven in the evening, another double back. The next day you worked another watch from three in the afternoon until eleven in the evening. You then supposedly got eighty hours off. The reality was that the watch officers only had two full days off because on the third day you were expected to spend some time at work catching up on the world events that had happened on your days off. This was called the 2-2-2/80.

MY NEW N2

For the last part of my orientation, my new commanding officer took me down to fleet headquarters in Yokosuka to meet the 7th Fleet intelligence officer (called the N2) and his staff. I was excited because it was one of the rare occasions in my career when I actually got to go on a Navy ship. The laws permitting women to serve on combat ships wouldn't come until the mid-1990s.

The N2 was very kind to me during the meeting. I gained a valuable insight into intelligence politics during the meeting, as the N2 and my boss discussed the professional performance of the junior intelligence officers assigned to the various aviation squadrons operating in the 7th Fleet area. Apparently one young officer wasn't living up to his potential because he was spending too much time drinking and chasing women. I made a mental note to remember how important this seemed to senior officers.

As I prepared to leave, the N2 asked, "Gail, if there is anything I can do to help you out, please don't hesitate to ask." I was part of the first group of women placed in the job, and I guess that was his way of making me feel welcome. Remembering how the use of humor had helped me fit in at my squadron, I mischievously replied, "Could you arrange to have a single black male officer assigned so I can have someone to date?" As I recall Commander Hegerman kicked me under the table, but thankfully the N2 laughed.

MY DEFINING CAREER MOMENT

I didn't realize it at the time, but that was the end of my down time and would prove to be my defining naval career moment. For the next two and a half years I would be running around in controlled states of panic with people screaming and yelling at me. What I would learn during this period of time would set the stage for my future success. This is where I really learned the value of persistence. I was really not prepared to do the job, so I would have to work hard and long to get myself up to speed.

The way the FOSIFs trained you was to throw you directly into the fire. You'd be assigned one of the four watch training positions. The most junior position was "plotter." A junior enlisted person filled this slot, and his or her job was to physically put on a map a "plot" of the locations of all Soviet navy ships and submarines that were operating in waters outside of their ports. The plots were based on information received from various intelligence reports that had to be analyzed carefully to figure out what information was most accurate. If you didn't understand the systems and processes used to collect the intelligence, you couldn't do your job well. The 7th Fleet would move their forces around in response to where you told them the Soviets were operating. I realized right away that this was like a high-stakes chess game.

The next senior position was "watch analyst." This was manned by a senior enlisted intelligence person who wrote the intelligence reports that were sent out to the fleet. The reports were very similar to newspaper articles and followed the old journalism format of answering who, what, where, why, when, and how. The focus was what the Soviet navy was doing today, what they did yesterday, and what are they going to do tomorrow. The reports were short but involved and written after screening hundreds and sometimes thousands of pieces of data in an eight-hour period.

The CSG member of the team was the only person authorized to analyze the SIGINT data and write reports on it, which again involved screening tons of data. Heading up the watch was a Navy lieutenant who had to read and edit all of the reports written by the watch, even those written by the CSG.

There was also an air analyst position that was manned about sixteen hours of the day. They usually weren't needed from midnight to seven in the morning unless the activity level was so intense it warranted bringing them on twenty-four hours a day, seven days a week as well. The Soviets had a very large air force, and their navy had a large air component. If they flew over water, you had to track them. The 7th Fleet units, particularly aircraft carriers operating in the region, did not like to be surprised by Soviet aircraft flying overhead. They liked lots of advance notice so they could launch aircraft in response. There's been more than one watch officer fired because they didn't provide sufficient warning to the fleet. This job also involved screening large amounts of intelligence traffic and plotting it on charts. You had to understand the strengths and limitations of the systems collecting the intelligence to figure out what information was most accurate.

ON-THE-JOB TRAINING

The training methodology was to get you up to speed on all of the watch positions by actually having you do each one. Usually you spent one watch cycle, or as we called it "watch string," being trained and then the next week you were left on your own as the person who trained you took a well-earned vacation. You were not allowed to advance to the next position until you mastered that job. At the end of your training period, you had to pass an oral board before you were assigned a watch team of your own.

My trainer was one of the most talented intelligence officers I've ever worked with, Jack Shankles. He was extremely knowledgeable and very patient with me. I gave him a lot of "deer in the headlights looks," but he never gave up on me. He was also one of the first people in the Navy to treat me as just another officer. My sex or race had no bearing for him. He and his wife, Bonnie, even made me an honorary member of their family.

Jack taught me a tremendous amount about the various types of intelligence reports we had to screen. There were five broad categories: signals intelligence (SIGINT), imagery intelligence (IMINT), human intelligence (HUMINT), open source intelligence (OSINT), and "other" technical intelligence (SOSUS is an example of this category).

The intelligence was collected from a variety of sources: satellites, aircraft, ships, humans, press reports, and so forth. The task of the watch was to screen all of the information and put together a picture of what was going on. There was a certain security within the insecurity of the Cold War. We had watched the Soviet military so closely and for so long that we had a good feel for what were normal training operations and what were not. The challenge was to figure out when the Soviet Union was doing something that wasn't normal so the 7th Fleet could move forces in place to counter their moves if it was deemed necessary. We had to figure out what was going on by analyzing the intelligence reports.

Jack gave me an excellent example to chew on during my training. About three months before my arrival, a watch team got intelligence indicating a single Soviet MiG-25 fighter aircraft was heading straight for Japan. It was not unusual for Soviet aircraft to conduct simulated attacks on Japanese or U.S. forces in the Sea of Japan, but these were normally done by more than one aircraft. Jack told me initially some of the watch thought it was faulty reporting. Turned out it was a Soviet pilot named Victor Belenko defecting to the west. He landed his aircraft at a Japanese military base. They apparently didn't shoot him down because the intelligence analysts were able to figure out what was going on.

As my on-the-job training went on, I continued to wonder if I was up to the job. The activity level we had to monitor was intense. The Soviets would launch aircraft and simulate attacks on our ships operating in the Sea of Japan or they would fly reconnaissance aircraft overhead or do both things on the same day. They might test the Japanese air defenses by flying close to Japanese air space or send submarines and surface ships to tail our ships. The watch had to anticipate the moves of the Soviet forces and make sure the 7th Fleet knew each move to keep ahead of the power curve. If the Soviets had military units on the move, our forces wanted to go out and monitor them. Guess you could call it controlled madness.

TIME FOR SOME PRODUCTIVE THINKING

One of the best things that happened to me was the fact that Jack prolonged my training past the usual time. My initial reaction when I was told I would need a longer training period was to revert to my usual negative habits of self-pity and depression. After a few miserable hours though, I began to re-member my father's advice about the two things you can do about a problem, *something or nothing.* I also remembered that during my first assignment, I had discovered that given a reasonable amount of time and a patient teacher, I could learn anything. I decided right then and there that it was time for some productive thinking instead of wasting my time wallowing in self-pity. What did I need to do to move forward and complete my training to the satisfaction of everyone concerned?

I determined that I needed to learn more about the intelligence sources than Jack had time to teach me during our time on watch together. I devised a three-pronged approach to remedy this problem, one I would use many times in my journey ahead. First, I read everything I could find on the history of operational intelligence (OPINTEL). I've always been an avid reader and loved history. I firmly believed you need to learn from the past, incorporate what's good, and avoid the bad to keep from making the same mistakes over and over.

My research gave me a lot of good insight. For example, I learned that OPINTEL had its historical roots in World War II. An excellent new resource on the subject written by Christopher Ford and David Rosenberg called *The Admiral's Advantage* came out in 2005. I wish it had been around back in the 1970s when I needed it. In their book, Ford and Rosenberg state, "Numerous historical accounts . . . attest to the vital role that intelligence played in mak-ing possible the Allies' overwhelming victory in 1945. For example, General Thomas Handy reportedly believed that Allied intelligence triumphs short-ened the war in Europe by at least a year, and General Dwight Eisenhower estimated that it saved thousands of British and American lives. Similarly, Admiral Chester Nimitz, commander in chief of Allied forces in the Pacific theater, believed that the good intelligence he received was worth as much as an entire fleet."[4]

I also learned that OSIS was based on what is referred to as "all-source analysis." Simply put it means it is not enough to just look at intelligence from the various obvious sources. You had to evaluate each report, discarding what was poor information, keeping what was good, fusing all the best information together to form a coherent picture of what was happening, and giving the de-cision makers the data they needed to develop a national security strategy and position military forces to gain the advantage over any potential adversary. The intent is to prevent hostilities and, if that doesn't work, be in a position to win should an actual conflict develop.

For example, if information indicates that a Soviet submarine is leaving port, you have to determine if it's going to train in local waters or be out looking for U.S. Navy ships. Either way you have to determine what type of submarine it is and whether it is carrying nuclear weapons. If so, does it appear to be positioning itself to attack U.S. targets? If that's the case, then the 7th Fleet would want to place assets in place to destroy it if the Cold War went hot. This is one of countless examples the watch officer had to recognize and analyze. If you overreacted or something was happening and you didn't recognize it, you could cause an international incident.

The analysis involved is an incredibly complex process. The best way to describe the working environment is to tell you to take five 1,000-piece puzzles, throw all of the pieces into one box, then add 5,000 pieces of various unrelated puzzles and give the mix to a four-man team. Give them eight hours to put them all back together again and have various people call them up every fifteen minutes and ask for a progress report. Then every so often send someone in to ask them why it is taking so long. At the end of the eight-hour period, whether they have the pieces together or not, they have to give a detailed analysis of what they think the pictures on all five puzzles look like.

The historical incident that most resonated with me and gave me insight into how to approach my new job was the role of intelligence in the Battle of Midway. The naval intelligence community had partially broken the Japanese navy communications codes. "Prior to the attack on Pearl Harbor, only 10 percent to 15 percent of the code was being read."[5] Typically, when transmitting sensitive military and diplomatic traffic, nations will put the messages in some sort of code. Since the naval intelligence community could in effect read portions of the Japanese mail, it allowed intelligence analysts to gain better insight into Japanese war plans.

In the days leading up to the Battle of Midway, the U.S. military knew without a doubt that a Japanese attack was imminent. The Japanese hoped to destroy the remainder of the U.S. forces in the Pacific and force the United States out of the war. What our military didn't know was where the attack would occur. Since the attack on Pearl Harbor had drastically reduced the forces available to counter any attack, it was critical that the warfighters

know where the main thrust of the attack would be so they could position
their forces for the best effect. "At the time of the battle . . . 3 aircraft carriers,
45 fighting ships, and 25 submarines were all that lay between Hawaii and
the West Coast and a large Japanese fleet that had yet to suffer a significant
defeat."[6]

As the Japanese began to position their forces, it appeared that the main
attack would be in one of two geographic regions—the Aleutian Island chain
and Midway Island. By reading Japanese mail, the intelligence community felt
the attack against the Aleutians was a diversionary tactic and that the main attack would be in the area of Midway Island. Admiral Nimitz, the Pacific Fleet
commander, believed the intelligence analysis, positioned his forces accordingly, and the rest is history. The Battle of Midway became the turning point
for U.S. forces in the Pacific.

SIGINT STUFF

The second prong in my strategy was to get tutored by the CSG guys concerning that SIGINT stuff. I knew their watch standers wrote those reports, but if
I was going to be a good watch officer, I still needed to know what the stuff
was all about. My bosses would hold me accountable for all of the intelligence
reporting on my watch, even the SIGINT stuff. According to the official NSA
website, "SIGINT is a category of intelligence that includes transmissions
associated with communications, radars, and weapons systems used by our
adversaries."[7]

I made appointments with the CSG day workers and took copious notes as
they tutored me on the ins and outs of SIGINT. I will never be able to thank
these individuals enough for taking the time to help me out. All of the CSG
folks looked out for me, but my three primary mentors were Chief Bob Baker,
Air Force Master Sergeant Frank Cotton, and Chief John Beard. I learned that
SIGINT has two major categories: communications intelligence (COMINT)
and electronic intelligence (ELINT). Chief Baker taught me about COMINT
and its various forms, Chief Beard taught me ELINT, and Master Sergeant
Cotton taught me about figuring out how to use all intelligence sources to
track Soviet aircraft. These guys were able to break it down into baby talk so
I could understand it. They made sure I understood the "so what" factor of
SIGINT.

For instance, you can learn a lot about a country's military intentions by studying how they are communicating. "The organization of a radio network and the manner in which messages are passed over this network reflect troop disposition, command relationships, and impending movements and preparations for military activity; therefore, an analysis of net structure, traffic contacts and patterns, traffic volumes, and similar communications features is of considerable assistance in building up a complete intelligence picture."[8]

Using my Midway example, when the naval intelligence officers went to Admiral Chester Nimitz with their estimate that Midway would be the main objective of the Japanese attack, the admiral initially questioned that conclusion. His intelligence staff gave him the background on how they came to that view. "In the spring of 1942, Japanese intercepts began to make references to a pending operation in which the objective was designated as 'AF' . . . Nimitz's fleet intelligence officer, believed 'AF' might be Midway since they had seen 'A' designators assigned to locations in the Hawaiian islands. Based on the information available, logic dictated that Midway would be the most probable place for the Japanese navy to make its next move."[9]

To give Nimitz further proof, the commanding officer of Midway was ordered to send a message in the clear saying he had some problems with his water distillation. Shortly after the transmission, an intercepted Japanese intelligence report indicated that "AF is short of water."

HF/DF AND ELINT
The CSG guys also educated me about high-frequency direction finding (HF/DF). Basically it involves getting a geographic fix on a radio transmission. This is the "idea of using two or more radio receivers to find the bearings of a radio transmitter and with the use of simple triangulation, find the approximate position of the transmitter that had been known and used since the invention of wireless communication."[10]

World War II provided me with lots of real-life examples for understanding this concept. "The Royal Navy . . . was the first to design an apparatus that could take bearings on the high-frequency radio transmitters employed by the German U-boats. Numerous shore-based installations were constructed on both sides of the Atlantic. . . . When the U-boats reported home . . . the HF/DF could get bearings on the approximate position of the boat. . . . In 1942 the allies began to install HF/DF equipment on ships. . . . After 1942 dozens of U-boats were sunk shortly afterward, being fixed after transmitting a radio message home."[11]

Electronic intelligence (ELINT) was also a major intelligence source. Chief John Beard was a walking encyclopedia on the subject. I had gained a rudimentary understanding of ELINT during my first job but did not have the depth of understanding I would need as a watch officer. "The earliest of the ELINT targets were World War II air defense radar systems. The objective was to gather sufficient information to identify the location and operating characteristics of the radars and then to circumvent or neutralize them during bombing raids." [12]

Early in my time at FOSIF, some NSA guys came around to brief us on a new system called *Classic Wizard*. Basically it was satellites collecting maritime related ELINT.[13] In *The Admiral's Advantage*, Ford and Rosenberg state, "By far the most significant innovation during the 1970s was the arrival of a new ELINT collection system in the autumn of 1976 . . . it soon allowed analysts to track virtually all ships and other ELINT 'emitters' at sea on a near-real-time basis . . . ELINT collection and analysis improved to such an extent that individual Soviet units could be tracked through entire deployments by following the radiation emitted by their navigation and surface-search radar sets."[14] Chief Beard was so knowledgeable on this stuff I nicknamed him The Wiz.

Other intelligence sources I had to get up to speed on included imagery intelligence (IMINT). I was familiar with the capabilities of imagery taken by aircraft, as we had taken lots of pictures of intelligence targets with our P3-C aircraft during my first assignment. There were lots of other military aircraft that took pictures of intelligence targets and sent out reports, like the U-2 and SR-71. I needed to become familiar with all of them.

In 1976, the intelligence community launched a space-based imagery system called KH-11.[15] The United States had other older systems, but the significance of the KH-11 over the older systems was it "could return its imagery in 'near real time.' . . . The KH-11's optical system converted images into electronic signals that were transmitted to elliptically orbiting relay satellites and back to a ground station for near-instantaneous reconstruction."[16]

If that wasn't enough, NOSIC, the OSIS node in the Washington, DC, area was working on developing a data base "correlating specific sound characteristics with specific . . . submarines, a process that became known as hull-toemitter correlation (HULTEC).[17] This had a powerful "so what" factor as well. For example, if you have intelligence that Yankee ballistic missile submarine (SSBN) A is leaving port and you know two months ago that particular submarine returned home from a six-month deployment off of the U.S. West Coast, then you know it's most likely that the submarine will be doing local training. If it has been operating at its home port for a long time, it may be en route to the U.S. West Coast, so you'd want to alert the 7th Fleet so they can get some military assets out to track it.

My head was already spinning, but I decided to add more hours to my training. As mentioned earlier, before you could head up a team you had to learn each position. I thought and still do think that is an excellent way to do business. The challenge was that the organization was so short-handed that you didn't get much guidance in the actual mechanics of your job during your training. The watch standers didn't get much vacation time, so having an extra body on your team, even one in a training status, was an opportunity to give people much-needed time off. Typically a trained watch member would spend one watch string showing you how to do a particular job, then he or she would take off for a couple of weeks for a well-earned rest and leave you on your own. If you didn't get it while the person was showing you the ropes, you had a rocky couple of weeks ahead of you.

MASTERING THE ART OF WRITING NEWS ARTICLES

The position I had the hardest time with was the one responsible for writing the news articles. In college and graduate school, they teach you how to write in an academic style. It's been my experience that the military writes more in the style of journalists. I had taken a journalism course in high school but, combined with my lack of knowledge of intelligence sources, I struggled mightily to do this aspect of the job.

I had to learn how to make the article pertinent to the needs of the warfighter. The admiral and his staff didn't want to read a book every day, so what they received had to be brief and to the point. I had to learn how to analyze developing situations and estimate what military units might do the next hour, the next few hours, and the next twenty-four hours and then report it in a way that gave the admiral and his staff everything they needed to know to handle the situation. The mantra was to cover what happened yesterday, what's happening today, and what's going to happen tomorrow and include it in each report.

Jack was a super teacher, but because of the intense demands of his job, he couldn't babysit me for the entire eight hours of his shift, so we came up with the perfect solution. One of the other watch officers, Chris "Corky" Corkill, invited me to also stand watch with his team; that way I could sit sidesaddle with his writer/analyst and ask questions. It was one of the best moves I could have made. Corky's team came on immediately after the team I was doing my official training with. It meant I was working a double shift and didn't get much rest, but that didn't matter to me. Corky was a walking encyclopedia on intelligence watch standing and freely shared all sorts of information with me. I became obsessed with wanting to learn everything possible about my new job. I also continued to spend a lot of my "off time" talking with the resident experts on various aspects of both Soviet and U.S. military warfare. The hard work paid off, and I was rewarded and given my own team.

I'M A WATCH OFFICER!

Once I finished my training and became a watch officer, my real rite of passage began. This was the toughest but ultimately the most satisfying time of my early professional life. The situations I faced in my first assignment paled in comparison. My bosses only cared about what was between my ears and that the analysis that came out of my team was timely and accurate. There was no quarter given if you failed to live up to their high expectations. If you or a member of your team failed in some area, you were verbally beaten about the head and shoulders. There was no praising in public or criticizing in private. They yelled at you in front of anyone. This wasn't about sparing feelings, it was all about providing the warfighter with the most relevant, timely, and accurate information available. It was all about support to the mission.

I had to get my ego and personal feelings out of the way. I learned when I dropped the ball not to expect my bosses to stop in the midst of some intense crisis, give me a hug, wipe away my tears, and say everything will be all right. Their attitude was to verbally kick you in the butt and tell you to shake off the mistake, get back up, and hit the watch floor again running, always giving your absolute best.

Essentially, what you were expected to do was account for what every Soviet military unit was doing each and every day, write it up in a newspaper-style bulletin, and write spot reports on late-breaking events. For the most part, the Soviets didn't have a lot of their naval and air forces deployed far away from their home base. The Soviet military readiness philosophy stressed being ready to deploy for combat on short notice.

As stated in NIE 11-15, "The Soviet navy emphasizes maintenance and in port/in area training rather than extended at sea operations."[18] NIE 11-15 was the first intelligence publication I saw that indicated the Soviets saw their navy as more defensive than offensive. I'll talk more about it in later chapters but essentially the number one mission of the Soviet navy was to protect their ballistic missile submarine force. (NIE stands for National Intelligence Estimate. According to the CIA website "A National Intelligence Estimate (NIE) is the most authoritative written judgment concerning a national security issue prepared by the Director of Central Intelligence. Unlike 'current intelligence' products, which describe the present, most NIEs forecast future developments and many address their implications for the United States. NIEs cover a wide range of issue—from military to technological to economic to political trends.")[19]

As a result, most of the Soviet units operated close to their home ports unless they were conducting their annual training exercises. The watch also spent a lot of mental energy keeping track of all of the Soviet submarines, but particularly their SSBNs. Even if we had no recent information on a submarine's location, we were expected to provide an educated guess of where it was.

Another big challenge was keeping track of the huge amount of aircraft the Soviets had in their Pacific Theater inventory. If they were flying, we had to track them geographically. The concern was that at any time they could leave their own air space and do a simulated attack or reconnaissance on one of our carriers. Aircraft carrier commanders wanted plenty of warning, so if the Soviets were flying a lot of aircraft, there were lots of reports. This was in addition to normally scheduled reports. I remember one time I ran to the lady's room right next to the watch floor and had one of my male watch team members follow me in and stick a message under the stall for me to review. We all knew the consequences of not providing the fleet with enough warning. At a minimum you were screamed and yelled at; at a maximum you would be fired. If that happened, your Navy career was over. None of us was willing to let that happen.

ALWAYS PREPARED FOR THE COLD WAR TO GO HOT

A few times a year the Soviets would try to sneak out and conduct major exercises in international waters. It was our job to recognize when it was happening so we could alert the 7th Fleet. The concern was that even though it was a Cold War, it could get hot without notice. We liked to monitor the exercises because it also gave us tremendous insight into how the Soviets would use their forces in an actual war. Generally speaking, military units train like they will fight. The Soviets would use exercises to test out their newest weapons, so we hoped to get some new intelligence on ranges and other operating characteristics of their military hardware.

At the end of each eight-hour watch we had something called a watch turnover. This was a formal presentation that was given to the oncoming watch. Your bosses as well as representatives from other military commands and any visiting VIPs would attend. It was very similar to the evening news on television in that you'd summarize what happened in the preceding eight hours. There was one major difference in that it was pretty standard that you'd undergo an intense grilling from your bosses like, "Why do you say that?" "What evidence do you have?" "Have you checked with other analysts from other organizations?" "Have we seen this type of activity before? When?" Heaven help you if you couldn't back up your report because you hadn't done your homework. You'd be yelled at and told to not leave your post until you sent out a revised report. No touchy feely political correctness here. Just get the job done and done right.

There were very good reasons for this intense treatment. First and foremost, this was the intelligence version of marine boot camp or Seal training, a process designed to develop and train an elite intelligence professional. Second, it may have been called a Cold War, but the potential for escalation into a hot crisis was very real. You didn't want to start a crisis through misinterpretation of information or miss the indicators that a crisis was developing. The day workers were the back up. They read all of the intelligence, and if they didn't agree with what you sent out, they would send out a revised report. All watch officers considered that a blow to our professional pride, so we constantly struggled to do the best job possible so that would not happen.

INTELLIGENCE IS AN ART, NOT A SCIENCE

This is where I learned that intelligence was an art not an exact science. We might have had a lot of high-tech intelligence collectors, but rarely did we have a 100 percent idea of what was going on or enough evidence to back it up in a court of law. We were lucky if we had enough information to give us a 40 percent certainty of what was really going on. We constantly struggled to do the best job possible so that the warfighters could make smart decisions for their military strategy. We had to be able to tell when a particular nation was merely training or if they were getting ready to attack.

Our bosses were chosen for their position because they were considered the best of the best in the naval intelligence profession. All of the watch officers were handpicked for the job by the senior members of the naval intelligence community; therefore, we were also considered the best of the best among the upcoming junior officers. During training, our bosses constantly drilled into our heads the serious nature of our job and the extreme challenges we faced in providing the warfighters with the best information possible.

THANK YOU OH GREAT MASTER OF OPINTEL

After I'd been on the job a few months, Commander Hegerman was promoted to captain and moved on to a new assignment as head of the Naval Criminal Investigative Service (NCIS) in Japan. He was replaced by another impressive individual, Commander Ted Sheafer. I didn't realize it or fully appreciate it at the time, but he would go out of his way to make sure I became one of the best Intelligence Watch officers ever. I am forever grateful to the tough love approach he took with me. He was brilliant and a master of OPINTEL. There were five key traits he beat into my head during this phase of my training:

1. the necessity to gain geographic/regional expertise
2. the need for understanding the concept of all-source analysis
3. the need for competitive analysis
4. the importance of collaboration with other intelligence agencies
5. the relevance of analysis to the decision makers

Geographic/Regional Expertise

One of the failures of the intelligence community and something they were always working hard to correct was the lack of a sustained program to educate their analysts. As I said earlier, it was generally on-the-job training with few opportunities to get advanced training or degrees. Whatever education or expertise you initially brought to the intelligence community was generally all the formal training you had. It was up to you to figure out how to make time in your busy job schedule to take additional courses or do professional research. In the small amount of off time I had, I continued my mentoring sessions with the CSG guys as well as studying any books on World War II that I could get my hands on.

Commander Sheafer taught me that as an intelligence analyst it was vitally important that I become skilled at discovering the goals and objectives of our country's potential friends and adversaries as well as strive to understand their history and determine their view of the world. I remember at one point I was on watch and he came and asked me to look closer at what the Soviets were doing with their military that day. He felt they were up to no good, so my team and I looked closely at everything but didn't see that anything unusual was going on. When I went into his office to give him my results, he said, "I wanted it to be true too bad. Watch out for that. Never let your own biased world view get in the way of what is actually going on. Keep checking the facts." In other words, don't let your personal biases determine the conclusions you make. Just because you're not getting along with or don't trust a country doesn't mean they are always up to no good.

All-Source Analysis

To do successful intelligence analysis, it is necessary to gain an understanding of the sources and methods of retrieval involved. For example, when a U.S. Navy ship is being refueled at sea, it sails parallel to the tanker; they call it underway replenishment. When the Soviets refuel at sea, the tanker sails in front of the navy ship with fuel lines going from the stern of the tanker to the bow of the ship it's refueling. I can't tell you how many intelligence reports I've gotten over the years saying a Soviet navy ship had broken down and was being towed home when in reality it was actually involved in a refueling maneuver.

Competitive Analysis

Competitive analysis is the concept of exploring several hypotheses to analyze an event, and it involves checking with other organizations to compare notes on late-breaking events. One of the first days I was assigned my own watch team I got an intelligence report that a North Korean submarine was operating in the southern Sea of Japan. It looked to me like it was heading out into the East China Sea. I thought, "Oh no, I've got a major crisis on my hands. A North Korean submarine is running wild! This must be the start of a crisis."

Commander Sheafer pounded into our heads that if we thought there was a crisis going on to be sure and check with other intelligence analysts before we send out a report. If it was a fast-moving event like an aircraft, send out an initial report stating the facts, but throw in a phrase like "analysis continues" until you have a better idea of the significance of the event.

I did have the presence of mind to call up the Intelligence Watch office at FOSIC Pac (The Pacific Fleet's OSIS watch) and ask him if he'd seen the intelligence report. I told him I was sending out a report to the fleet. I'll always remember his words: "I can't tell you not to, but I think you should wait. I don't believe the report. There is nothing going on in the world that would indicate or cause the North Koreans to deploy a submarine to the Pacific." I disagreed and decided to send out the report. Later we received verification that indeed the FOSIC Pac guy was right, and it was a faulty report. But in the meantime, the 7th Fleet had reacted by sending out military units to look for it. When your analysis is proven wrong, the Pacific Fleet yells at the 7th Fleet, who yells at FOSIF Boss, who yells at me.

I should have done a competitive analysis which means:

1. Call the Intelligence Watch at U.S. Naval Forces Korea. They were the region experts on the North Korean navy. They would have had an excellent grasp on what was normal and not normal and would have known the likelihood of the North Koreans deploying a submarine outside of the Sea of Japan.
2. Have my CSGer call the NSA. The NSA maintained a twenty-four hours a day, seven days a week Intelligence Watch. Ask if they had any intelligence suggesting that the North Koreans were deploying a submarine out of area.
3. Call the Defense Intelligence Agency, who also maintains a twenty-four hours a day, seven days a week Intelligence Watch. Ask them what they thought.
4. Have my watch team recheck all incoming information to see if there was other intelligence supporting this.

All of this calling around really doesn't take much time and in the long run, it's better to get your facts straight first than to send military forces off on a wild goose chase.

Collaboration

In spite of the impression given by the media, there has actually been quite a lot of collaboration on analysis within the intelligence community. At times the problem has been the huge volume of information available, not the lack thereof. At the start of every watch, we were expected to check in with analysts from other intelligence organizations. We'd make sure that none of us had information that the other had not seen. As your watch progressed, you were to stay in frequent communication with these other organizations.

Computers were a tremendous help with this. In the mid-1970s, we had such technology as instant messaging, making it easy to contact other analysts. I would also frequently call up the organizations actually putting out the intelligence reports and ask them how good they thought the information was. There were five ground stations associated with the Classic Wizard system: Diego Garcia, British Indian Ocean Territory; Guam; Adak, Alaska; Winter Harbor, Maine; and Edzell, Scotland.[20] All of them sent out tons of intelligence reports. Officially the organizations came under the NSA, so my CSG on watch was supposed to talk with them, not me. But they were usually so busy they didn't mind if I called. It got so that I'd get a report that seemed a little off and I'd call and get, "Gail, we were expecting your call and we were just putting out a correction to the report." I made a lot of great friends with people that I never got to meet face to face, like the people at the NSA.

RELEVANCE OF ANALYSIS TO THE DECISION MAKERS

One of the key principals Commander Sheafer stressed was that intelligence exists only to support the decision maker. Your goal was to provide information to him or her in the manner needed and in the time they needed it to affect the decision-making process. I like the way General Colin Powell described what he needed from intelligence officers: "Tell me what you know. Tell me what you don't know, and then tell me the significance of it for me." In all of the training programs I've set up over the years and in all the mentoring I've done, I too have stressed this vitally important point.

How do you put this all together to do your job as a watch officer? See the supplements at the end of this chapter for some real examples of how this all works.

NOT FOR THE FAINT OF HEART

This was not a job for the faint of heart. We were trained to always give 110 percent. We learned that ours was a lonely job, as we could never discuss the details of the job with friends and family. Intelligence was often a thankless job where we only got noticed when something went wrong. All of this made for high stress, but I think the end results in my growth as an intelligence professional made it all worthwhile. I remember the bosses telling all the watch officers that because of what we were learning and the work ethic we were developing, we would all one day rise to the rank of captain.

Since the naval intelligence community only picks one person to reach the rank of admiral every two or three years, becoming a captain is usually the highest rank you can expect to attain. That rank seemed pretty far away and unattainable for most of us; however, of the three other watch officers during my time there, one made admiral; one became commanding officer of the Maritime Intelligence Center, which is the number two position in all of naval intelligence; and then there's me. Commander Sheafer not only went on to make admiral but became the intelligence officer for the Joint Chiefs of Staff.

Even though I was tired and stressed a lot of the time, I've never enjoyed a job more or had more responsibility. As a young lieutenant, I had far more responsibility and leeway than a lot of senior military intelligence officers do today. The caliber of my coworkers was exceptional, plus they were a whole lot of fun. Humor was frequently used to bring the stress level down, and practical jokes ran rampant.

During one of my night watches, we were really working hard on a crisis when I thought I heard a woman's voice screaming, but the pace was so intense I immediately forgot about it and pressed on. Later I went into the ladies' room and found one of the communication ladies dabbing at small spots of blood on her arms. Seems she had fallen asleep at work and her coworkers had taped her to the chair while she was sleeping. Lest you think this was mean, falling asleep on watch is a court martial offense in the Navy. I'm sure she was happier being the victim of a practical joke than facing jail time.

My favorite practical joke revolved around a little black doll I gave to The Wiz as a farewell gift. The neat thing about this doll was you could feed it real baby food. Her lips would actually suck the food in, and then the food would filter through her stomach and into her diaper. I discovered you could stick a lit cigarette in her mouth and that the sucking motions of her mouth would actually have the doll puffing on the cigarette. That night when The Wiz came in for our last watch together, there stood "Little Gail," cigarette in mouth with smoke coming out of her diaper. From that time on, whenever visiting dignitaries came for a tour, they were likely to find "Little Gail" around doing her thing. A few years ago I ran into The Wiz while visiting the NSA. He said "Little Gail" was gone now; her guts had finally given out, but she had a good run.

MAKING THE GRADE
In spite of everything, I constantly wondered if I was making the grade. We never really knew until our performance evaluations came out. I was devastated to learn I was ranked dead last in terms of professional competence among the watch officers. To be considered for good follow-on assignments and future promotions, it's crucial to do really well on these performance evaluations. I figured there was no way I would be able to get promoted with a grade like that, so I seriously considered quitting the Navy and going to the University of Denver to finish my masters work. After giving it some serious thought, I decided to wait and see what my follow-on assignment would be and then make my final decision.

If the OSIS masters perceived that you were performing well, you got a good follow-on assignment, if not you were assigned a mediocre or dead-end job. For my follow-on assignment, I was chosen to put together the Navy's first course on how to do OSIS-type intelligence analysis. I would be assigned to the staff at the Naval Intelligence Training Center at Lowry Air Force Base in Denver, Colorado. I was to develop the course that would be used to teach new intelligence officers the skill sets needed to become "all-source" intelligence analysts. Initial work on the course had been done, but they wanted me to more fully develop it.

I never would have been sent to that job if my command did not think I was a superstar. After the Navy offered me that assignment, I decided to stay on. Because the school was located in Denver, I would still be able to finish my master's degree in international studies at the University of Denver. I was very glad I had taken the time to wait instead of making a decision based on my initial response to the performance evaluations. Note to self: Don't make snap, emotionally based decisions.

I'm forever grateful to the OSIS masters. This was only my first encounter with this group of geniuses. I would meet several others along my professional journey, and after each encounter I would emerge somewhat battered but a stronger, smarter intelligence professional. It is only in recent times that material from World War II has been declassified enabling the brilliant intelligence work done by these men and women to be written about. My hope and expectation is that one day we will be able to fully discuss the Cold War achievements of these OSIS masters, and everyone will probably feel as I do. Guys, well done! Or as we say in the Navy, Bravo Zulu!!!!

Takeaway: Persist through every challenge.

Key principles I learned about persistence:

1. I had to get my ego and personal feelings out of the way.
2. I learned when I dropped the ball not to expect my bosses to stop in the midst of some intense crisis to give me a hug, wipe away my tears, and say everything will be all right.
3. I learned that naval intelligence was an art, not a science.
4. I learned not to make snap decisions based on an emotional response to what I perceived as bad news.
5. I'm forever grateful to the OSIS masters.

CHAPTER 3 SUPPLEMENT

Example 1

As mentioned in this chapter, during the height of the Cold War, the Soviet Union typically kept two nuclear submarines armed with nuclear tipped missiles off of our East Coast and two off our West Coast. One day, with no advance notice, they increased the number to four and five off of each coast. We tried to figure out what was going on using all of the principles the OSIS masters had taught us. My graduate background in international studies, along with the mentoring by the CSGers, gave me the skills to determine there were no foreign affairs problems or crises that might have caused this situation. The Soviet military did not appear to be in an increased defense alert status nor were there any new defense issues that seemed to be the cause of this increase. The U.S. military was not conducting an exercise that they might have been reacting to. There was extensive collaboration within the intelligence community.

We sent a report to the decision makers that, based on analysis of all intelligence sources, the rest of the Soviet forces were not on alert or in an increased defense posture, so we did not believe an attack on the United States was imminent. We engaged in continuing competitive analysis and couldn't figure it out until one young air force captain came up with the solution.

It seemed that the Soviet Union was doing maintenance on some of their land-based ballistic missiles and had apparently deployed more submarines equipped with nuclear missiles to keep the number of nuclear weapons aimed on U.S. targets the same in case the Cold War went hot. Imagine what could have happened if the intelligence community had misread the Soviet intentions. Based on our analysis and recommendations, the U.S. military didn't go on alert or launch a preemptive strike. This is only one of countless events that never made it to the public eye because the intelligence analysts got it right.

Example 2

It was a Sunday, and I came in for a day watch expecting an uneventful shift. The Soviets may not have been big on God, but they rarely did much with their military on Sundays. As I leisurely reviewed the intelligence traffic, I suddenly felt the hairs stand up on the back of my neck. It looked like for some reason they were flying reconnaissance aircraft. My team and I sprung into action, calling up the NSA and other intelligence agencies. We also started to get intelligence reports that when fused together indicated the Soviets were not only flying reconnaissance aircraft out of the Sea of Japan and into the South China Sea but were also deploying a large number of naval ships from Vladivostok, their fleet headquarters. Ultimately they would deploy thirteen ships plus their fleet flagship, the cruiser *Admiral Senyavin*.[21]

There was one major current event I hadn't taken into account as I began my watch. The day before, February 17, 1979, the Chinese had invaded Vietnam with "100,000 to 170,000 Chinese soldiers supported by tanks, artillery, and aircraft . . . 'to teach the Vietnamese a lesson.'" I had forgotten that about three or four months earlier the Soviet Union had signed a Peace and Co-operation Treaty with Vietnam. As I remembered all this, I wondered if the Soviet Union was going to intervene militarily.

I didn't consider it a major concern to U.S. interests because as near as I knew the Chinese were mad at them over "something" the Vietnamese had done in Cambodia. I had watched the events unfold over the preceding weeks but didn't see any threats to U.S. interests and had a "so what" attitude as my watch started. We had extra people from the day workers who were putting out summaries of the Chinese/Vietnamese situation, so I had not expected to be involved. Not one of my better analytical conclusions.

After doing all the steps Commander Sheafer had drummed into me, my initial take was that it didn't look like the Soviets were going to enter a conflict but were probably going to do diplomatic trash talk and flex their military muscles to back it up. That was just my initial call, as it was very common for the United States to send an aircraft carrier to a region to "show the flag" during a crisis. So it didn't seem out of the realm of possibility to me that the Soviets would do something similar.

My team and I put out our initial reports on the Soviet movements. I didn't think the Soviets would intervene militarily, but I also knew I could be wrong so in my reports I focused on what we knew. I relied on the Chinese and Vietnamese experts in the intelligence community for the in-depth geo-political analysis. We would spend the next few days and weeks watching the situation closely. The conflict only lasted a month, but we were even busier than usual as we tracked this potential flashpoint.

NOTES

1. Available at www.dictionary-quotes.com/our-greatest-glory-is.

2. Dennis Kimbro and Napoleon Hill, *Think and Grow Rich: A Black Choice.* (New York: Fawcett Crest, 1991), 146–147.

3. Available at http://www.c7f.navy.mil/about.htm.

4. Christopher Ford and David Rosenberg, *The Admiral's Advantage: U.S. Navy Operational Intelligence in World War II and the Cold War.* (Annapolis, MD: United States Naval Institute Press, 2005), pp. 2–3.

5. Patrick D. Weadon, National Security Agency Historical Publications, "Battle of Midway." Available at http://www.nsa.gov/about/cryptologic_heritage/center_crypt_history/publications/battle_midway.shtml

6. Weadon, National Security Agency Historical Publications, "Battle of Midway," p. 10.

7. National Security Agency, "Signals Intelligence." Available at www.nsa.gov/sigint/index.shtml.

8. Lambros D. Callimahos, "Introduction to Traffic Analysis." Declassified by NSA 1-7-2008 pursuant to E.O. 12958 as amended, FOIA Case#51551. At http://www.nsa.gov/public_info/_files/cryptologic_spectrum/intro_traffic_analysis.pdf

9. Weadon, National Security Agency Historical Publications, "Battle of Midway," p. 2.

10. Wikipedia, "Huff-Duff." Available at http://en.wikipedia.org/wiki/Huff-Duff, p. 1.

11. Uboat.net, "HF/DF: The High-Frequency Direction Finder." Available at www.uboat.net/allies/technical/hfdf.htm, pp. 1–2.

12. Jeffrey T. Richelson, *The U.S. Intelligence Community*, 5th ed. (Boulder, CO: Westview Press, 2008), p. 211.

13. Richelson, *The U.S. Intelligence Community*, p. 215.

14. Ford and Rosenberg, *The Admiral's Advantage*, pp. 61–62.

15. Richelson, *The U.S. Intelligence Community*, p. 177.

16. Richelson, *The U.S. Intelligence Community*, p. 178.

17. Ford and Rosenberg, *The Admiral's Advantage*, p. 62.

18. Director Central Intelligence, *NIE 11-15-82/DSoviet Naval Strategy and Programs Through the 1990s* (Washington, DC: Director Central Intelligence, 19 October 1982), 13–14.

19. Available at www.foia.cia.gov/soviet_estimates.asp.

20. Richelson, *The U.S. Intelligence Community*, p. 216.

21. "A War of Angry Cousins." *Time* 113, no. 10 (March 5, 1979). Available at www.time.com/time/printout/0,8816,916622,00.html.

4

Faith

God is a very present help in time of trouble.

—*Psalm 46:1*[1]

But looking at them, Jesus said, "With men it is impossible, but not with God; for with God all things are possible."

—*Mark 10:27*[2]

And all things whatever you ask in prayer, believing, you will receive.

—*Matthew 21:22*[3]

I have been driven many times to my knees by the overwhelming conviction that I had no where else to go. My own wisdom and that of all about me seemed insufficient for the day.

—*Abraham Lincoln*[4]

As I look back over the ups and downs of my life and my career, I don't believe my life really started to move on a more even keel until I started consciously working with and trying to understand spiritual principles. In retrospect, it's very apparent to me that God guided and protected me as I pursued my life-long dream of a career in naval intelligence. It's also painfully apparent to me that at times I blocked my own blessings through ignorance, a lack of faith, and an underdeveloped spiritual awareness.

I've always envied people who say they've had a sudden flash of insight concerning God that caused their life to immediately change in wondrous ways. That's certainly not been the case with me. My religious and spiritual growth came in spurts and generally happened right after some tremendous low point in my life. I've learned the hard way that successful work habits and a magnificent obsession with your dream will only take you so far. One of the greatest discoveries of my life was the realization that if I really wanted to soar, I had to learn to tap into and develop my relationship with God.

By working on becoming more spiritually aware, I found I was better able to recognize when God was helping and guiding me. Knowing I was not alone gave me the strength and emotional stamina to successfully deal with crises as they came up. Instead of always feeling helpless and hopeless, I began overcoming each problem that came my way in a steadier more forward-moving way. I believe by sharing this portion of my story I can help others to discover this important truth earlier in their life's walk and not have to suffer the setbacks and personal struggles I did.

MY SPIRITUAL ROOTS

My spiritual journey began shortly after birth as my mom followed her own family's tradition of ensuring all her children attended church and Sunday school until they reached the age of twenty-one. We all knew her stand on this, as she counteracted any of our protests by saying, "After you turn twenty-one, you can do what you want, but you will know and learn about God as long as you're in my house."

My dad, on the other hand, was not a churchgoer. In fact, it was hard to know what he really thought, as he seemed to gain great pleasure in taking the opposing view on whatever subject we were discussing just to get a heated interchange going with anyone who dared to take him on. When my mom hosted the minister for dinner, Dad would spend the evening asking the minister such challenging questions as, "Adam and Eve had two sons, Cain and Abel. One brother killed the other. So where did all the rest of the people in the world come from?"

The one time I did directly ask my dad about religion, he got this sad expression on his face and proceeded to tell me a story from his childhood. "Your Uncle Sam, Aunt Bea, and I lived with our Grandmother on her farm in Alabama, while my mom was getting herself set up in New Jersey with a job and a home for us there. Times on the farm were hard, and one day we ran out of food and had no wood or coal to warm our house. When I went to bed that night, I prayed hard for God to help us and give us something to eat. When I got up the next morning, there was still no food in the house. That was the day I lost my faith." Then he got up and left the room indicating that was the end of the discussion. I was puzzled and wanted to question him more, but out of love and respect I never pursued the subject again with him.

Dad always said his favorite movie was *A Razor's Edge,* starring Tyrone Power. Power played a character who had survived fighting in World War I. He spent the rest of his life traveling the world on a quest trying to find a meaning for his existence. He wondered why he survived when so many others had died. At the end of the picture, Power's character had found peace. He was working as a common seaman on a merchant ship. My dad often wistfully described the look of utter peace and serenity on the character's face as he worked on the deck in the midst of a severe storm, which is the final scene in the movie. I've seen the picture several times and agreed with my dad about the powerful effect. As I write this, I can still see the expression of bliss on the actor's face.

Years later, I would remember those conversations and the movie scene as my brother and I signed the hospital paperwork for my father's body to be transferred to a funeral home after he died of lung cancer. The nurse asked if we wanted to view his body, and though I wanted to remember him as he was when he was alive, I said yes. As I looked at my father for the last time, my grief and guilt were suddenly replaced with an overwhelming peace. The expression on his face was the same one that I'd seen on Tyrone Power in that movie long ago—a combination of serenity and bliss. What wonders had he seen with his final breath? I thanked God right then and there for giving me that gift of peace as I said goodbye to my beloved father.

MY SPIRITUAL TURNING POINT

After leaving home, I seldom went to church, as I just didn't see the relevance of the far away God I had learned about as a child. The real spiritual turning point for me was when I became exposed to the concept of "practical Christianity." In simple terms, it's more than just attending church on Sunday. It involves using spiritual principles to help us deal with the everyday challenges of life, not just when a crisis occurs. This was a new way of thinking for me, and it proved to be the life-changing spiritual experience I was seeking.

Many times my mom had tried to tell me that God was everywhere, but I wasn't listening or didn't understand what she was trying to tell me. She said in her mother's time it was the custom for a child to attend church but not actually join until they had a personal experience with God. I knew my grandmother had a life-changing religious experience with God in the woods one day, but it wasn't until years later that I was able to see the significance and importance of a personal experience with God.

My first conscious exposure to practical Christianity was when a good friend and coworker invited me to attend his family's church in Denver, Colorado. The minister preached a lot of sermons revolving around faith and the power of prayer. I enjoyed his sermons, but I didn't see any major changes happening in my life. What I didn't realize then was it would take more than just attending church every Sunday and listening to powerful sermons to bring about the major spiritual awakening and better life circumstances I was seeking. It wasn't until I learned how to use the principles I was being taught on Sunday in my every day life that my life really began to change.

As I said, this minister taught a lot about prayer and faith, so when it was time for me to be reassigned to a new job, I decided to use prayer to ask God for a good assignment. This was going to be a tall order, I thought, even for God. I was at a place where, to advance in my career field, every other assignment had to be operational in nature. The Navy refers to this as sea duty, which means I needed to be assigned to a unit that would be at a homeport, such as Norfolk, Virginia, or San Diego, California, for a year and then operate at an overseas location for six months. At the end of this period, the unit would return to its homeport for another year, at the end of which it would deploy for another six months. This cycle would repeat for a three-year period, and then I would be assigned to what's referred to as shore duty. The outcome of this next assignment would virtually affect not only the next three years of my life but also my future in naval intelligence.

The problem was the Navy didn't know what to do with me. This was 1982, and the law that prohibited women from serving on a ship classified as combatant wouldn't be changed until 1994. The naval intelligence community was as proactive as the law would allow in assigning women to jobs so that they could remain competitive for promotion using assignments that were categorized as "sea duty equivalent." These were jobs in the land-based aviation squadrons or remote overseas locations, but they were few and far between.

LOOKING THROUGH HEAVEN'S EYES

At the time when I needed this good assignment, the Navy had four fleets, the 3rd Fleet, which operated in the Eastern Pacific; the 7th Fleet, which operated in the Western Pacific and Indian Oceans; the 2nd Fleet, which operated in the Atlantic; and the 6th Fleet, which operated in the Mediterranean. Initially, the intelligence community thought they could assign me to the 6th Fleet staff through a legal loophole. The fleet headquarters was onboard a destroyer *Tender*, a ship that was not classified as combatant; however, the admiral turned me down, saying that when he moved his flag (personal location) to a combatant location, I wouldn't be able to go with him. He did not want to be in a situation where a key staff member had to be left behind, leaving him shorthanded. I reminded God that I had asked Him for a good assignment as I continued to pray.

I next asked to be assigned to one of the Navy's land-based aviation squadrons. The P-3 squadrons were out of the question since I had already done that, and it was a first tour job. I hoped that I could be assigned to an EP-3 squadron, which was land-based and focused on intelligence collection. The Navy only had two of these squadrons, and only one opening was available during the time period I was due to be reassigned. As I prayed, I pointed out to God the obvious benefits of this being my next assignment. The job was given to a good friend of mine instead.

I began to waver wondering why my life wasn't getting better now that I had started back going to church and praying. After all, I had prayed asking God for a good assignment, and from my point of view there were no more good options left. I still had a few more lessons to learn on how God sometimes answers our prayers. I was about to learn that God had a sense of humor, as one of my future pastors was fond of saying.

Right about this time, I was requested by name to go to United States Southern Command (SOUTHCOM) stationed in Panama. I was horrified and dismayed. Why didn't I see it as an answer to prayer? First off I hate hot, humid climates, and I have a snake phobia. I'd heard all sorts of horror tales about encounters people stationed there had had with poisonous snakes.

Second, it was not even a Navy command. The military has several organizations that are composed of people from all of the services. These commands are known as Joint Commands. Although multiservice means people from each segment of the military are involved, one of the services usually has the largest number of people and is in charge of one of these Joint Commands. The Army dominated SOUTHCOM with an Army commander in chief and Army personnel in most of the key staff positions. If I'd wanted to be around the Army, I would have joined the Army. Besides, the feeling among many in the Navy was a joint assignment was the kiss of death for your career.

My first reaction was I didn't care if they did ask for me by name, if the Navy really thought highly of me they wouldn't make me go there; however, I later discovered that my view was very shortsighted. God had a blessing in disguise waiting for me within this particular assignment. One of my favorite songs is from the soundtrack for the animated movie *Prince of Egypt*, which tells the story of Moses. The theme of the song is you have to look at your life through heaven's eyes. It is only through a larger view that you can obtain a true perspective of whether the events in your life at any particular time are good or bad. Thankfully, God's ways are not bound by the shortsightedness of His children.

GOD'S WAYS ARE HIGHER THAN MAN'S
God, of course, knew the bigger picture and what was going to happen in the future. In 1982, many did not believe the future of the military was joint warfare. But the 1986 Goldwater-Nichols Act would completely change the way the military did business. Instead of each service operating independently of each other, the military services would be forced to operate more as a team rather than as separate entities moving in sometimes divergent directions. The 1986 act also made Joint Command experience one of the requirements for getting promoted to admiral or general, which ensured they would begin to assign their best and their brightest to these Joint Commands. Joint warfare now consists of all of the services fighting a conflict together as a team under one commander. There's a popular slogan that refers to this: "One Team, One Fight."

Four years before this change came about; I was being educated and prepared to do business in a new way. If I had been spiritually aware, I would have known my prayers for a good assignment had been answered. God works in ways that are mysterious to the human mind. On the surface, my SOUTHCOM assignment appeared not to be a good one, but my attitude of faith should have been, "God, I don't understand why I'm being sent to such an undesirable assignment, but I'm going to walk forward in faith and trust your judgment knowing I'm only looking at the trees but you see the whole forest."

This was the beginning of an educational process for me that would later allow me to excel at providing intelligence support in several major conflicts without the benefit of having served at sea. My prayers for a good assignment had been answered; I just didn't realize it at the time. Joint warfare is how we eventually fought the Gulf War, the war in Kosovo, and many other smaller conflicts. It's also how we're fighting the current crises in Afghanistan and Iraq.

There is a belief among some members of the senior naval intelligence community that says if you never went to sea you can't excel at providing intelligence support because you don't have the right background. I disagree. I would have loved to have gone to sea, but I couldn't because of the legal restrictions. Having several assignments at Joint Commands, however, allowed me to learn and master the concepts that would be used in fighting future conflicts, even without the experience of going to sea.

It's interesting that each time I was sent to a Joint Command, it was during a time when a crisis or war was going on in that command's area of responsibility. During my time at SOUTHCOM, the command was involved in monitoring crises in El Salvador and Nicaragua, as well as the Falklands War.

While assigned to the United States Naval Forces Central Command (NAVCENT), the naval component of United States Central Command (CENTCOM) the crisis with Iraq in the aftermath of the Gulf War heated up. While at the United States Strategic Command (STRATCOM) I was hand-picked for a new position as deputy director of the organization's 500-person Joint Intelligence Center (JIC). I was also placed in charge of intelligence support in which STRATCOM was asked to support other military commands in combat operations. In support of CENTCOM's Operation Desert Fox, my organization provided threat information in support of 415 air-launched cruise missile strikes versus 100 targets in Iraq.

For Operation Allied Force in support of the United States European Command (USEUCOM), my organization was responsible for providing imagery analysis and battle damage assessment for 300 plus targets. The efforts of my organization were much praised by EUCOM and called "masterful" by the Joint Staff in the Pentagon. I was dragged to all of my joint assignments kicking and screaming, but they made me a joint intelligence warrior extraordinaire. In fact, because God had been preparing me every step of the way, my time on active duty as a captain was comparable to any of my naval intelligence peers, and I believe my record reflects this. I believe God knew what was in my future and, even though I couldn't always see it, He was using each assignment to broaden my education and prepare me for the job ahead.

WITH GOD ALL THINGS ARE POSSIBLE

I do have to admit that it took a few years for the good in my Panama situation to sink in, but while there I did have a major spurt in spiritual growth. I had to hit rock bottom for it to happen, though. It was at this point I saw the truth of the biblical quote, "With men it is impossible, but not with God; for with God all things are possible."[5]

I also came to realize that my problems were often a result of my bad attitude. If I thought I had a bad attitude when told I was going to Panama, it only worsened after I arrived. The day I arrived at the airport in Panama, I had a bad case of the flu, the airlines lost my luggage, and the man who picked me up at the airport told me my new command had not made reservations for me with the base housing people as they had said they would. I was sick, only had the clothes on my back, and had no place to live.

The Navy guy, Jim, who met me at the airport, was great, though. After I did the lost luggage paperwork, he took me to his car, where he had a chilled bottle of wine waiting for me. Seeing how sick and discouraged I was, he put me up in his room for the night, and the next day he took me to the housing office, where he bullied them into giving me a place to stay. It was a pigsty and hadn't been cleaned from the previous occupant, but at that point I didn't care. Jim drove me around so I could buy some cleaning supplies, clean sheets, and cold medicine. When I finally got back to my new room, I was so sick I didn't have the energy to put the sheets properly on the bed. I just threw them on top of the bed, swallowed a bunch of medicine, and passed out.

Things marginally improved when I was well enough to go to work, as I found I had been assigned a job that only required about fifteen minutes of effort a day. It seems the intelligence staff was in chaos and being "reorganized."

I saw it as a challenge that gave purpose to my life. I made a few enemies when I started suggesting better ways things could be done, but the bosses liked most of my suggestions and started giving me more responsibilities.

It's my nature that when I see a problem I work to come up with a solution. Sometimes my coworkers thought I had some kind of ulterior motive because of the way I attacked each problem, so I found myself the target of office politics feeling like I did in junior high when the "other kids" didn't like me because I worked hard to get good grades. Over time, I've learned to present new ideas and concepts in a manner that not too many people feel threatened; however, I've also learned that if you're going to break new ground, it's inevitable that you'll make enemies among those people who are not as forward thinking and have an aversion to change. My advice to those like me is keep your heart and intentions pure and stay prayed up. If you do that, you will eventually overcome the backlash.

Unfortunately at this point in my life, I had not learned that lesson. One day someone threw away a bunch of papers I needed to finish writing an important report on the situation in Nicaragua. Earlier in the day, I had told folks not to touch them and that I would be back in the evening to update and send out the report so it would be in Washington, DC, first thing the next morning. One of the "other kids" threw out the papers anyway hoping to get a rise out of me. It did. I called him up at home, cursed him out, and then threw his coffee cup against the wall, breaking it. The seniors in the command figured he was wrong, but I was more in the wrong because of my unprofessional response. I found myself deep in the doghouse with no apparent way out. What a dumb way to end my career.

Feeling sorry for me, my good buddy Jim took me for a picnic at one of the most beautiful spots in the world, a bluff overlooking the Panama Canal. He gave me great advice that day, suggesting I take the energy that I normally put into working and get fit and fabulous. I was overweight at the time and would have to lose weight for the Navy's upcoming physical fitness test anyway. It sounded like a good idea to me, and I certainly didn't have anything else productive to do with my life, so I found an Army guy who agreed to be my personal trainer.

After the first day of my new regimen, I was totally wiped out and feeling very discouraged. I crawled up the stairs to my room and sat in the middle of the floor chugging down ice water. Sweat was pouring off me as I flipped on the TV to take my mind off of myself. There was a religious program on, and I almost switched it off. I didn't like to watch programs like that, figuring those guys where all con men, but for some reason this time, I listened and my life was forever changed.

The show was *The Hour of Power* with Dr. Robert Schuller. His sermon that day was on using prayer to help you with all of your problems. The example he talked about was how he used prayer to help him with a lifelong struggle with his weight. I was glued to the set, not believing this was just a coincidence. I resolved from that moment onward to try prayer again and searched through one of my religious books until I found a good generic prayer that I began to repeat out loud every morning before I went to work. I just prayed to be divinely guided and for everything I did to turn out for the good of myself and others. I didn't address any other specific topics.

PRAYER WORKS

The results were almost immediate and astounding to me. One of my primary critics was suddenly ordered to apologize to me, I lost weight easier than I ever have before, and I found myself no longer in the doghouse at work. In fact, I was chosen to be the command briefer, which entailed giving the commanding general and his staff a current events brief several times a week. I was even allowed to do my own analysis for the presentation, which was very unusual at major commands. For most jobs like this, the briefer is just a mouth piece with a separate analyst who actually writes the briefs. Whenever VIPs, like senators and congressmen visited, I gave them briefings as well.

Some may think this was not the result of prayer and that I would have redeemed myself eventually, but when I was detaching from that command, my boss, a marine colonel, told me he'd been prepared to write me an adverse performance report recommending I be kicked out of the Navy but for some reason changed his mind. His last words to me were, "You done good kid!" I also received a medal that the command normally only awards to someone much more senior than me.

I kept up my daily prayers for the next three years, and my life went fairly smoothly. I had one of my favorite jobs of my whole career during this time— I was assigned to the war gaming staff of the Naval War College in Newport, Rhode Island. It was a great job, great location, and super coworkers.

Even though things were going well, I still felt the need to get deeper yet into understanding my spiritual nature, so I devoured books by Dr. Norman Vincent Peale and Dr. Robert Schuller. I also started reading a monthly magazine put out by a nondenominational religious group and was so impressed with what they taught I decided to see if there was a church of that type near Newport. To my disappointment the nearest church of that particular denomination was in Boston. Even more frustrating was the fact that I was getting ready to be reassigned to Hawaii and, as far as I'd been able to tell, there was no church of that denomination there either. I really wanted a teacher to study with, and I liked what these people were teaching.

WHEN THE STUDENT IS READY, THE TEACHER APPEARS

Shortly before I was due to move to Hawaii, I decided to go up to Boston to attend the church I had found in connection to the magazine. At the beginning of the service, the minister said, "Our opening prayer is written by that dynamic Honolulu, Hawaii minister, the Reverend Helen Street." I was floored! After the service, I went up to the minister and asked him if he could give me any details on the Hawaii church. He said he couldn't but directed me to two other attendees who had just moved from Hawaii and had been members of that church.

My first Sunday in Hawaii I made a beeline for that church. Any doubt I had about the rightness of my choice of churches evaporated immediately. One of my favorite Broadway show tunes is from the show *Flora the Red Menace*, which starred Liza Minnelli. It's called, "A Quiet Thing" and speaks of how happiness often does not come in with bands playing and people cheering. It most often comes in on tiptoe, it's a quiet thing. I have always played that song when something significant has happened in my life, like when I graduated from high school and college. As I walked into church that day, the pianist was playing that song.

I thought my Mother would be upset that I wasn't attending a more traditional church but she was just happy that I had found a spiritual home. She urged me to get involved by attending religious classes and volunteering to do things like ushering. Reverend Helen Street, or Reverend Helen as she was called, was everything I had hoped for and more. She was spiritual but also down to earth and had a great sense of humor. She became a great friend and mentor to me.

She's no longer with us. She died at the end of the Gulf War, but under her tutelage, I grew spiritually by leaps and bounds. She herself lived, ate, and breathed the religious principles she taught. It was from her that I truly learned the tenants of practical Christianity. Reverend Helen called miracles "ordinaries." She said if we really lived the principles in the Bible, miracles would be ordinary occurrences. Another term she used was "rubber duckies." During the week between her classes, she expected us to use the religious principles we were learning in everyday life. At the beginning of class she'd ask the question, "Does anyone have any rubber duckies they'd like to share?"

I heard a lot of great stories in her classes that helped us build our faith. One guy, an avid runner, needed new sneakers. He was experiencing a cash flow problem and couldn't afford to buy them. He also had an interesting issue; one of his feet was larger than the other, so he would need one sneaker in one size and the second in another. One day he was jogging and saw a pair of sneakers in the middle of the road. He picked them up. They were brand new. What really got his attention was each shoe was a different size and they were exactly the sizes he needed.

In another class, one lady said she had prayed for growth. When she went for a scheduled physical and got weighed and measured, she found she had grown one inch taller. I'll always remember Reverend Helen's response to that story: "God is such a giggle." I never asked the lady who told the story, but I'm sure the next time she prayed she asked more specifically for "spiritual" growth.

PRACTICAL CHRISTIANITY

I have to confess that I was slow in putting the principles to work in my life. At first I just sat quietly and soaked everything in, afraid that if I tried and it didn't work I might be tempted to leave the spiritual path. One Saturday I finally decided to pray to God for something specific. Reverend Helen taught that God's love for us was so all-encompassing that He even cared whether we got a parking space in a crowded lot.

The catalyst for trying the principles for me was a dry spot in my social life. I'd been in Hawaii several months and had been so busy at work I hadn't put much time and effort into my social life. Normally I worked on Saturday, but one Saturday for some reason I had the day off and I was at a loss what to do with my time. I went to an early movie, browsed in the bookstore, then wondered what to do with the rest of the day. While driving home I had an epiphany and thought, I've been attending these classes for months and haven't used any of the powerful principles in my own life. I asked myself what I would ideally like to have happen that day and decided to ask for something frivolous. I wanted an incredibly attractive man to call me up and take me to dinner.

I got home and started pacing around thinking that was a silly thing to use as my first application of these principles I had been learning. I was hungry but wondered if I made myself a sandwich would I be showing a lack of faith. Hunger won out, and I made myself a chicken sandwich. By that time it was only about two in the afternoon, and I didn't want to spend the rest of the day staring at the phone, so I decided to take a nap. I was exhausted from the long hours I had been putting in at work, so I slept until about six that evening. I was bummed out when I woke up and discovered the phone hadn't rang.

I decided to take a shower and get ready for bed. As I was walking up the stairs I said, "Well God, I guess this praying for specific things stuff doesn't work." Right at that moment, the phone rang. It was an incredibly attractive man I'd met several weeks earlier. We spent about a half hour talking on the phone. Finally, he asked if I were busy later that evening. I had a town home right on the water and told him we could go sit on the beach.

I decided I would still shower and put on some nicer clothes. As the water was running, I leaned back and said, "God you forgot the dinner part." Right at that instant the phone rang again. The guy said, "Instead of the beach would you like to go to dinner?" Reverend Helen loved that story. She asked for permission to tell it in church. I expressed concern that some people might be offended because I prayed for something so superficial. She said, "Not that bunch!" She was right. There were a couple of people who didn't like it, but most people thought it was funny.

THE REAL TEST

The real test for me, though, came when I failed to be selected for promotion to commander. I'll go into more detail in a later chapter but will briefly explain where my spiritual growth came into play during this critical junction in my journey. For officers, the military is an up or out organization. If you don't get promoted at a certain point, you have to get out. You have two chances for promotion. If you fail to get selected one year, you will come up for promotion again the next year, but if you don't make it that time, you're history. On top of that, it's extremely rare to make it on the second try because of the intense competition.

When my time came up, I was expected to make it and, in fact, the people in naval personnel had been working on my next assignment under that assumption. I felt like my world had come to an end when the news came down that I had not made it. It was like thinking you were in a happy marriage and suddenly your spouse asks for a divorce.

I decided to go for a counseling session with Reverend Helen. She was great. She let me do my crying thing, and after that we prayed that I would beat the odds and get promoted the next year. The interesting thing was not only did I get promoted, but I also assumed the rank as if I had promoted on time. I also stayed on the career fast track. I was handpicked and pulled out of my assignment eighteen months early to go to Korea and head up intelligence support for the 1988 Olympics, a move that required approval by the secretary of defense. Truly with God, all things are possible.

I also attribute the fact that I successfully battled my weight, my own battle of the bulge, to the help of God. After having most of my thyroid surgically removed because of Graves' disease, I found that I had a difficult time controlling my weight. I'll go into more in the next chapter, "My Battle of the Bulge," but the end result of my health challenge was that I spent a good portion of my career fearful of being kicked out of the Navy for being overweight. Their policies are very strict in that area, and the only medically acceptable excuse for being overweight is pregnancy. I had many close calls, but God was always there, giving me just what I needed to overcome the challenge one more time.

One such instance was when I had been sent to Bahrain to help out during one of the many Iraq crises in the 1990s. I managed to find time to exercise but was still worried about gaining more weight. I knew my boss would start the paperwork to kick me out of the Navy if I was overweight when I returned to my parent command in Tampa, Florida. I found a store that sold diet TV dinners. I had a microwave in my room but no eating utensils. One night after I came home from work I couldn't sleep because of obsessing over my situation. I kept wondering how I could get a hold of a fork so I could implement my new diet strategy.

The next morning when I went into work, there in the middle of my desk was a fork. I had been using the desk of a guy who was on vacation, so when he returned I asked him about the fork. Since he was also a friend, I confided my story to him. He smiled and said, "God sent you that fork." I think the fork was God's way of saying, "Have Faith. Before you even ask, I will provide. I'm always here. Pay attention!"

DIVINE SIGNPOSTS

As I've gotten older, I've become a firm believer in divine signposts. The catalyst was reading a book by Doreen Virtue called *Divine Guidance*. Basically it puts forth the argument that God is a constant presence in our lives and sends us evidence and guidance in different ways. Some will open a book at random and notice a phrase or passage that helps them with a current problem. Some will hear the same song over and over again. Some will get an inner knowing. Everyone is different, and each situation is different.

That book validated and explained some unusual experiences I was having. One day while driving to work, I prayed out loud, "God, I really need your help. I'm depressed and mentally and physically exhausted. I need some inspiration to get me through the day." After my prayer, I put a tape of uplifting songs into my car stereo. I lived close to the base and only had time for one song. I played the song from the movie *Flashdance*, "Oh What a Feeling." As I drove up to the base gate, I turned off the tape, and the radio automatically came on and the same song was playing. Thank you, God, for even caring about the little things.

The most dramatic instance of this happened at one of the lowest points in my military career. It was during my time at USSTRATCOM. I was leading the command efforts to support USEUCOM combat in Kosovo operations. We had also taken over support of USEUCOM's part in enforcing the sanctions against Iraq. One night there was a mistake in intelligence analysis that resulted in the loss of innocent life. Aircraft thought they were dropping weapons on a surface-to-air missile sight. Turns out it was a water trough. Some innocent Iraqi farmers and farm animals were killed. I was accused of trying to cover it up.

Since we had reported the incident right after it happened, I didn't understand how someone thought I had covered it up. A preliminary investigation was held. One of the admirals on the staff had everyone who had been on watch during the incident plus their supervisors in one room. Before the investigation, the senior intelligence officer had stated he had overall responsibility for the incident since he was the J2. He said the investigation was not going to be "a blame game" but only carried out to see what procedures we had in place and if they needed to be changed so that nothing like that would happen again.

About ten minutes before the start of the meeting, one of the officers who had been in charge of some of the analysts and had been on watch during the incident came running into my office. "Ma'am, you have to look at this; it explains what happened." He showed me a memo that one of the senior enlisted men had distributed that changed one of the procedures I had put in place. We were providing intelligence support for the aircraft supporting sanctions against Iraq in the northern part of that country. If my folks detected what they thought was a potential threat to the aircraft, such as a surface-to-air missile or artillery, they were directed by me to call up intelligence personnel in Washington, DC, and get a second pair of eyes on the potential target. The Washington command had more experienced imagery analysts, and I wanted to make sure my guys were collaborating with other intelligence agencies. It would not take up too much additional time and may help avert a mistake in our report.

The rules of engagement in place authorized the aircraft to bomb surface-to-air missiles or artillery if they believed it was directed at them. The memo written by one of my subordinates had changed that procedure, saying there was no need to have the Washington folks look at the imagery. My heart skipped a beat. I had not seen or approved those changes, and under Navy rules that meant a court marshal for the senior enlisted man involved.

I looked at the young officer and said, "Sergeant X was not authorized to make this change." The officer replied, "He's a senior enlisted man in the Air Force, and he can change procedures if he wants." My response was I was a captain and therefore senior to the sergeant, and no one was authorized to change the rules or procedures without my knowledge or permission.

The admiral grilled us about our procedures and asked if we had changed things during the incident in question. The man who had changed the rules was honorable and raised his arm and acknowledged his mistake. As expected, no adverse action was taken against him or anyone else. We were just told to make sure we followed all the procedures in the future.

There was one incident during the meeting that should have raised flags with me. At the start of the investigation, the admiral asked us to go over the procedures that had been put in place. I thought it was my place to review them since I was in charge of the efforts and had been the one to come up with the procedures, but shortly after I started talking the admiral glared at me and said, "Shut up captain." Puzzled, I sat back in my chair wondering why he didn't want me to explain my procedures. I'd been down the road of people not liking me or considering me professionally incompetent so many times, I thought this was just another issue of proving my credibility. The officers and enlisted people who worked for me went on to answer his questions. Both the admiral and J2 seemed satisfied by the answers. I was okay with it because my folks had covered everything very efficiently.

I thought that was the end of it until a few days later my immediate superior casually mentioned that one of the people present at the meeting said I tried to cover the incident up and had prevented everyone from giving the admiral the full story. I immediately called a meeting of everyone who had been at the meeting. I told them that apparently someone thought the full story had not been told and if that was true to speak up and I would go immediately to the commander and chief and tell them whatever information someone thought had not been talked about during the investigation.

They all said they thought all of the facts had been talked about, so I left it at that. What I didn't know at the time was I was already being investigated. I got called into the J2's office a few days later, read the riot act, and handed a counseling letter accusing me of a cover up. He said when the enlisted man had spoken up at the meeting and accepted responsibility for changing my procedures; I should have spoken up and said it was my fault. He said I had not lived up to my responsibility. He also said he had considered beginning court marshal proceedings but changed his mind. He then said he had not lost confidence in me and was keeping me in charge of the command's intelligence support to combat operations in Kosovo and the sanctions against Iraq. He ordered me to hold a meeting with all who had been present at the admiral's investigation and apologize to them for covering up the incident. Scenes from the movie *Patton* where he had been forced to apologize to everyone who worked for him for slapping a soldier flashed though my mind, but I gave him a respectful, "Yes, Sir!"

Mentally I dropped to my knees. I was devastated. I was being transferred in a few weeks. My immediate supervisor had been in the room with me while the J2 was going off on me and had tried to support me. I realized afterward that it was probably due to his influence behind the scenes that I only got a counseling letter. As we walked back to our offices, I asked him how I could continue working the hours and putting forth the effort involved in supporting combat operations after being falsely accused and punished. He told me he believed me and that the J2 had also chewed out my accusers for attacking my integrity. I'd gotten the letter because the J2 believed I had called the follow-on meeting with my folks only after I found out I was being investigated. I asked my boss how that could be since I didn't know I was being investigated. Friends in Naval Criminal Investigative Service (NCIS) later told me they operated that way so the person being investigated doesn't get alerted and try to flee.

I was furious and reminded my boss that the J2 had told us no one was going to get in trouble. I had not been interviewed or questioned by whomever it was doing the investigation, so I never got a chance to tell my side of the story. It was only when the J2 handed me the counseling letter that I found out what it was they thought I had done wrong. That off my chest, I promised him I would continue my job out of respect for him and sense of duty in supporting the Kosovo operations.

I was scheduled to take a brief break and leave later in the day to drive to Colorado and look for a home since I was being transferred there in a few weeks. As ordered, I called all of the people involved in the investigation meeting that day and apologized for giving anyone the perception I had tried to cover up the incident. I was not going to apologize for something I didn't do. I had to sign the counseling letter, but in my mind I wasn't agreeing with what was written, only that I'd seen it. My only legal recourse would have been to request a court martial or bring discrimination charges against the command. I didn't have the emotional energy to go that route, plus since the court martial board would probably be made up of people from that command, what would be the point.

I realized my only real action plan was to intensify my prayer life and follow my Mother's advice to trust God to get me through this situation. She always told me she thought my depression was showing lack of faith. She was probably right. Like Abraham Lincoln, I knew I had nowhere else to go.

I had been reading a book about a guy who was undergoing a spiritual transformation. Every time he had a mystical experience it involved the numbers 444. He'd wake up at 4:44 A.M. or someone would tell him of a strange experience that took place at 4:44 A.M. He said that many believe the numbers signify that your guardian angels are looking out for you. As I was driving off base that day en route to Colorado, I glanced at the sign by the gate that normally displayed time, data, and temperature. In letters that appeared larger than normal to me were the numbers 444.

It took a while for me to recover emotionally from both the analysis failure that caused the loss of life and the false charges that had been leveled against me. When I returned from Colorado, I held my head up high, kept working as hard as I could, and did my best not to dwell on the past. It was one of the hardest things I've ever had to do.

I kept seeing the 444s. I'd be driving down the road and notice the numbers on the car in front of me. One time I was driving on the highway, and the car in front of me had the 444s. My eyes popped out when I noticed the car in the other lane also had 444 on its license plate. I'd be watching a television program and notice those same numbers were part of phone numbers being displayed on the screen.

I believe the numbers were a divine guidepost—a signal that all would be well . . . and eventually it was. The same J2 that almost court marshaled me a few weeks later gave me one of the best performance reports I've ever received and a medal as I was being transferred. As he handed me my medal, he said, "The thing I'll remember most about Captain Harris is her unrelenting honesty . . . even when I didn't want to hear it." I believed there was only one possible explanation for his turnaround—the hand of God.

Takeaway: Guidance doesn't always come in the form of lightning from heaven.

Key principles I learned in the area of faith:

1. If you can conceive it, you can achieve it, but the feeling gets the healing, meaning you have to not only visualize the wanted outcome but feel the way you would if it was happening right now.

2. Thoughts are things that affect the outcome of your life. If you think bad
   things are going to happen, they will. If you think good things are going
   to happen, they will.
3. God answers prayers and is a very present help in time of trouble. There is
   no problem that cannot be overcome with his help.
4. There will be divine signposts along the way to direct you. It's up to you
   whether you take their directions.

NOTES

1. Robert H. Schuller and Paul David Dunn, *The New Possibility Thinkers Bible*.
(Nashville: Thomas Nelson Publishers, 1996) Psalm 46:1, p. 638.

2. Schuller et al., *The New Possibility Thinkers Bible*, Mark 10:27, p. 1174.

3. Schuller et al., *The New Possibility Thinkers Bible*, Matthew 21:22, p.1142.

4. At www.famousquotesandauthors.com/authors/abraham_lincolnquotes.html.

5. Schuller et al., *The New Possibility Thinkers Bible*, Mark 10:27.

So I'm Fat . . . At Least My Uniform Fits: My Personal Battle of the Bulge

A sound mind in a sound body.

—*ancient Greek Saying*

There are two things you can do about a problem: something or nothing.

—*James Harris*

Oprah never would have made it in the Navy, not because she doesn't have what it takes to succeed in the military but because I don't believe she would have put up with all the crap they throw at you if you're overweight. I can't mince words, the Navy's weight-control program was the most frustrating and incompetent system I've ever encountered. My weight challenges were caused by my problems with thyroid disease, but according to Navy policy the only accepted medical reason for being overweight was pregnancy. Of all the challenges I faced during my career, this was the one that frequently brought me to my knees emotionally and several times nearly got me thrown out of the Navy.

A TASTE OF THINGS TO COME

I got my first hint of what was to come when my dad and I arrived to be sworn in at the Navy's recruiting office in New York City on a Friday morning a couple of weeks after Thanksgiving in 1972. I thought I'd just raise my right hand and swear I was prepared to give my life for God and my country, like they did in the World War II movies I'd loved and been raised on. Lieutenant Clair, the gracious lady who'd recruited me, had promised to take my dad and me out to lunch to celebrate after I was officially sworn in.

When we arrived, Lieutenant Clair told me they had to weigh me before giving me the oath to make sure I was within Navy standards. I started to feel uncomfortable, not remembering them doing that to new recruits in any of the movies I'd seen. I shrugged and stepped on the scale. It was one of those scales with the sliding metal things. I watched them move those things around and saw it stabilize at 136. I suddenly remembered that my Navy paperwork said for my height I couldn't weigh more than 131 pounds. Was this going to be a problem?

My weight normally fluctuated between 125 and 130 and since it was right after Thanksgiving I told myself that 136 wasn't that much over. I noticed the room suddenly seemed really quiet, and all the Navy people had those "we have a problem" expressions on their faces. I looked over at my dad and he shrugged his shoulders and gave me a "wait and see" look. Lieutenant Clair had a concerned look on her face as she muttered, "Excuse me, I have to call Washington."

She came back in about fifteen minutes and said, "Whew, that was close. They almost canceled your enlistment, but I convinced them to give you some time to lose the weight. If you can lose the extra weight by Monday you can still join the Navy. If not . . ."

I started to say something real smart like, "Are you kidding, lose five pounds in two days! You people are nuts! What's the big deal over five pounds?" but my dad gave me one of those "keep your mouth shut" looks. His face was grim, but he looked the Navy folks straight in the eye and in a calm voice declared, "We'll be back on Monday." He took my arm and escorted me out of the recruiting office like I was a princess.

WELCOME TO THE MILITARY MINDSET

As we walked back to the bus terminal, my dad explained the military mindset to me. Speaking with a quiet confidence honed by years of experience, he began to educate me to the ways of the military world: "Welcome to the military mindset. You're going to have to deal with a lot of rules and regulations you think are silly or stupid. That's the way it is. Most of the time they strictly enforce them, but in times of crisis or war when they're desperate for people, they'll lower their standards or waive the rules. When the crisis is over and they don't need large numbers of people anymore, they'll use any excuse to kick you out to bring down the numbers. There are two things you can do about a problem: something or nothing. If you still want to follow your dream, cut back on what you eat this weekend and come back and let them weigh you Monday."

I still didn't understand why being five pounds over weight was such a big deal, but I ate nothing but soup and salad all weekend. On Monday morning, my family's bathroom scale showed I was still one pound overweight. I didn't figure there was much point in going to the recruiting office, but my mom and dad cheered me on. "Don't worry. Don't eat or drink anything this morning. By the time you get to New York, you'll probably have lost another pound."

My mom was escorting me this time because my dad couldn't get out of work. I went to my room and picked out an outfit to wear. When I came out, my mom took one look at me and went ballistic, "Take that off. It makes you look fat. Why do you keep wearing those loose fitting clothes? Quit hiding your beauty." She marched me back into my room and picked out another dress and, after dressing me, she pulled me in front of the mirror and said, "See, look how much better you look. Get rid of those loose clothes in your closet. No wonder the Navy thought you were fat. Go on look at yourself."

Surprise, surprise. When I looked in the mirror, even I had to admit she was right, and I looked hot. I still thought my goose was cooked, thinking it didn't matter what I looked like if I was still a pound overweight. My mom insisted we go to the recruiting office.

"Where's your faith? You're not trusting in God." As we rode the bus over to New York, my mom kept pumping me up, "Don't give up. If it's for you, it's for you." When we arrived at the recruiting office, we learned Lieutenant Clair was out sick and one of her male counterparts would be in charge of enlisting me. After shaking his hand, I took off my winter coat. His eyes widened and his jaw dropped, "I'm not going to weigh you. You're not overweight. Raise your right hand and let's do your oath." I heard my mom muttering, "Thank you, Jesus!"

MUCH ADO ABOUT NOTHING
This experience should have put me on notice but it didn't. Have you ever looked back and realized how many times you had to learn things the hard

way? Well, I definitely joined that club thinking this whole weight thing was much ado about nothing. In basic officer training, they weighed us every Monday morning. Most of us pigged out on weekends, enjoying the great restaurants in Newport, Rhode Island. On top of that, the food in the Navy chow hall we ate in during the week was fantastic. Steaks, lobsters, cake, and ice cream, including all the fixings, like whipped cream, cherries, and nuts. It sure was better than the stuff I'd been eating in the college cafeterias, but it wasn't long before I learned about the consequences of not paying attention to what and how much I was eating.

If we were overweight Monday morning, we had to get up an hour early for the rest of the week, go down to the gym, and run a mile. We were on the honor system, and most of my Officer Candidate School (OCS) classmates just ran down to the gym and signed the list they had left out for us fatties, supposedly proving we did the run. I figured since I had to get up early, I might as well do the run. I was usually only one or two pounds overweight, so I honestly didn't give my weight much thought. It didn't seem to be a big deal, and no one actually said we wouldn't be allowed to graduate if we were overweight.

For my first six years in the Navy, the only rules regarding weight revolved around a height and weight chart. You had to maintain the standards for your height and that was it. I experienced no negative consequences other than an occasional lecture from the higher ups about my weight. Once, while stationed in Japan, my boss, Commander Sheafer, called me in for my annual career counseling session, gave me one of those "you need to shape up or ship out" looks, and in a stern voice without an ounce of sympathy informed me, "If you want to succeed as an intelligence officer you'll need to lose weight and comb your hair."

Hindsight is 20/20, and I see now he was correct. I should have paid closer attention to his warning. I had started to gain weight in the aftermath of my 1976 thyroid surgery. I had cut back on what I was eating but had achieved only limited results. I didn't like my weight gain, but I made all the right responses when told I needed to get a handle on it. Inwardly, however, I was confused. Why weren't my superiors giving me feedback on my job performance instead of how I looked? I found out years later that Commander Sheafer considered me one of his best Intelligence Watch officers and was trying to motivate me to meet the Navy standards so it couldn't be used against me.

TIME FOR A WAKE UP CALL

I got my real wake up call on this issue of weight at the start of my third job in the Navy. I was assigned as a teacher to the Navy's intelligence training school. After I'd been there a few months, my department head called me in and told me, "Gail, some of the enlisted instructors have complained about you. They say you're fat and shouldn't be allowed to teach because you're setting a bad example." I knew I was about fifteen pounds overweight at the time, but I jumped up out of my seat yelling, "That's crazy! Have they complained about anyone else?"

Right about that time, Bud, one of the other instructors and a good friend of mine, wandered into the office. He looked at the expression on my face and then looked at my boss and asked, "What's wrong with her?" "Oh, she's just upset because some of the enlisted instructors said she's fat." Bud laughed and looked at me and spat out, "Gail, that's no big deal!" I got on great with these guys, but I was irked by their apparent indifference to my weight issues. "How would you feel if they said that about you?" Their advice to me was, "Get over it. Just get the weight off."

I was shocked by all this focus on weight until some of my air force girl friends told me the Air Force had an unwritten policy that they would only accept beautiful women. Supposedly it came to a head when one lady won a lawsuit against them saying she hadn't gotten in because the Air Force considered her ugly. When I first joined the Navy, I do remember thinking that all the Air Force women looked like models, but I never connected the dots as it applied to my personal battle of the bulge. I was to learn over the years that in the Navy workplace, appearance was everything. If you didn't look good, you'd have a hard time getting promoted. Thus began my personal battle of the bulge.

MY BATTLE OF THE BULGE

The year was 1980, and the Navy decided to go hard core on the weight and fitness thing. When I first joined, I had the false assumption that the military would be on the cutting edge of diet, fitness regimens, and sports medicine. The Washington folks would come up with a policy and then disseminate it to all Navy commands; presumably under the assumption the commands would develop local plans to carry it out. The reality was that individuals were left to their own devices to figure out what to do to get and stay fit. It was all aimed at passing the required physical fitness test.

A command would typically assign one person as "fitness coordinator," but most had little or no experience in exercise and nutrition and in most instances received no special training. The base gym might have one person assigned as a fitness expert, but since they had to service an entire base, they could not give much individual attention. The Navy could learn an awful lot from the Marines and the Army guys, who not only talk the talk but walk the walk of fitness. They make it part of their daily work regimen to go to the gym or jog around the base. They also generally work out together as a unit several times a week. The end result is that you rarely see an overweight Marine or Army guy. With the exception of the Seals, I found the Navy units I was assigned to just gave lip service to fitness. You were expected to do what you needed to do, whatever that was, on your own and on your own time, but make sure you pass the fitness exam.

The Navy method of monitoring fitness levels was to test you twice a year. First they weighed you, then you went out and did the timed run and other physical parts of the tests, like sit-ups and push-ups. At first, I struggled with the physical part of the test. The first time I took it I failed the run. I had been so focused on starving myself to make the weigh-in part I hadn't worked enough on the physical stuff. I could do the mile and a half distance but not in the time I needed it.

I didn't want to fail again, so I started running every day. Several of the students at the intelligence school went running with me and gave me tips on how to improve my technique. They had just graduated from OCS in Pensacola, Florida, where marine drill instructors were in charge of a lot of their training. Since they had been trained in fitness by the best in the world, they were able to give me some good pointers. After they had worked with me a few weeks, I took the test again and made it within the required time frame. The help and support of these students gave me a tremendous morale boost as I continued to fight my personal battle of the bulge.

I did everything I could think of to try to stop the weight gain. I cut back on the amount of food I was eating; gave up stuff like cookies, donuts, and potato chips; and consulted the base nutritionist for diet tips. They gave me an

1,800–2,000-calorie-a-day diet plan that not only didn't help me lose weight but caused me to gain instead. In fact, I continued gaining until I dropped my intake down to 500 calories daily. I also incorporated a daily three-mile run and joined an aerobic exercise class as part of my fitness regimen. I really felt I was doing everything I could to win this ongoing battle of the bulge.

I was usually still overweight as test time approached, so a few weeks ahead of time I'd go on my apple/diet soda fast until the weight came off. I got the apple thing out of a New Age metaphysical book and added Diet Coke in later years once the Coca-Cola folks started selling it to help me feel full. I was desperate to overcome my weight problem and willing to try almost anything to accomplish it.

While still in intelligence training school, I mentioned my ongoing weight problem to the base doctor and asked if he thought my thyroid had anything to do with it. Instead of giving me the normal diet advice I had come to expect, he told me nothing was wrong with my thyroid but I needed to have breast reduction surgery. I was shocked and offended. He ignored my protests and said if I didn't have the surgery my big breasts would cause me back and shoulder problems in the future. I had never heard of such surgery.

It turned out that the very day of my physical one of my longtime girl friends was in town. I invited her to my house for dinner but ended up crying on her shoulder all evening, moaning and complaining about what the doctor told me. She sided with the doctor, telling me she had had the surgery herself and was glad she did. Based on what my girlfriend told me, I had the surgery hoping my battle with bulge would now come to a victorious end.

LOSE THE WEIGHT OR LEAVE THE NAVY
Ultimately though, no matter what I did to fight my battle of the bulge, the end result was the same. I just kept getting fatter, and now the weight issue began to seriously affect my career. The commanding officer of the intelligence training unit marked me down because of it on my performance reports. During our counseling session, he told me that in terms of talent I was the best instructor he had, but because of my weight problems, my stats dropped all the way to the bottom in overall ratings. He concluded by saying if I didn't lose the weight, I would get thrown out of the Navy.

My self esteem started to dive. I'd always thought of myself as average looking, but after the complaint by the enlisted instructors and the poor grades on my performance report, I started to believe my physical appearance was repulsive. I felt like everyone was looking at me and finding me fat and un-attractive, which was fed by the fact I was not dating either. Now, with the Navy officially threatening to throw me out because they considered me fat and ugly, it looked like it was unanimous—I was officially losing the battle of the bulge.

I kept going back and forth to the doctor, continually suggesting my weight problems could be caused by my Graves' disease. They refused to believe I was subsisting on as little as 500 calories a day and generally gave me the "you just need to control your eating" lecture. In my heart, I knew it had something to do with my thyroid, but because the Navy doctors didn't agree, I had to suck it up and figure out how to solve the problem on my own.

WHY WON'T SOMEONE HELP ME?

Most of my Navy peers were supportive and sympathetic to my plight and even tried to help my morale by fixing me up with blind dates. In preparation for one of these blind dates with an African American dentist friend of a col-league, one of my girl friends, a slim, drop-dead gorgeous Air Force captain, took me out shopping. She took me to one of her favorite places, where the sales girl smiled and eagerly asked my friend Linda if she needed help. But when Linda pointed at me saying I needed a nice outfit for a hot date, the sales clerk's smile was quickly replaced by a disgusted look as she haughtily declared, "We don't sell clothes for people *her size*."

I was shocked by her statement, but that shock quickly escalated to anger. Linda, having seen this happen before, moved us swiftly toward the store door. "Did you hear what that girl just said about me?" I sputtered. "Don't worry about it," Linda calmly said, "I know plenty of other better places to shop." We did find a nice outfit that even my mom would have approved of, but the incident did little for my self-esteem. On the night of my scheduled dinner date, Linda came over to help me dress and make sure my hair looked good. The dentist showed up on time, sat and talked with me for about fifteen minutes, and then looked at his watch and said, "I know we were supposed to go to dinner but my son is sick and I have to leave."

Apparently the guy found me so unattractive I wasn't even worth a couple of hours over dinner. I called my parents, crying and totally devastated by what had just happened. My dad was great, saying that man left because he knew I wouldn't have sex with him on the first date. My mom had been listening in on an extension and added her two cents about not hiding my beauty and wearing nice-fitting clothes. I decided all I could do was be the best I could at my work and hope everyone would forget how badly I was losing this battle of the bulge.

While I was still at my teaching assignment, the Navy added a fat rehab program to their alcohol and drug program. As soon as I heard about it, I applied. I thought surely the powers that be would be impressed that I was doing everything I could to overcome what they considered to be my weight problem. To my surprise, I was turned down for the program. At the time I was about twenty pounds overweight, so I requested an appointment with my commanding officer and asked him why I had been turned down. In a tone heavy with sarcasm he sneered, "You're not fat enough for that program. Get your act together and cut back on what you're eating."

I was determined to stand up for myself, knowing my weight was hurting my career. Why wouldn't somebody help me instead of always just pointing out the obvious problem? "First you tell me if I don't lose the excess weight you'll throw me out. Now you're saying I'm not fat enough to qualify for the fat rehab program. What am I supposed to do?" My pleas for help fell on deaf ears, as he dismissed me indicating the discussion was over. I was on my own again, feeling destined to lose this constant battle of the bulge.

In tackling this problem by myself, I kept in mind my father's saying that there were two things you could do about a problem: something or nothing. I continued with my daily intake of 500 calories or less, did high-impact aerobic classes, and jogged three miles five or six times a week. As needed, I'd go on my apples and Diet Coke fast. When that didn't work, I would go on a total liquid fast for thirty days and always managed to get the weight off in time to pass my test, but it was a brutal, self-destructive way to live.

Most of the people I interacted with didn't know about my eating habits. When I went out with them, I'd eat "normally" and then compensate for it later in the privacy of my own home. In my mind, I wasn't suffering from bulimia or anorexia, so I didn't think I was doing anything wrong. I remember reading articles about women with eating disorders and wondering how someone could get so screwed up. I didn't realize that I had a very serious problem and was on a self-destructive path that could eventually affect more than my career if I didn't start getting the right kind of help.

FINALLY, THE RIGHT KIND OF HELP

In spite of the negativity about my appearance, I was able to maintain a healthy professional self-image. I honestly believed that my professional performance was more important than my weight, and since I always passed the fitness part of the test, I believed I'd done all that I could to meet the Navy physical fitness standards. I just kept pounding away trying to make myself one of the best intelligence officers in history.

It was not until 1989, thirteen years after my thyroid surgery, that I finally found a doctor who listened to me and consulted with a specialist and put me on a thyroid supplement medicine. Graves' disease had caused my metabolism to go into overdrive and would have eventually caused my death. Thyroid medicine is designed to stabilize and normalize a body's metabolism, so after being put on the right medication, it became easier to keep my weight under control. Finally, I was getting the right kind of help. I still had incidences when my weight would shoot up, but the doctor would adjust my medication and I would be able to lose it without the extreme 500-calorie a day diet I had always used in the past. It seemed I was finally gaining ground against the enemy, and maybe I'd even win this lifelong battle of the bulge.

A few years ago, I consulted with a specialist at the University of Nebraska Medical School. She was horrified at my medical treatment history and told me I should have been on the thyroid medication immediately after my surgery, which is generally considered standard procedure. She said if I had, I probably would not have experienced all the weight problems I'd had to suffer through for so many years. She also said it was a miracle that I hadn't experienced such other serious health problems as depression, vision problems, hair loss, insanity, or heart disease not only due to the lack of proper medication but from the destructive lifestyle I had been living to overcompensate for the weight problem.

While I sometimes had problems with depression, the only other major problem I noticed during those years was occasional hair loss. One night, while in Egypt, I was in front of a mirror brushing and admiring my glorious mane when most of it suddenly fell out. I freaked and nearly had a nervous breakdown right then and there. I kept getting up during the night to count the strands of hair on my pillow. Thankfully, it was only temporary and grew back, but it took several months.

I've since learned that thyroid disease is one of the most misdiagnosed health problems and one a lot of people don't even know exists. It was years later that a movie was released based on the struggles Olympic athlete Gail Deavers had with Graves' disease. Having lived it myself, I thought it was pretty accurate in the depiction of the trials and tribulations of the disease, except for one scene. The actress portraying Gail was taking a shower when a lot of her hair suddenly fell out. I didn't feel she showed enough panic, fear, and despair, as it brought back vivid memories of when that very thing had happened to me. Thank goodness there is now more awareness about this potentially dangerous health problem.

ONE MORE ROUND WITH THE BATTLE OF THE BULGE

During the first Gulf War, the Navy waived the twice-yearly physical fitness tests and weigh-ins just as my dad had predicted so many years before. I spent part of the war in the Middle East and didn't have a safe place to exercise, as I was staying in a hotel in town that didn't have a gym. We were told that women shouldn't go outside wearing scanty clothes, so I couldn't do my normal daily three-mile runs either. I ended up doing what exercises I could in my hotel room, like jogging in place for thirty minutes and practicing sit-ups and push-ups. I watched what I ate, and the thyroid medication really seemed to be helping me maintain my weight. I felt pretty good that I was only five pounds overweight at the war's end. When it came time for my boss to sign the performance report, he pointed out he'd given me top grades in professional and personal appearance. I thought that meant that the five extra pounds wasn't an issue for him. Obviously I still hadn't learned from past experience that omission of the facts does not mean it is not an issue.

A couple of weeks later, I was in the Officer's Club after work waiting for my friend Dave so we could go out to do dinner. He was also my command's flight surgeon and the doctor who'd finally put me on thyroid medication. He came up to me at the bar with a concerned expression on his face. "I just talked to the commanding officer, who told me you have to lose those five extra pounds by next week or he'll have to mark you down in your performance report."

I immediately erupted with rage, picked up the movie I had bought for Dave to borrow, and threw it at his head as hard as I could. Dave followed me as I stormed out of the club yelling and cursing like a sailor. When we got to my car, Dave took my purse from me saying, "I'm not going to let you drive. You'll get in an accident if I let you drive in this condition." I grabbed my purse out of his hand and flung it out into the parking lot while all of my built-up frustration over the weight issue erupted in a tidal wave of fury.

"If he wanted me to lose the five pounds why didn't he tell me two weeks ago when I signed the report? I thought he wasn't going to make an issue of the five pounds because of the war. Haven't I done everything in my power to maintain my weight? Does being five pounds overweight make me a terrible person? Does my professional competence mean nothing? Is this really an issue of national security?"

When I finally stopped raving and pacing around the parking lot, I noticed Dave quietly watching me with tears in his eyes. I took a few deep breaths willing myself to calm down, then told him I was better and could drive home. He helped me pick up the contents of my purse that had spilled out when I had thrown it across the parking lot and gently put me into my car.

I drove home, opened a bottle of cheap red wine, put on some sad music, and had a really great pity party. Fortunately, a couple of glasses of wine on an empty stomach knocked me out, and I had the rest of the weekend to pull myself together. I kept remembering what my dad said about there being two things you can do about a problem: *something or nothing*. I decided it was time to do something.

By Monday morning, I'd come up with a game plan. I swaggered into my commanding officer's office, hands on hips and with as much arrogance and righteous anger as I could muster and declared, "It's obvious to me the Navy is more concerned with my weight than my professional performance. Obviously my job is relatively unimportant; therefore, I will spend most of my workday at the gym until my weight is within acceptable standards. If you need me, you know where to find me."

To his credit he let me get away with it. He would have been perfectly within his right to court-martial me for insubordination, but he was also a good friend and knew I was saving face in a situation I found unbearably humiliating. I suspect Dave had already given him a heads up on my reaction, and both of them were trying to save my career and keep me from any more self-destructive temper tantrums.

I got back on my apples and diet soda regime and would go in to work early, do most of my work, delegate what was left to my staff, and head out to the gym. At the end of the day, I'd go back to work and take care of whatever was left for me to do. Because I was simultaneously subsisting on apples and diet soda, I was really grumpy and not a joy to be around. The really positive thing that sustained me through this time was the support of the folks that worked for me. They gave me a card one day that they'd all signed that said, "Don't Give Up." I managed to lose the five pounds and for a brief moment in time was allowed by my bosses to rest in peace.

TURNING POINT

I found that there are a lot of prejudgments toward people who are overweight. Many of my bosses and a few of my coworkers over the years seemed to think I was spending my entire spare time overeating. This was true early in my career before I was diagnosed with Graves' disease, but it wasn't the case once I knew I was going to have an ongoing problem with weight gain.

One particular example of this that I will always remember was when one of my coworkers, an always in shape Marine, decided I was a disgrace to my uniform. He figured me for a couch potato with bad eating and exercise habits. He apparently observed my behavior for a few months to prove he was justified in his prejudgment of me. After a few weeks, he joined me one day on my daily jog around base. "I just want to shake your hand. You've got an exercise regime that would do a Marine proud!" That's the second best compliment I've ever received and a definite boost to my so-often low self-esteem.

The turning point for me with my personal battle of the bulge came while I was stationed at Naval Forces Central Command (NAVCENT). One of the senior staff members seemed to have it in for all the females and ethnic minorities on the staff. He decided to try and use my weight as an excuse to kick me out of the Navy. When I told him I had Graves' disease, he called me a liar. I told him to check with my doctor, who could verify my medical condition, but he didn't bother. I remembered my father's advice early in my Navy career about trying to handle the situation by filing discrimination charges against him. I decided that even though I believed he was a bigot, I'd try and handle this in another way.

Before I could put a plan into motion, I was sent to Bahrain to help out during one of the many crises with Iraq. When I returned to Tampa, I still hadn't lost all the weight I needed to, but I received an unexpected reprieve. I didn't have to take the fitness portion of the test for six months because I had injured my back during an exercise routine while in Bahrain. This, of course, antagonized the office bigot even more.

One day, I was sitting at my desk working when one of the chiefs, an African American female, came into my office upset and almost in tears. "Bigot just called me into his office saying he wanted me to weigh you again, even though you don't have to take the test for another six months. He said he wanted to document his records, but I refused to do it. This isn't right! A lot of us know you have a medical problem, and he shouldn't be allowed to get away with treating you like this."

Stunned but not surprised I got up and headed to his office. I walked right past his secretary, pushed open his door, and barged right in asking, "Why did you send the chief to weigh me again? I already weighed in over at the hospital, and I don't even have to take the test right now because of my back problems." Looking extremely uncomfortable, he backed away from me saying, "Calm down. I'm on your side. I don't believe you're as overweight as the hospital says. I was just trying to help prove them wrong." He obviously didn't know that the senior Navy intelligence folks had given me a heads up about a call he'd made to them saying I was overweight and a disgrace to the command.

Having made my point, I decided to back off and just thanked him for his concern. As I left his office, I devised an interesting idea to beat this constant battle of the bulge and get the "bigot" off my back once and for all.

I had been doing some light exercise and running short distances as part of my back rehabilitation program with the help of one of my coworkers, Steve, a nationally ranked runner and member of the Navy track team. Steve had me running a quarter of a mile, then walking a quarter of a mile for a total distance of three miles, five times a week. I wondered, if I volunteered to take the Navy physical fitness test even though I had the medical exemption, if it would put this thing behind me. It still wouldn't count on the records, but if I passed it I would be making a powerful statement to anyone who still thought I was a lazy, overeating couch potato.

The test was scheduled for the next morning, so I ran my idea by Steve. He looked me straight in the eye and said, "You can do it. I'll run it with you to pace you." The next day as we walked over to the test location my legs felt weak, but Steve kept telling me we could do it. He had me do about twenty minutes of vigorous stretching before the test and told me, "I think part of your back problem might be caused by your hamstrings. If we stretch those out real good, you should be able to pass your sit-ups and still do the run. We'll stretch you out again before we run. Don't worry, you can do it."

Steve was right. I was able to do the minimum number of sit-ups and push-ups to pass that section. I was real nervous when we started the run, but Steve kept giving me pep talks all along the way. "Looking good. Keep it up! Imagine there's a good-looking guy at the finish line who wants to take you on a romantic date when you finish!" I made it with just a few seconds to spare. Instead of going to take a shower, I marched into bigot's office in my exercise clothes with sweat dripping everywhere and pointed to the scar on my neck. "See that? That's where they took most of my thyroid out. I told you I had a medical problem and that I really do exercise, which I just proved by passing the test this morning." He never bothered me again. I had done something about the problem and enjoyed the taste of victory. Thank you, Dad, for the great advice.

Takeaway: You only get one body, you'd better learn to take care of it.

Key principles I learned in my own personal battle of the bulge:

1. There are two things you can do about a problem: something or nothing.
2. I needed to quit hiding my beauty and build up my self-esteem.
3. I realized how many times I had to learn things the hard way.
4. I should have paid closer attention when those who cared about me gave me good advice, like "If you want to succeed as an intelligence officer, you'll need to lose weight and comb your hair."
5. Hindsight is 20/20. I needed to begin to learn from the past and make the necessary changes to improve my future.
6. I didn't realize that I had a very serious problem and needed someone who could give me the right kind of help.
7. I've since learned that thyroid disease is one of the most misdiagnosed health problems and one a lot of people don't even know exists.

6

You're Going to Lose a Few Battles . . . Focus on Winning the War

And I'm telling you, I'm not going.

—*Effie* (from *Dreamgirls*)[1]

I think I can, I think I can.

—*The Little Engine That Could*[2]

I had begun to wonder if it was time to get out of the Navy. I had reached the twenty-year retirement point and would be coming up for promotion to captain soon. My original goal had been to reach that twenty-year mark and attain the rank of commander, which was considered by most to be a successful Navy career. I could hold my head up if I did decide to retire. I knew that competition for promotion to captain was very fierce, plus I didn't think it would be fair for me to keep my name on the list if I believed I would still have problems making the Navy's weight standards. I really believed I had done all in my power to keep my weight within standards, and frankly I was getting tired of the constant battle.

WHEN IN DOUBT, ASK DAD AND MOM

I was also getting mixed signals from my parents. My dad was fighting a losing battle with lung cancer, and I was home for what would be his last Christmas. I don't know if it's true for everyone who knows they are dying, but my dad seemed to be able to look into the soul of his loved ones and see all the good, the bad, and everything in between. I was lying on the couch watching TV when my father came into the room and sat down in his favorite chair. I felt him staring at me, so I took my eyes off of the TV and looked in his direction.

He had a strange look on his face, like he had just figured out something very important. His eyes were full of compassion, and he looked like he was weighing what he was about to say very carefully. In a surprisingly quiet voice he simply stated, "You're very depressed." I had allowed my weight struggles to cast a negative cloud over all areas of my life, and Dad had apparently seen through my façade. I saw no need to hide the truth, so I nodded and admitted I'd been that way for some time now.

In addition to my battle of the bulge, I was dealing with a less-than-exciting social life. I had made several good friends in the Navy, but they were spread out all over the world, so most of my social interactions were through catch-up phone calls. My coworkers were mostly married and didn't include me in on their social scene. I dated some but felt like a failure in that area of my life because I hadn't found that special someone to spend the rest of my life with. When I told one of my friends that I was tired of the dating scene, she scoffed at my feelings of failure and commented on how many wild and fun romantic adventures I'd had over the years.

I stopped my depressing reminiscing and focused on what my father was saying. "You've not had much of a life. It's actually been kind of sad. I think it's time you left the Navy and got a life. You've done enough, now it's time for others to finish what you started." I didn't know what to say. Dad had always been my biggest supporter as he walked me through all of the up and down, love-hate times of my Navy career. As my dad left the room, I thought to myself, I do love the Navy, but apparently it doesn't love me back. Maybe my dad was right.

I began to think this was a confirmation of what I had been thinking about retirement when my mom stopped what she was doing and came in to talk to me. My mom had been in the kitchen as usual, cooking up a storm, but had apparently overhead our conversation. As soon as my dad left the room to go to bed, she came over to me saying, "I don't fully agree with your father on this. If you decide to leave the Navy, make sure it's for a reason unique to the Navy. Every job has its trials and tribulations, so don't think if you get a job

out here you won't have any more problems." Well, it seems I had two different opinions from my parents, now what?

THEN SEEK THE COUNSEL OF A TRUE FRIEND
After the holidays, I returned to Tampa still undecided about what to do. One
evening I called my beloved mentor, Drew Simpson, who came right to the
point when I explained my dilemma. "I think you should stay and see if you
make captain, if you think you can handle the rejection if you don't."

My thoughts turned to the series of Rocky movies I had watched over the
years. In the first one, Rocky didn't think he could defeat the champ, so his
goal was not to win but to last for fifteen rounds. No one had ever gone fifteen
rounds with the champ, but Rocky reached his goal, badly beat up but he
made it. In *Rocky II*, he realized he had set his goal too low. He came to believe
he could win and so he did. Maybe, like Rocky, I had set the goal for my Navy
career too low. Maybe, just maybe, in spite of losing some battles, I could win
my war with weight and get promoted to captain. If I did, I would only be like
the third or fourth African American female in Navy history to achieve that
rank. At the time, no black woman had ever made it to admiral, so getting
promoted to captain would definitely be a win in my personal "war."

As I pondered the issue, I began to ask myself, what did winning my war really mean to me? It would mean that in spite of my physical struggles I would
work through each battle and ultimately meet the challenge, no matter how
unattainable it might seem. More importantly, it would validate my belief
that it didn't matter whether I was an ideal physical model of a naval officer.
What really mattered was whether I could meet the intellectual challenge of
being a professional Navy intelligence officer. My body might have had some
physical weaknesses, but I knew my mind and spirit were strong enough to
achieve my goal and win.

AMAZING TRACY
My thoughts turned to my niece, Tracy, who was born with sickle cell anemia.
At the age of five she had already had two strokes and an extensive procedure
done on her heart. Once a month she had to have all of the blood in her body
replaced. She'd had many medical crises over the years, yet 99 percent of the
time she maintained a positive radiant attitude. Not once did I ever hear her
complain. As a matter of fact, I remember the time I was home on vacation

and my brother called and asked me to take Tracy to her monthly blood replacement procedure so he and his wife wouldn't have to take off work. "I would be happy to," I responded, "but the Houston Medical Complex is huge, and I don't know where to go." My brother laughed as he assured me that Tracy could show me the way.

I was a little leery, as Tracy was about six at the time, but I wanted to help out and so agreed to do it. I was amazed as Tracy not only knew her way around the huge complex, but she even pointed out the best and most convenient place to park my rental car. I totally lost track of all the places we had to go through to set up her procedure, but she guided us through without one wrong turn. She was obviously a favorite with the medical people, as lots of doctors and nurses stopped what they were doing to say hello and give her a kiss as we made the required rounds. By the time we got to our final destination, she had lipstick all over her face.

We started at about eight in the morning, but Tracy wasn't set up in her room until about four that afternoon. When she was all settled in and hooked up to a bunch of machines, I asked her if she was hungry. I had noticed we had passed a McDonald's in the hospital somewhere along the way. In spite of having one machine pumping blood out of her and another pumping new blood in, Tracy seemed to be calmly taking it all in stride. I would have needed to be sedated to go through what she was experiencing, but she responded in a sweet calm voice, "Aunt Gail, could you get me a fish sandwich?" "Well Miss Tracy," I replied trying to cover up my own discomfort, "I don't know how I will be able to find my way around without you, but I'll do my best to go get you that fish sandwich."

I found my way back to McDonald's without too many problems, but the lines were long so it took longer than I had thought. When I got back to Tracy's floor, there was my amazing niece, standing bare foot in the middle of the hall looking worried and anxious. When she saw me, an expression of relief passed over her old young features. "Aunt Gail, I was worried about you. I was afraid you'd gotten lost, so I was going to come and find you." Fighting back tears, I looked away and cleared my throat before speaking. "Thank you, Tracy. The lines were long. Let's get you settled back in your room so you can eat your sandwich." Some how she had managed to unhook herself from the blood machine and had wheeled the IV equipment out with her into the hall to come looking for me. What a truly amazing little girl!

Remembering that incident forced me to put my Graves' disease issues back into proper perspective. So I had a disease that made me fat, that was nothing compared to what Tracy and millions of others with life-threatening illnesses were going through. I realized I was basing both my professional and personal self-worth on what the bathroom scale said I weighed. I resolved not to waste another minute obsessing over what my scale told me. I truly aspired to keep that vow, and now that I'm retired from the Navy I never weigh myself. I let how my clothes fit or don't fit be my guide as to whether I need to lose a little weight. Thank you, dear Tracy, for your amazing positive attitude toward the wars of life! I learned a lot from you!

WHAT I NEEDED WAS A LIFESTYLE CHANGE

I was still wondering what actions I needed to take to further my Navy career when I saw an advertisement for the next afternoon's Oprah show. The ad said she was going to reveal her weight loss secrets. I had a sudden thought that maybe I hadn't done everything I could to win my battle of the bulge and that there was something to be learned from another lady who had major issues with weight. So the next day I decided to leave work early to watch the show. I confided my intent to several of my female coworkers who cheered me on, assuring me I was going to hear something useful and ask me to take notes for them as well.

This turned out to be the episode where Oprah and her trainer, Bob Greene, discussed exercise regimens and the benefits of a low-fat diet. I felt like I had been hit over the head. The information on that show was so simple, yet it made so much sense to me. Don't diet, this experienced personal trainer advised, make a lifestyle change by getting a professional to help design a fitness program tailored to your needs and your lifestyle.

Now I had tried the trainer thing once a few years earlier while I was stationed in Panama, but it had been a very negative experience. An army coworker had offered to help me and several of my friends lose weight, but he turned out to be a sadistic jerk. He'd scream and yell at us and make us do extreme stuff, like 200 sit-ups several times during the workout and then take us on long runs afterward.

The final straw was the day he took us through an hour of heavy aerobic exercises in a poorly air-conditioned gym. I was on my knees sweating like a pig and wondering if I was getting heat stroke because my breathing was so labored I couldn't get the words out to ask for help. Our so-called coach came over to me and, instead of seeing if I was alright, started yelling at me, causing my volcanic temper to rise quickly to tantrum level. Before I erupted and said or did something I'd probably regret for the rest of my life, two of my exercise classmates discerned the murderous look in my eyes, grabbed my arms, helped me stand, and then pushed me toward the door. Literally dragging me outside, they whispered in my ear to calm down and not take it personally. I just wanted to throw something at him or at least give him a good cursing out.

ONE BAD APPLE DOESN'T SPOIL THE WHOLE BUCKET

Even though my anger boiled as I remembered this episode, I decided not to let one bad experience sour me on the whole personal training profession. I went out and joined the best and most expensive gym in town and requested a personal trainer to get me started. They assigned me a young lady named Amy Johnson, who was just out of college. She was fun and enthusiastic and, because she was new in the fitness business, had no preconceived notions or prejudices. I also went to the health club nutritionist and showed her my medical records, asking for a low-fat diet regime. She was shocked at how the Navy had mishandled my medical treatment, and I thought her eyes would pop out of her head when I told her about my 500-calorie-a-day diet.

She explained that the more I cut back on calories, the more inclined my body was to slow my metabolism and shift into survival mode. I was literally starving my body to death, so it began storing fat to keep me alive. She explained that because of my thyroid disease I needed to eat five or six small meals a day and keep my metabolism revved up. I told her I didn't want a new diet, I wanted a lifestyle change I could live with.

She agreed and said a low-fat eating regime would probably work the best and limited me to no more than twenty grams of fat a day. I was to eat three basic meals and two snacks each day. I usually had a bagel and orange juice for breakfast, a turkey or chicken sandwich for lunch, and a diet TV dinner in the evening. The nutritionist also gave me lots of ideas for low-fat meals that I could cook myself and suggested eating only at restaurants that served low-fat items on their menus. For snacks, I ate fruit or something low-fat. I was to strictly stick with this for six days a week, then choose one day to eat whatever I wanted, within reason of course. I found this to be a very easy regimen and made Friday my free day when I would thoroughly enjoy a steak and a baked potato with lots of sour cream accompanied by a couple glasses of wine.

Amy, my new fitness trainer, was phenomenal. She developed a dynamite program for me that revolved around the concept of cross training. I had first heard that concept from one of my doctors because of my slew of running-related injuries. After one rather painful episode, the doctor sat me on the table, leaned close, and looked me directly in the eyes saying, "I've got two words for you: cross training." I was clueless as to what that really meant, but thank God Amy knew exactly what it meant and what I needed. She developed a program that incorporated weight training, biking, low-impact aerobic classes, and jogging.

Instead of running five or six times a week, I ran three and on alternate days did some other aerobic exercise, like biking, which I had loved as a child. I especially enjoyed long rides on the weekend. I was, however, a little leery of the weight training thing, thinking that was just for guys. I let Amy coach me through, although very reluctantly, always threatening her bodily harm if she made me look like a man. I did have one moment that I put my foot down. I was doing squats with a heavy barbell on the back of my shoulders when I looked in the mirror and noticed that every muscle in my legs was outlined. Amy commented on my great muscle definition, but I thought I looked like a man. We laughed, then compromised by backing off some of my leg work.

My instances of sports-related injuries dropped dramatically as I moved into this new fitness lifestyle. From Amy, I learned that especially as you got older, it is extremely important to do stretching exercises before and after you work out. Even for those in their twenties or thirties, not warming up your muscles before and cooling them down after is one of the primary causes of sports-related injuries. When I first started working out with Amy, I had problems with my knees, hamstrings, lower back, and right shoulder. After just a couple of months of working with her, I felt great and had suffered no negative side effects from my new regimen.

Steve continued to be an invaluable friend and ally as well. He gave me many valuable running and diet tips and helped me gradually get back into my jogging form after one of my many running-related injuries. He also turned me on to the benefit of massage therapy to keep the body toned and tuned up. I can't thank him enough for all the help he gave me over the years.

I kept telling him when he retired from the navy he was a natural and should get into sports medicine.

This fitness program combined with the low-fat diet completely transformed my appearance. I only lost about fifteen or twenty pounds, but by doing it right and toning the areas where I lost, it looked like I'd lost double that. Amy explained to me that muscle weighed more than fat, so I might not lose as many pounds, but the overall effect was amazing. I was still a few pounds over the Navy's weight standards but was able to pass the body fat option. Even though Amy was a civilian, my command let her take the fitness test along with me. She was working on a paper and wanted to observe and participate in a military fitness test firsthand. I passed with flying colors, so I decided to give myself a fitness challenge as a way of celebrating my new fit condition.

WHAT HAVE I GOTTEN MYSELF INTO

I made plans to hike the Inca Trail in Peru with my friend Dave to celebrate my new fit condition. I've learned the hard way that even though you're good friends with someone, that doesn't mean you'll make good travel companions. Dave and I had taken many trips across Europe together while stationed in Spain, so I knew we were on the same wavelength, at least in the area of travel.

We started out sightseeing in Peru's capitol, Lima, for a couple of days, then headed for our departure point, the city of Cusco. Cusco is at 11,000 feet above sea level, which is something I should have taken note of at the beginning of this adventure. Our group totaled eleven people, half of whom were experienced hikers from Europe. They had spent several days in Cusco so they could acclimate to the higher altitude before starting our climb. We Americans only spent a day or so in the city, which I was to find out very soon wasn't nearly enough. I had been spending most of my time in either Florida or the Middle East, both of which were not good climates to prepare my body for what was to come.

I really had no idea what I was getting into. About 400 hundred years ago, the Inca tribe carved a bunch of steps out of mountains that led to a hidden city called Machu Picchu. It's a four- or five-day hike where you travel over steep valleys in the Andes and then go over three passes, all of which are more than 12,000 feet above sea level, with the highest one more than 15,000 feet above sea level. Not as high as Mt. Everest to be sure but a challenge to novice hikers like me nonetheless.

At the start of our hike, I took Dave aside and said, "Dave, you run marathons, I run 5Ks. You're in better shape than I am, so please don't feel you have to stay with me during the hike. Go at a comfortable pace for you, and I'll see you at the end of the day." Unfortunately, I had neglected to take into account the fact that men and women communicate differently. If I had been traveling with one of my girlfriends and said that, she would have known that I was also saying, "But if I start to have problems, please don't leave me!" Dave took me at my word and, when I did find myself in trouble, he was nowhere in sight. Ultimately, it was the best thing to happen and became an unexpected forum for me to learn some very valuable lessons.

In our group, there were a couple of doctors and a nurse, which was of some comfort to me. Edwin, our guide, had been in the Peruvian Army, so he was tough as nails. There were twenty-five native Peruvians to carry our bags, set up our tents, and cook our meals, so all we had to carry was a light backpack with a raincoat and whatever else we wanted on our person. I was in the best shape of my life, but I had not properly trained to do this kind of journey. I've since learned that even experienced mountain hikers consider this a tough hike. There's that 20/20 hindsight again.

"I THINK I CAN, I THINK I CAN," SAID THE LITTLE ENGINE THAT COULD

My toughest days were the second and last day of the hike. The morning of the second day we had to travel up a steep path that was more than a mile in length and appeared to me to be almost straight up. The path consisted mostly of carved steps that seemed pretty large to me. I kept asking our guide, "I thought people were shorter than us 400 years ago. How tall were these guys? Why did they make these steps so high and wide?"

I was really struggling and constantly bringing up the rear while doing lots of huffing and puffing and thinking to myself, this is only day two. At one point, another American woman and I were lagging very far behind the others. She looked at me with tears of frustration welling up in her eyes and fearfully said, "We're not going to make it." I suddenly felt righteous determination bubbling up from inside me. I looked past her eyes and deep into her soul and declared, "Oh, yes we are!" I looked a couple of feet in front of us and said, "See that bush? Let's make it to there."

As we moved forward, I reminded her of the childhood book *The Little Engine That Could*. As I recalled, the normal train that would take toys to the children in a town over a mountain pass had broken down. In desperation, the people turned to a little blue engine and asked it to help. The little engine, much smaller that the usual one, didn't know if it had enough power to make it over the high pass, but they talked it into trying. As The Little Engine That Could huffed and puffed toward the pass, it repeated to itself over and over, "I think I can, I think I can" until he finally made it.

We kept going, targeting a location a few feet ahead and making that our next goal. Each time we'd reach our destination, we'd stop for a brief rest, choose another spot a few feet ahead, and move forward. As we trudged up the mountain we chanted, "I think I can, I think I can." Like that little engine in the storybook, we made it. Our guide took a picture of us lying on the ground panting and wheezing, but we had enormous satisfied grins on our faces. We had helped and supported each other up that mountain. Unfortunately though, the rest of the group had made it a long time before and were finishing up a leisurely lunch. By the time we joined them, it was time to push off again.

The last day was supposed to be relatively easy in comparison to most of the trip. We were going to descend a few thousand feet and have lunch in the first small village we would come to. Then we would have a fairly level hike that would bring us to Machu Picchu. The problem I had was that by the morning of the last day, I could barely walk. I had severely sprained one of my ankles, and my knees and feet were sore due to the lack of support my mediocre hiking boots provided me. Edwin asked me why I hadn't brought my military boots, and the only answer I could come up with was I was too inexperienced to know any better. I asked him what would happen if I couldn't hike out, and he told me I would have to hire a helicopter to come get me. That sounded much too expensive, so I figured I was going to have to gut it out somehow.

Edwin made a big staff for me out of a piece of bamboo, so the beginning of the day it wasn't too bad. I fell several times but made adequate progress limping and sliding down several areas of the mountain on my butt. During the last part of that portion of the descent to the village, I was in severe duress. I had asked Edwin to have one of the twenty-five porters bring up the rear to keep the slower hikers like me company, but my request had been ignored.

Dave continued to take me at my word, so suddenly I found myself all alone in the Peruvian mountains, none of my fellow hikers anywhere in sight. I was at the point where the pain was so bad and my legs were so weak that the only way I was able to make any progress at all was to plant the staff about a foot in front of me, lean on it, and drag one leg forward at a time. At each step, I got madder and madder that no one bothered to come back to check on me.

WHATEVER HAPPENED TO NOBODY LEFT BEHIND?

When I finally made it to the village, I collapsed on the ground and looked around for the rest of my group. They were laughing and eating lunch, obviously having been there for quite some time. As Edwin came over to me, I grabbed my staff and tried to smack him upside the head with it, but he backed off out of my reach. I struggled to rein in my temper, asking myself if I really wanted to go to jail for murder. I finally looked at him and snapped, "Go get me a coke!"

The running joke between Edwin and me had been that no matter how remote of an area we were in, I always found some Peruvian woman with a bunch of sodas chilling in a cool stream, waiting for some dumb American like me to pay whatever price she asked to get one. I never found Diet Coke but figured with all the calories I was burning it shouldn't be a problem. The day before had been different, as I had not been able to get one. Not only was I sore, I was starting to go into caffeine withdrawal. Edwin had promised I could get one in the village the next day. True to his word, Edwin bought me a Coke.

Dave came with some cold compresses for my knees and went to work on the rest of my legs. He reached into his medical bag and pulled out a handful of Motrin. Before he could stop me, I grabbed the entire bunch out of his hand, threw them in my mouth, and washed them down with Coke. Dave was horrified. "Gail, you're going to OD!" I looked at him and snarled. Dave and Edwin dragged me over to a bench by the rest of our party and propped me up. Some of the group tried to get me to eat something, but in my foul mood all I wanted was another Coke and to sit by myself and steam. I knew I was acting like a two-year-old child, but at that point I really didn't care what anybody thought of me.

CHARIOTS OF FIRE

The rest of the group went back to finishing their lunch and prepared to leave for the last part of the hike. Edwin told me he was leaving Hector, the assistant cook, with me to guide me to Machu Picchu and then on to our final camp-site. I could tell by his tone he didn't think I would make it. I sat quietly sip-ping my Coke and watched the others head off. I was tempted to jump right into a massive pity party when I remembered once again my dad's advice on handling a problem. I couldn't call him up for a pep talk, so I said to myself, "There are two things you can do about a problem: something or nothing. What are you going to do about this one?"

I began to assess my situation with an eye toward doing something con-structive about it. I needed to finish the hike, that was painfully obvious. Quitting was not an option. On the negative side, I was stranded in the middle of nowhere with a group of people who, other than Dave, didn't know me and apparently could care less what happened to me. As bad as some of my Navy assignments had been, I was used to the military code of teamwork and the mindset of never leaving a buddy behind. It was apparent this group had no concept of that or even of teamwork. I could have fallen off a cliff, got bitten by a snake, or killed by terrorists for all those folks cared. It was going to be up to me to get myself out of this fix.

On the positive side, I finally had a guide who would stick by my side and who knew the last part of the route. The Motrin had taken the edge of the worst of the pain; in fact, my legs and feet were numb. I was still so mad it felt like steam was coming out of my ears, but all of a sudden a scene from the movie *Chariots of Fire* popped into my mind. It was the story of an Olym-pic runner, a Scottish missionary actually, who was participating in a race in Paris. At the start of the race one of the other runners pushed him and knocked him to the ground. The look on the face of that fallen Olympian, one of pure rage and determination, flashed across my mind's eye. I watched the scene as if I was seeing it on the movie screen. He determinedly picked himself up, brushed the gravel off his legs, and went on against all odds to win the race. Seeing myself as that runner, I stood up, grabbed my stick in my left hand, threw down my empty Coke bottle, and set off down the trail in a slow jog with that image of that Olympic runner edging me on.

Hector looked totally stunned but followed along at my pace. I had to stop, lean on my stick, and catch my breath a couple of times, but even though my group had left half an hour before me, I made Machu Picchu only a few minutes behind them. I was done in and could barely walk, but I was there. Dave and one of the other ladies helped me the rest of the way to the campsite.

The very kind lady told me it was her way of apologizing for not appearing to care earlier.

That night Dave and I went out to eat in a restaurant, and as we waited for our dinner, the theme from the movie *Chariots of Fire* began to play over the restaurant radio. I believe that was God's way of letting me know that although I had felt abandoned by my travel companions, He had been with me every step of the way. With God on my side, how could I not have completed the hike? I believe the fact that my companions had appeared uncaring was the best thing that could have happened. If they had coddled me, I don't believe I would have finished the hike.

It was ultimately my positive use of anger that gave me the emotional and physical strength to finish. This whole adventure was a tremendous boost to my self-esteem, which had taken a licking during my battle of the bulge. I had consistently exceeded what I thought were my intellectual limits as I dealt with the demands of a career in military intelligence, but I had never before overcome my perceived physical limitations. I would never want to hike the Inca Trail again, but I will be forever grateful for the experience. When I returned, one Army general came up to me and said, "Gail, I heard about what you did. You don't have to pay for something like that. Come hang with the Army the next time you want to give yourself a physical challenge."

Lest you think ill of Dave, for most of the trip the poor guy was experiencing severe vomiting and diarrhea. I was so self-absorbed I didn't even notice how sick he was. Truthfully, I don't know how he completed the hike. Many of the other hikers fell ill as well. As a matter of fact, I was the only member of the group that didn't get sick during the hike. I waited until I got back to the States and was having a great dinner with Dave in Miami before flying back to Tampa. A couple of hours after dinner it started and lasted all night long. Dave and I have never gone on another vacation together; however, since that time, most of my vacations have revolved around fitness themes, like biking around western Ireland and through the Loire Valley in France.

HELLO, CAPTAIN GAIL HARRIS, GOODBYE DADDY

After all of my adventures, I decided to leave my name on the promotion list for captain. A couple of days before the promotion board was scheduled to meet, I got a panic phone call from a good friend of mine who was working in the naval personnel office. "Gail, I was reviewing your record for the board and saw you didn't have a recent picture in your record. I need a recent picture of you as a commander so they can see you're not fat. They'll be showing the photo as the board reviews your record." I knew I couldn't get an appointment in time to get a new one, but I remembered I did have one fairly recent picture that was taken of Dave and me at a formal navy party. I was concerned that my date in the picture was white, but my friend said no one would care. He was right, I received the promotion. I couldn't wait to tell my dad!

Once I knew the date of my promotion ceremony, I called and asked my dad if he would be able to fly to Tampa for the event. He said he didn't think so. I knew his time on earth must be coming to an end for him to not feel he could be there with me on this important day. My command said I could make whatever promotion arrangements I wanted to, so I contacted the Navy recruiting office in Houston where my family lived. They told me they would be honored to have my ceremony in their office. I didn't make it home in time to see my dad, but I received my captain's eagles at my father's funeral. He was there with me, and I know he was proud of the way I had persevered through each battle. Goodbye, Daddy, thank you for seeing me through and helping me to win my private war.

Takeaway: Focus on winning the war, not just waging war.

Key principles I learned about dealing with trials and tribulations:

1. Every job has its trials and tribulations, so don't think if you change jobs you won't have any more problems. Make sure you are leaving for the right reasons.
2. I decided to not let one bad experience sour me on the whole personal training profession.
3. I had neglected to take into account the fact that men and women communicate differently.
4. With God on my side, how could I not have completed the hike?
5. It was ultimately my positive use of anger that gave me the emotional and physical strength to finish.
6. I discovered the importance of adopting a healthy eating plan as early in your life as possible.

7. I learned to develop an eating plan that's tailor-made for me and takes into consideration my health and family medical history.

8. I saw the value of investing time and money to obtain a personalized exercise plan with exercises I liked and were convenient for me to do.

9. I'm so thankful for my support group. I would have thrown in the towel long ago if people hadn't supported me along the way.

10. The benefits of a healthy exercise and diet plan are so great; I encourage everyone to make them a key part of their life.

NOTES

1. Written by Henry Krieger and Tom Eyen, from the Broadway musical *Dreamgirls*. Original Broadway Cast Recording 1982, Decca U.S.

2. Watty Piper, *The Little Engine That Could*. (New York: Platt&Munk, 1976), 33.

Living in Foreign Lands: Stuff They Don't Tell You in the Travel Books

The ancient Greeks had a saying that "Laughter was of the Gods." Humor has been one of the primary tools I've used over the years to get me through those exceptionally tough times. Humor has been particularly useful for dealing with the challenges of living in foreign lands. The military isn't the only job that requires foreign travel. It has become a major requirement for many of the jobs in today's world. Admittedly it's not easy being on the other side of the world away from family and friends or living in conditions or cultures that make you fearful or uncomfortable, but the bottom line is many jobs in today's world require just that.

Through years of doing career counseling, I've talked to many young people who expect to advance in their jobs but are not willing to do the geographic relocation or travel that might entail. If you're not willing or able to do that, make sure you choose a career that allows you to live where you want. If you find yourself in a job that requires travel and/or foreign living and you fail to learn how to adjust to it, it can have a negative effect on your job. I personally found humor and a little good old American adaptability took me a long way when my Navy career took me to foreign lands.

JOIN THE NAVY AND SEE THE WORLD!

When I was growing up, the Navy's recruiting slogan was, "Join the Navy and See the World." In this case and at that time, there was indeed truth in advertising. By the time my first assignment ended, I had seen many of the countries ringing the western Pacific Ocean. By the time I retired, I had visited or lived in most every part of the world. I found this fun and educational but also a mixed blessing.

When I'm speaking to young people about the pros and cons of a career in the military, they always ask me what I liked the most and what was the least appealing. The answer for both questions is the same, the frequent moves and extensive travel. I know that sounds contradictory, but I actually have a very simple explanation. When I first started out, I enjoyed the adventure and experience of seeing foreign lands and experiencing different cultures. As I got older, I became more set in my ways and wanted my central heat and air conditioning. I wanted American TV and to be able to watch all of the episodes of my favorite soap opera, *Days of Our Lives.* I wanted to be able to watch football games live, and I missed my family terribly.

During my first assignment, when I visited a foreign country, I flew in on one of my squadron's aircraft. I usually stayed on a U.S. military base, which was essentially the same as living in the United States. I had heat and air conditioning, and all my electrical appliances worked on the same current as at home. There were even stores on base where I could buy U.S. products and services. It was only when I stepped outside the gates of the base that I truly experienced the culture of whatever country I was living in.

I was usually so busy with the demands of my job that I didn't spend a great deal of time sightseeing. Occasionally I'd get an opportunity go out to dinner with some of the guys and do some shopping but those occasions were few and far between.

SETTING UP HOUSEKEEPING IN JAPAN

It was my second assignment, when I was assigned to FOSIF Westpac in Japan, that I got a true taste of what it was like to live in a foreign country. I considered myself an experienced traveler since I spent my junior year of college living in Great Britain and Belgium, where my biggest challenge was learning to drink warm Coca-Cola. There were a few cultural differences but nothing like I was to experience during my tour in the Far East.

Most of the housing facilities on overseas military bases were reserved for families of military members who worked on that particular base. There were usually facilities called Bachelor Officer Quarters (BOQ) for single people or those married men and women who came on overseas assignments alone. When I arrived in Japan, I found there was no room in those spaces and that I could only stay in the BOQ for one night while I located a suitable place to live off base.

Finding that an impossible mission, I badgered the housing administrators until they found me temporary quarters sharing a Quonset hut on the naval base at Atsugi about five miles from my work location. I've never liked having a roommate, particularly having to live with someone I didn't know. Turned out though that my roommate was a very nice teacher working at one of the schools on base, but as with any single female around a lot of sailors, she had a very active social life. I'd often be trying to sleep when she was entertaining. The final straw for me was one night when she'd fixed dinner for a group of the guys. Some of them had too much to drink and climbed on top of the hut's roof and started yelling and jumping up and down. I started looking for a place to rent off base the very next day.

My coworkers tipped me off to what I needed to do and, after giving a bottle of expensive whiskey as a "gift" to one of the base housing personnel, I found a three–bedroom, two-bath house in a good location and for a price I could afford. I was over the first hurdle, now on to the second hurdle. I had no furniture. You could always tell the married Navy person over a single one, even if the married ones didn't have their families with them. The married ones had furniture, dishes, lamps, silverware, and everything else you needed to made a house a home. A single person always had a fantastic stereo, a great color television, something to sit on, and something to sleep on. They generally lived under the mindset that these were the essentials for a comfortable lifestyle.

I, of course, was single and true to form, except I didn't even have a bed. As a junior officer, I didn't make much money, but I bought a bed and one of my new coworkers gave me a couch. I paid $30 each for a set of dishes and set of eating utensils. I also bought a set of cooking pots for about $40. There were some tremendous shopping bargains in the Far East at the time, and the quality of most of it was incredible. I still use the same dishes, pots, and utensils that I purchased way back when.

WELCOME TO THE LAND OF OZ

Once I finally found a place to live, I decided to do as I had done in Adak and learn all I could about this place I would call home for this tour of duty.

Japan was a fascinating country, but I felt like Dorothy must have when she found herself in the Land of Oz. Everything was upside down and backward in comparison to what I was used to. My house, for example, had no heating, no air conditioning, and little or no insulation. If it was seventeen degrees outside, it was seventeen degrees in my house. For heat you could have portable kerosene or propane heaters, but the base safety experts warned against leaving these things on while you slept, because without a good ventilation system you could die in your sleep from the fumes.

As a single person with no one home during the day to warm up the place, I came home to a very cold house and a frozen toilet. Being the intelligent, innovative person my dad was so proud of, I came up with a workable solution. When I got home, the only things I took off were my hat and shoes. Then I turned on electric space heaters in my downstairs bathroom and my bedroom and cranked my electric blanket up to the maximum setting. I put my pajamas on the heater to warm up, grabbed a couple of pop tarts for dinner, and crawled under my electric blanket in my uniform and winter coat.

When I smelled the pajamas starting to burn on the heater, I'd get up, throw off my coat and uniform, throw on the smoking pajamas and crawl back under the electric blanket. I left a small space heater on all night in my downstairs bathroom, so when I woke up I'd grab clean clothes, run down stairs through my freezing house, go into the reasonably warm bathroom, take a quick shower, get dressed, and head off to work where it was warm. Some of those living off base told me they'd just take their clean clothes on base, shower, and get dressed at the base gym.

Another coping mechanism during the cold months was to become one of those nightmare dinner guests who come to dinner and then wouldn't go home. To their credit, I had friends on base who felt sorry for me and often invited me to dinner in their homes and let me stay the night. There were four wonderful families that adopted me and to whom I will be forever grateful: Jack and Bonnie Shankles, Chris and Merrie Corkill, Frank and Margo Cotton, and Chris and Barry Flynn. I owe you much. Thanks guys!

Another challenge I faced was what to do with my garbage. A couple of times a week, I noticed my Japanese neighbors leaving neatly wrapped packages outside on the street in front of their homes. At first I thought they were leaving stuff to be picked up by the Japanese equivalent of Goodwill or the Salvation Army. Turned out that was how they prepared their garbage to be picked up. I asked some of the other singles living off base for advice. I really couldn't see myself taking the time to wrap my garbage up like Christmas presents several times a week. Their advice was to throw the garbage in the trunk of my car and dump it in garbage cans on the base. Worked for me!

DRIVING: THE ULTIMATE CHALLENGE

Driving for me was the ultimate challenge. Like the British, the Japanese drive on the left side of the road, and because I'd lived in England that wasn't quite as foreign to me as it was to other first timers. There were, however, some other real scary aspects to driving in Japan. I had what we in the United States considered a small Toyota, which may have been small by U.S. standards, but it was huge by Japanese standards. The roads were very narrow, and even my small car took up most of the road. Most of the roads were considered two–way, but I frequently encountered cars parked along the side, making the available driving space even smaller.

The real fun started when I would meet a car coming at me from the opposite direction. The space was often not big enough for both of us to drive through at the same time, so one of us would have to either pull over or back up. Sounds simple but apparently in their driving culture, the first one to move over or back up "lost face." As near as I could figure out, that meant losing your dignity and/or self-respect. This frequently led to a stand off that could last for hours. The best story I ever heard involved a friend of mine who told me that he and another driver sat there for several minutes with each refusing to give an inch. Finally, my friend calmly opened up his lunch and started eating. The other driver finally gave way.

The Japanese are also very aggressive drivers. They'd cut in front of each other all the time and speed whenever the bumper-to-bumper traffic would allow. Pedestrians were another problem, particularly the children. In a lot of the neighborhoods, the houses weren't set too far back from the street, and the Japanese children would run out of their houses directly into the street without looking to the left or right. They would just throw up one of their hands, warning you they were crossing the street. Usually by the time I'd see them, they were already in the middle of the street. If you accidentally hit and killed one of them, you would have to pay their family the cost of what it would have taken to educate them for their chosen profession, which was generally medicine or engineering.

The end result of all this was most Americans had at least one car accident some time during their stay in Japan. The good news was because of the heavy traffic, they were usually just fender benders with no serious injuries to either party. If someone was hurt in the accident, you had to go see the person in the hospital, bring him or her a gift, and apologize profusely. If you didn't, you risked being sued.

I had my accident while trailing several other friends in their cars en route to a Formula One race in Tokyo. At one intersection, three of the cars ahead of me made right hand turns, but as I prepared to follow them I saw a car fast approaching from the opposite direction. We both slammed on our brakes. My car slid to a stop, but his slid out of control and appeared to slam into a tree at the side of the road. Fortunately his car slid into a sewage ditch just before it would have hit the tree. When an American was involved in an accident, we all had to stand around and wait while the police called in interpreters. I started to pace back and forth, so one of my friends broke out some sandwiches and cookies in hopes of calming my nerves. When the interpreter finally showed up, he took both of our statements and then went to confer with the police. I started sweating and pacing again, but much to my relief, the police decided we were both in the wrong and just made us bow to each other, shake hands, and apologize.

HELP, I'M LOST AND I CAN'T READ THE SIGNS

Another challenge was you could never predict how long it would take to get from one place to another because of the horrific traffic jams. I've driven in California, New York City, and Washington, DC, traffic, but traffic jams in Japan are the worst I've ever experienced. There were two small U.S. Navy bases in the vicinity of my job. Each were like mini cities and had stores and movie theaters. Sometimes we'd want to go to the largest Navy (Yokosuka) or Air Force (Yokota) bases in the area because of the larger military stores. They were both filled with great shopping bargains, and the Navy base even had a Baskin Robbins. The drive to Yokosuka could take any where from thirty minutes to seven hours, depending on the traffic.

Compounding the traffic problem for me was the fact that I couldn't read the street signs. Most of the signs were in Japanese characters. We Americans developed our own methods for giving directions. If someone invited you off base, they would give directions based on landmarks, not the names of streets.

The directions would go something like, "Go out the front gate, drive until you see the advertising posters with two babies on it, make a right, go three blocks, and turn right at the gravel pit." After getting lost for hours numerous times, I came up with a plan. I started carrying around a large wad of Japanese money. When I had given it my best shot, I found a taxi, got out of my car, walked over to him, gave him the name of the U.S. base I was trying to find, pointed to my car, gave him the money, and then followed him to my destination. Good old American ingenuity at work.

DON'T DRIVE, TAKE THE TRAIN

Since driving was so stressful, most of us used the excellent Japanese train system whenever we could. You could get almost anywhere you wanted by train, but this too presented some interesting challenges. As the train approached each stop, the Japanese conductor announced the name of that stop. Sounds simple enough, but the problem we ran into was there is a big difference in the way the Japanese and the Americans pronounced the names of these stops. The solution was to count the number of stops you had from where you got on to where you wanted to get off. Heaven help you if you fell asleep.

If you took the train into Tokyo, your next problem was to figure out how to exit the station. The Japanese have built a huge underground subcity directly under Tokyo that is filled with shops and restaurants. When I first started going there, I'd just follow the crowd, figuring eventually I'd find my way out. After I wandered around for a while, some kindly soul would see that "I'm lost" look on my face and offer their help. A lot of the Japanese learn English in school, and they actually look for opportunities to practice their English on poor lost American tourists. Always on the alert for a solution, I took to hanging out with a military girlfriend that actually learned the language. I had a great time following her around to restaurants, museums, and plays.

Eating out was another challenge, since the menus were in Japanese. There was an easy way around this problem, though, because most Japanese restaurants had plastic replicas of everything on the menu displayed in their front window. I'd just grab my waitress or waiter, drag them outside, and point at what I wanted.

One of the many neat things about Tokyo was that their movie theaters played the latest American movies in English with Japanese subtitles. The first time I went, as we were waiting in line for the theater doors to open, my friend said, "When the doors open stay close to me." I didn't know what she was talking about until the doors opened, and all those people who had been waiting patiently in line suddenly turned into a mob running as fast as they could for the nearest seat. Turns out the theaters sold more tickets than there were seats available, so if you were unlucky or not fast enough, you had to stand while watching the movie.

KOREA: BARGAIN CENTRAL

I've also spent a great deal of time in Korea, which, though located in Asia, is entirely different from Japan. Where the Japanese were very polite but very formal and reserved, the Koreans were warm, friendly, and very open. I was fortunate enough to live on base in Korea, but friends who lived on the economy said Korean homes had a heating system that involved pipes under the floors, which kept them warm and cozy.

The big thing about Korea was the shopping. I don't usually shop for anything but books and music, but in Korea I was out of control. You could buy complete sets of luggage for $11.00, thick sweaters for $3.00, and brand name sneakers for $5.00. You could have tailor-made clothes done for $20.00. It was incredible. With all those bargains, I had to come up with a way to control my spending. The first thing I did when I arrived at my shopping destination was buy two return bus tickets, one for me and one for whatever I'd end up buying. I would only take a certain sum of cash money and one credit card. I would shop until I ran out of cash, switch to my charge card, and keep going until I couldn't carry anymore in my arms. I'd stagger back to the bus station and take the ride back to my home base. Sometimes I'd just buy a new suitcase with wheels to stuff all of my purchases into. At the end of my assignment, I had a lot of suitcases.

The year I was there I went home for Christmas dragging three huge suitcases filled with stuff. When I went through U.S. customs, the official looked at my stuff in amazement and asked how long I was planning on being in the States. I told him ten days, and I thought his eyes were going to pop out of his head. I flashed him my military ID and he obviously decided to cut me a break. He let me through without any further problems.

When I got home to Houston, my family went hog wild. I had bought Christmas presents for everyone. I had also brought my young nephews leather flight jackets and brand name sneakers. I had thick, furry blankets, sweaters, custom-made sweat suits, and designer jeans, which Mom and my sister immediately laid claim to. They even took the stuff I had bought home for myself, reasoning I was going back and could buy more when I returned. The end result was I went back with only one small carry-on.

THE KOREAN CULTURAL CHALLENGE

Korea did have one cultural challenge for me. As part of my job, I was expected to socialize with my Korean military counterparts. Since the senior Korean military members were all male, the Navy had been reluctant to send senior female officers to jobs in that country. About 50 percent of the social obligation involved interacting with the Koreans and their families, while the other 50 percent involved going to dinner with just the males and then on to the nightclubs until the wee hours of the morning. The U.S. military guys were concerned that the Koreans would have a problem with female officers participating.

This actually posed no problem for me. After dinner, my Korean counterpart would politely escort me outside, find me a cab, and then all the guys would continue on with whatever they did for the rest of the evening. I considered myself blessed, as the next morning my American counterparts came into work looking heavily hungover while I was bright-eyed and bushy-tailed. It was apparent to me that the Koreans frowned on women drinking in public, so during dinner I usually only drank soda or water. Once I got daring and had a small shot glass of their national drink, called Soju. I forget what it's made of, but the next day I felt awful and broke out in hives. Once was enough for me.

The Koreans did have a hard time understanding why I was single, though. When I told them I had been engaged twice and jilted each time, they could not understand how a man would have so little honor that he would promise to marry a woman and then back out. When I left that country, I was honored by having a professional call with the number one and number two highest-ranking men in their military intelligence organization. I had a half-hour session with each one and was politely grilled on why I was single. When I told my father about it later, he was furious, but I was flattered by their concern. They obviously thought I was a nice lady and couldn't understand why some man hadn't snapped me up.

THE MIDDLE EAST AND PERSIAN GULF

I've also spent a great deal of time in the Middle East and Persian Gulf. The first time I went to that part of the world was during the first Gulf War when I was stationed in Bahrain, an island nation located in the Persian Gulf off the coast of Saudi Arabia. My first impression was that I'd stepped onto a movie set. It was gorgeous and exotic, and everyone was decked out in beautiful flowing robes. I was very self-conscious about my Western dress, as every woman was dressed in conservative black robes. Many were covered from head to toe with only their eyes showing.

I always tried to respect the culture of whatever country I was in. I was really concerned that I was offending these people by the way I dressed, so I was very reluctant to venture out except when I went to work. I dressed as conservatively as I could and stayed in my room on my few days off. One day my mom called and was surprised to find me in my hotel room. She knew it was my day off and had just planned to leave a message for me to call her later. I told her I was afraid to go out because all I had were Western-style clothes. She said, "You know if you go out you'll probably find other women out and about in Western-style dress." I took her advice and went shopping at one of their malls. She was right, as mothers often are.

I ended up spending so much time there that I had a Bahraini driver's license. After the first Gulf War, I was assigned to the Naval Forces Central Command (NAVCENT). I was part of the command's small planning staff colocated with United States Central Command (USCENTCOM) at MacDill Air Force Base in Tampa, Florida, but Bahrain was actually the fleet headquarters. Because the crisis with Iraq didn't end with the Gulf War, I ended up spending more time in Bahrain than I did in Tampa. Whenever the crisis heated up, I went over to Bahrain to augment the intelligence staff there. I didn't mind; I liked being in the thick of things. Bahrain has a strong British influence, so gradually I began to feel more comfortable mingling in their culture.

My command strongly recommended that when socializing off base, both men and women dress in conservative clothes. I only violated that rule once. At the time, one of my favorite activities was jogging. I enjoyed it, and it helped me control my weight. The winters weren't too bad, but in the summer the heat could go up to 115 degrees. Jogging in that hot, dry desert climate was difficult for me. It was considered a real no-no for a woman to go outside in shorts and a tee shirt, so I just ran around the small available space on the base doing multiple laps to make my miles. It was somewhat boring, but it worked for me since I could wear shorts and tee shirts while jogging on base. There was no way I was going to jog around in that climate all covered up, especially when I was on a U.S. base.

One of the neat things about overseas assignments is that U.S. military folks tend to socialize together more than when assigned to a U.S. location. Small things like dining out and sightseeing become major social events, so once folks found out I liked to jog, that became a social event as well. A group of us would jog together, then clean up and go out to eat.

One day I was going jogging with the command chaplain and a Marine colonel but found out they were going off base. I knew it was probably not a good idea, but I went along with and did it anyway. Everything went well until we were about a half mile away from the base. All of a sudden a car with four women in it started following us. They were all dressed in the traditional black robes, and my first thought was I was going to cause an international incident violating the off-base dress code. I really started to feel anxious but decided it was best if I kept running and stayed close to my coworkers. At the end of the run the women stopped their car and applauded me. I guess they were thinking that this old woman was actually keeping up with those two men. In actuality, the guys had slowed their pace so I could keep up with them. I usually jogged along at a ten- to twelve-minute-per-mile pace, but running with these guys I had run at a nine-minute-per-mile pace. In spite of that reaction, I never jogged off base again. It wasn't worth the risk. I could see the headlines in the paper: "Sight of middle-aged American woman's legs causes riot in Arab country."

EGYPT

I didn't actually interact socially with people from the Arab world until I spent about five months filling in as the naval attaché in Egypt. I was initially told that the embassy had turned me down because there had never been a female military attaché in the Middle East. There was concern that the military men of those countries wouldn't deal with a female. Turned out the embassy's concerns were unfounded, as I have never been treated better or with more professional respect or courtesy. As far as my Middle Eastern counterparts were concerned, if the embassy said I was the one they dealt with for naval matters, it was okay with them.

On my first day there, I was taken over to the Egyptian Ministry of Defense. One of the senior Egyptian military guys came over and introduced himself. He gave me a big grin and said, "You don't know this but today you are the most famous woman in Cairo!" Unlike my experience with U.S. military males, my credibility was never a problem. They assumed if I had made the rank, I was competent. I never experienced any of the negative issues I frequently experienced dealing with U.S. military men.

I understand there was intense speculation of how I would handle the dinner parties, but there were no cultural problems at all while I was there. In Egypt, the men and women would mingle during the cocktail hour and sit down at the same dinner table; but after dinner the men would go into one room and the women into another. People wondered where I would go. It was a no-brainer for me. It actually reminded me of growing up in a southern-values African American home. During the dinner parties in my family, after dinner the men went into one room and the women the other. I chose to hang out with the Egyptian women. They loved it and took me under their wings and made sure I was invited to all of the parties. A big part of the attaché job was socializing. If the wives hadn't liked me, I would not have been able to do a big part of my job. I found the women warm, smart, elegant, and charming.

The other thing that struck me about the Arab world was the religious thing. I knew very little about Islam, so I was surprised to find out their religion shared reverence for many of the same biblical characters as Christianity. I find it interesting that three of the world's major religions—Judaism, Christianity, and Islam—share the same patriarch, Abraham, and many of the same religious values. Odd isn't it that we all can't seem to get along.

MY PERSONAL FAVORITE, IRELAND

I loved living in Spain, but when asked which country was my favorite place to live outside of the United States, I'd have to say Ireland was my all-time favorite. As corny as it sounds, something about the place calls to my soul, which is why when offered the opportunity to go there as part of a writer's retreat a few years after I retired, I grabbed my credit card and threw financial caution to the wind. That was my fourth trip to Ireland.

Midway through the nine-day trip, I plunked myself down in the hotel bar in front of a roaring peat fire with a glass of Jameson whiskey in hand. I don't usually drink hard liquor. My idea of a strong drink is regular Coca-Cola as opposed to diet. Throughout the trip, tour guides had kept talking about how much some of the more famous Irish writers drank. I was suffering from writer's block. I'd only written one of the two articles I needed to do before I returned home to Durango, Colorado. I figured if whiskey was good enough for famous writers, I'd see what it could do for me and my creative process.

After a few sips of that potent brew, I felt my face begin to go numb. I didn't panic, figuring I couldn't get alcohol poisoning from three sips of whiskey. I put the glass down, closed my eyes, and sank down further into my chair while letting my mind roam. What was it about Ireland that kept drawing me back? I came up with two trains of thought, one personal and one political.

On the personal front, my journeys to Ireland were reflected in the name of my favorite soap opera, *The Days of My Life*. My first trip had occurred as I was turning twenty, the second as I was going into my 40s, and counting the current trip, I made two trips in my 50s. As I got older and more financially prosperous, my trips got more lavish, but there was one thing that never changed. Ireland was the first place I ever went as an adult where I was made to feel my skin color was irrelevant. I always felt welcome in Ireland.

My first trip to Ireland was as part of a junior year abroad program. We were studying in London, and since most of us didn't have much money we broke up into groups of fours to split travel expenses and keep costs down. We usually went in groups of two guys and two girls so we'd have someone to share lodging costs with. As fate would have it on this trip, the two guys were white and the two women black. We didn't have enough money to stay at hotels but could afford the cheaper bed-and-breakfast establishments. Our Irish hosts seemed genuinely surprised when the women stayed in one room and the guys the other. They'd always ask, "There now, did ya' have a fight?" Linda and I would always giggle and say, "We did and we're not speaking to them!" Apparently the Irish had no issues with interracial dating, which in the United States in the 1960s was the "gay marriage rights" issue of the time.

IRISH HOSPITALITY

The other thing I've always liked about the Irish is their overall friendliness. They go out of their way to help you out and make you feel welcome. On my first trip to Ireland, my travel companions and I actually spent our first night in jail. Our only crime was stupidity. We'd flown into Belfast airport and rented a car with a standard shift. None of us knew how to drive a standard shift, but it was that or walk. The guys did the macho thing and said they would do all the driving. Linda and I had no problem with it. Neither of us felt up to the challenge of trying to drive on the left-hand side of the road while simultaneously learning to shift gears.

I knew we were in for trouble before we even got out of the airport parking lot. It was freezing cold, so the guys had to spray some defrosting stuff on the car lock just to be able to get the key in the door to open it. Then they couldn't figure out how to drive the car forward. The rental car attendant saw what was happening, took pity on us, and came out to give them a quick lesson on shifting gears.

We had four days and wanted to see as much of Ireland as possible, so we decided to circle the country. After about an hour of driving, the car stopped moving and we noticed a rather strong smell emulating from it. The guys opened the hood, presumably trying to give the impression they knew about cars. Nothing the guys did worked. It was so cold they finally gave up and got back in the car. We didn't know what to do, so we just sat there shivering, getting colder and colder until we heard a tap on the window. It was a couple of policemen. We explained our situation, and the police looked under the hood and crawled under the car, then came back with a twinkle in their eyes. "You burned out the clutch!"

They took us over to the jail and let us use their phone to call the car rental company. We wouldn't be able to get a replacement car until the next morning, so they invited us to spend the night, made us some hot chocolate, and let us sleep on chairs in front of the fireplace. We burned out two more cars before that trip ended, but each time someone was there to rescue the dumb American students. They took us in, let us use their phone, and gave us food and drink while we waited.

My second memory of Irish friendliness happened on my next trip nearly twenty years later. I was traveling with my good buddy Dave. We were both single and unattached and worked for the same organization in Spain. We had an unspoken agreement to keep our relationship platonic. We enjoyed each other's company so much we didn't want to jinx it by adding the complications of romantic dating. We decided to share hotel rooms during the trip, figuring if we combined our financial resources we could afford to stay at the finest hotels and eat at the best restaurants.

I had just been dumped by my boyfriend, just turned forty, and considered myself over the hill. To ease any potential concerns Dave may have had about me being on the rebound and having newly developed romantic intentions toward him, I started the trip off by saying, "Normally I sleep in the nude . . . but I just know you're the type of man who's attracted to midriff bulge and cellulite, so I'll sleep in pajamas so you don't lose control of yourself."

On one of our last nights in country, we went to dinner at Bunratty Castle and then decided to have a nightcap in the hotel bar before we retired. As we entered the bar, a good-looking man sitting at the bar waved hello. It didn't raise any flags for me since it was a common occurrence during our trip. Next thing I knew, he was standing at our table with a pint of Guinness in hand. "Glory be if it tisn't my dream woman in the flesh. I've always wanted to have sex with a black woman." Pointing at Dave he continued, "Darlin' what are you doing with him? Come away with me now and put me out of my misery." Laughing I looked at Dave and winked, "Thank you for the complement, but I'm very happy with my friend."

Seems he couldn't take no for an answer. Pulling up a chair, my new admirer sat down and said, "Don't look at me. I can't stand it. I just want to kiss your luscious black lips. Come away with me darlin'." He continued on for about twenty minutes. He was so charming even Dave was cracking up. We finally made our excuses and retired to our room. As we were leaving he screamed after me, "Darlin' don't tell me what room you're in. I don't think I'd be able to control myself." The next morning, Dave looked at me and asked, "Why didn't you run off with that man?"

"Performance anxiety," I replied, "No mortal woman could live up to his dreams." I may not have run off with him, but he certainly gave me back my womanly self-confidence. I may have been dumped by my boyfriend, but here in Ireland at least one man thought I was a goddess.

POLITICS AND HISTORY

Snapping back to the present, I took another sip of whiskey and let my thoughts drift off to politics and history, which was the second thing that kept drawing me back to Ireland. All of the issues being discussed as world problems today can be found in Irish history: religious persecutions, poverty, famine, immigration, emigration, slavery, the dot-com boom, and the list could go on and on.

I knew about King Henry VIII of England dropping out of the Catholic Church because it wouldn't approve of him dumping his wife so he could marry Anne Boleyn, but I had no idea of how it affected the average person until I looked closer at Irish history. Catholics were denied property and the right to vote. In the 1600s, "many women and children, defeated soldiers, and priests were shipped off to the West Indies and sold as slaves. These were to be the ancestors of the so-called 'Black Irish' of Montserrat, the Caribbean island where Irish was still spoken up to 100 years ago by a mixed-race people."[1] Religious discrimination remains a hot topic well into present times.

During the nineteenth century, when the potato crop failed in Ireland, it triggered a widespread famine that lasted from 1845 until 1849. By 1900, almost half of Ireland's estimated nine million people had immigrated to other countries. Today Ireland has bounced back and is the largest exporter of software in the world. Now they have people immigrating there for a better life. This isn't the first time Ireland has experienced an influx of foreigners. The Vikings, Normans, and British are all part of the rich Irish history.

As I drifted out of my relaxed revelry, I was reminded of the importance of studying the history of any place we may be called to visit overseas. I gained so many insights from my stays in foreign countries and through exposure to their cultures. God bless the Navy for allowing me to live a life of travel. I joined the Navy and saw the world.

Takeaway: Many jobs today require foreign travel and living—deal with it.

Key principles I learned from living in foreign lands:

1. Humor has been one of the primary tools I've used over the years to get me through those exceptionally tough times and has been particularly useful for dealing with the challenges of living in foreign lands.
2. I needed to take the time to learn about the place I would call home for each tour of duty, which paid off in such richly rewarding dividends.

NOTE

1. Seamas Mac Annaidh, *Irish History*. (Bath BA 1 1 HE, UK:Parragon Book, 2005), p. 114.

8

What If You're the Problem?

Knowing yourself is the beginning of all wisdom.

—*Aristotle*[1]

When the sun is shining I can do anything; no mountain is too high, no trouble too difficult to overcome.

—*Wilma Rudolph*[2]

I believe every one of us has a good side and a bad side. One of the most important things a person can do during the course of his or her life is identify their personal strengths as well as their weaknesses. To succeed in life, we have to learn to play to and build on our strengths, while at the same time accepting or making peace with our weaknesses. We only need to follow the news to see what happens to people who let their bad side dominate. Unchecked negative character traits can wreak havoc on both our personal lives and our careers. The sad truth, though, is that too often our friends aren't honest with us, and our oversight neglects to tell us that the real reason we were passed over for promotion was an uncontrolled character flaw.

UP FRONT AND PERSONAL

As I moved up in rank, I sat in on many meetings with supervisors where we had to evaluate workers for performance reports or decide who was going to get the best jobs in an organization. Long ago my dad had told me I'd be surprised at how often bosses or superiors talked about your job performance behind the scenes. I found out he was correct, as usual. Many times in meetings I've heard such comments as, "She's immature. No way she's leadership material," or, "He whined about his divorce for weeks. He's not leadership material," or, "He doesn't know how to interact with people."

I frequently asked my fellow evaluators if they'd ever talked to these people about what they considered a negative character flaw. The response was always the same: "He or she should know." As true as that may be, I would then encourage them to talk to the person being discussed concerning these negative character traits in case he or she wasn't aware of them. It always seemed to me that bringing them out in the open and giving each person a chance to deal with these negatives was only fair. I've always made it a practice to call people in and chew them out over their negative work habits. They usually start out thinking I'm just being a witch, but later many have thanked me for giving them the chance to rectify the situation before it ruined their chances for promotion.

Intelligence professionals don't get much management experience, but I've had several jobs where I had to manage other analysts. The pattern I followed was always the same. I'd call everyone together and be totally up front about what I expected from every member of my team. I'd say,

> I'm pretty simple to figure out. All I ask is you do what I ask, when I ask. If there is a problem with carrying out my orders or completing any projects you're working on, please let me know so we can revisit the time lines and I can help you solve those problems. I'm into microknowledge, not micromanagement. If you do this, you will find me one of the best bosses you've ever had. If you don't, you'll find me one of the meanest, most obnoxious people you've ever worked for. It's up to you.

Almost without exception, they would start out challenging every decision I'd make but come around eventually and even admit my management style worked.

CASE IN POINT: ASSIGNMENT KOREA

My assignment in South Korea involved overseeing the intelligence support for the 1988 Olympics as head of the Indications and Warning Watch. It was an organization similar to an Ocean Surveillance Information System (OSIS) node, except it was joint. We were responsible for providing South Korea and the United States with updated information on any potential attack or negative actions being carried out by North Korea. I had people from all the services plus a Cryptologic Support Group (CSG) working for me, and it was also multinational. My deputy was a South Korean colonel, and I had a separate intelligence watch made up of all South Korean military personnel.

The guy I replaced had been dealing with some serious family issues and hadn't done much to prepare the organization for the upcoming Olympics. The event was going to start just a few weeks after my arrival, so the members of my new organization wanted me to start making major changes the day I arrived. During our initial meeting, I told them my first moves would be focused on learning how they were organized, because I didn't believe I could improve an organization without firsthand knowledge of how it worked. I needed to learn what was working and what was not and then make my changes based on what I learned.

One young Air Force officer stormed into my office after the meeting, full of righteous concern and furious at what he considered was wasting time we did not have. I patiently explained my methodology, but he wasn't having any of it and started yelling at me. I stood up, looked him in the eye, and challenged him. "If you think there are problems, I want you to write me a paper, identify them, and give me proposed solutions." He did just that and I implemented many of his suggestions, but only after I had taken the time to examine the way the organization was set up. In spite of that shaky beginning, he would become one of my biggest supporters and one of my most valuable workers.

I also initially had problems with the CSG. On one of my first days there, I asked them to research a signals intelligence (SIGINT) issue for me, but the senior CSG enlisted man refused, saying, "With all due respect, I don't work for you, I work for NSA [National Security Agency]." I didn't say a word to him as I picked up his phone and called the CSG watch in Hawaii. I had great relations with them, so I simply asked my questions, they answered each one, and they encouraged me to call again if I had any other questions. I hung up the phone, gave the CSG guy a "don't you ever even think of messing with me again" look, and left the room. I never had trouble with the CSG in Korea again. I would never be their favorite person, but during the year I was there they gave me great support.

SEEING THE POTENTIAL, NOT JUST THE PROBLEM

My results as a manager were almost always the same. The first few weeks on the job, my people couldn't stand me, but when it was time for me to be transferred they didn't want me to go. They found it unique that I meant what I said and would call them on any negative traits, and if they changed I'd give them excellent performance reports. Some young workers think if you criticize their performance you either don't like them or you're just being mean. I paraphrase a famous George Bernard quote when explaining my management style to them:

> Some people look at poorly performing workers and say why? I look at you and see the potentially great intelligence analyst within you and say why not? The intent of my criticism is to make you into the analyst I know you can be.

I've got several negative traits that I've spent a lot of time and effort trying to overcome. I haven't always been successful, and several times it was only through the grace of God that my career survived. One of the major lessons I've learned is if I maintain the right mental attitude I can soar with the eagles, but if I don't I'll crash and burn. By right mental attitude, I mean seeing the glass as half full instead of half empty. It means keeping my faith strong and persevering, even if it means crawling on my hands and knees if that's what it takes. It means getting up and dusting myself off when I stumble, no matter how embarrassed or humiliated I feel about a particular situation.

This is no simple task for me, especially since I have a lifelong history of dealing with depression. Depression is one of the side effects of thyroid disease, though I've been fortunate in that I never needed to use antidepressants. The pattern I've discovered in my life is that when I have a specific goal I'm working toward and things are going along smoothly, when something I think is bad happens, I start to head for that black hole of depression. If I allow myself to remain in this negative mindset, bad things continue to happen. As soon as I start to pick myself up enough to reevaluate the situation and come up with a new approach, the tide starts to turn in my favor.

DEALING WITH DEPRESSION

I've developed several techniques to deal with the type of depression caused by Graves' disease and the high-stress job challenges, apparent failures, and personal setbacks I've experienced. The first one is reading biographies of successful people. Without exception, these folks had to overcome multiple perceived failures before achieving ultimate success. Their stories always inspire me and give me the strength to keep trying.

One of my favorite stories is about a young woman born on June 23, the same day I was but a few years earlier, in 1940. She was premature and very sickly, causing her to develop scarlet fever, double pneumonia, and finally polio. The doctor told her family she'd never walk, but by the time she was nine years old she was walking with the help of a brace, and at thirteen she no longer even needed the brace. She had a rolling gait, but she was walking unassisted. That was not enough for this determined young lady. She joined her high school basketball team, setting the state record for scoring and leading her team to the state championships. She started running track, even though people told her she was making a fool of herself. At age sixteen she made the Olympic team and won a bronze medal. Four years later she became the first American woman to win three gold medals in the Olympics.

After reading Wilma Rudolph's story, how could I stay depressed? If she could overcome all that she had to deal with, how could I not find the inner strength to deal with whatever challenges I was facing? I've collected many such stories over the years, and when I'm feeling like I don't have anything left to give, I pick up one those stories and read them again. They never fail to motivate me.

I've also found that a physical work out makes the depression go away. If I go for a run or a bike ride or do some weight training, my mood is suddenly elevated. I've read that the medical reason for this is that exercise causes a mood-elevating chemical to be secreted in your brain. All I can say is it works for me.

THE "AIN'T IT AWFUL GAME"

Another technique I often use is the "Ain't It Awful Game," which was given to me by my beloved spiritual mentor Reverend Helen. She taught me that when I was faced with a problem, I was to call up a trusted friend and follow these simple rules. They have to listen to you whine and complain for at least ten minutes without criticism. While you're complaining they are to mutter such soothing and sympathetic comments as, "That's awful," "Poor baby," or "You poor thing." After ten minutes, they can begin to offer such constructive criticism as, "Gail, don't you think that when you threw that man's coffee cup against the wall, most people would feel you were not only behaving unprofessionally but were way out of control?"

I'm not a trained psychologist, but I find it relieves a lot of stress and tension if I can rant and rave about a situation and get all those negative, ugly thoughts and emotions out of my system. Once I do that, I'm better able to rationally accept constructive criticism and move on to actually deal with the problem in a constructive way. The secret to success when using this technique is to carefully choose your game partners.

I have several categories of "Ain't It Awful Game" partners. I choose whom to call depending on the situation at hand. If it's a career problem, I'll call someone in my profession. If I think I'm being dumped on because I'm a woman, I'll call one of my girlfriends who is in the same career field. If I think I'm being dumped on because I'm African American, I'll call another African American in my career field.

The deductive reasoning behind my choice of game partners is very simple. Since I'm always into solutions, if I think the failure or setback may, and I emphasize "may," be because I'm a woman, I don't want to call some guy who's going to think that I'm being overly sensitive or emotional. Since I'm already stressed, the last thing I want or need to deal with is convincing a man that although there has been great progress made, the workplace is still not always an equal playing field. By calling up another professional female, she already knows this, and we can cut to the chase.

What I would be looking for in this particular situation would be help in deciding if my problem was resulting from being a female in a nontraditional career field or because I've done something wrong that needs to be corrected. If she's ever faced that situation herself, she can tell me how she dealt with it. She can candidly say if she thinks it was my fault or if the other person was in the wrong and make suggestions and recommendations to help me to improve the situation.

All of this to say, if you're going to play this game, it is crucial that you choose someone who knows you well and whose opinion you respect; otherwise, it will turn into a nonproductive whining session, and you will be no better off than you were before you made the call.

TEMPER, TEMPER!

My worst trait is absolutely my temper. It's not that I have a short fuse and fly into a rage for little or nothing. It actually takes a lot to make me angry, but when it happens I turn into a female version of the Incredible Hulk. I don't turn green, but I'm told the veins pop out on my forehead and I start yelling and using bad language. Whenever I have found myself in professional trouble, it was almost always because I lost control of my temper. I might not have even done anything wrong, but I left myself open for someone who didn't like me to exploit the situation and ignite the flame of my explosive temper. In other words, several times I ended up shooting myself in the foot.

One instance that comes to mind happened while I was assigned to the Pacific Fleet staff. I was temporarily put in charge of the Soviet Navy Analysis Shop, which was one of the most prestigious jobs in the naval intelligence community, especially for someone like me with the rank of lieutenant commander. My new department was part of the OSIS node that provided intelligence support for the operational staff, the Fleet Ocean Information Center (FOSIC).

I was happy to be in Hawaii with some of my favorite people in the world. It was a great working environment; I had a fabulous town home on the water and was a member of a great church. Even though I knew it was only temporary, life was good. Then into my Garden of Eden came a snake, though I didn't recognize that at first.

People this guy had served with had given me a heads up, telling me that he had been an egomaniac even before his recently completed prestigious embassy assignment. He also had a reputation of lying about others to superiors and stabbing people in the back to get ahead. What made him even more dangerous, they warned me, was he was the kind of guy who smiled in your face as he was stabbing you in the back. I decided to withhold judgment though until I had a chance to see for myself. Because I have frequently been the victim of prejudgment, I tried to keep an open mind and judge people by how they treated me rather than what I may have heard about them from others. I've had many experiences where I got along very well with someone who other people had problems with.

My initial impressions of him were that he was a nice guy and knew a lot about the Soviet Union. In fact, he was the first person I heard predict the fall of the Soviet Union based on what he'd learned about their economic problems. I decided to give him the benefit of the doubt. What I didn't know at the time, though, was he thought he was going to get my job when the new boss came in; however, when the new boss arrived, he liked me and decided to keep me in the job and have "Mr. Ego" work for me. "Mr. Ego" was not happy with this arrangement and proceeded to become everyone's worst nightmare to work with. Without exception, everyone in my shop couldn't stand him. There were several occasions where I had to physically restrain someone from decking him. I tried to deal with the situation with my usual humor, but it just wasn't working for me this time.

The final straw came when I came into work one day to find all of my people in an unscheduled staff meeting with "Mr. Ego." He had taken it upon himself to inform my staff how terribly screwed up our department was and how we could all be doing things better. After the meeting, each of my people came to me complaining about his management style, and once again I had to physically restrain one guy from punching his lights out. That was bad enough, but then "Mr. Ego" decided to tell me what I was doing wrong and what I needed to do that day to fix it. This was it as far as I was concerned, this guy had to go. I gave in to my anger, turned into the Incredible Hulk, and cursed him out in front of everyone which, unbeknownst to me, included the senior intelligence officer who had come in at the height of my verbal outburst.

ERROR, ERROR!

I should have listened to that little inner alarm saying, error, error, error. It's true I had a legitimate complaint about "Mr. Ego," but I made a couple of critical errors in judgment. I should have gone to my boss as soon as it was apparent that this guy was going to be a problem. This would have at least alerted him that there was a potential situation in the works. Instead, I tried to handle the situation myself, thinking I didn't want to get anyone in trouble; however, when I lost my temper in a very public forum, it caused the senior leadership to start thinking there was something wrong with me since they didn't know the background leading up to the blow out. "Mr. Ego" was smart enough not to respond to me publicly when I was yelling at him, but it gave him just what he needed to lay the ground work to ruin my reputation with the senior staff.

I was pulled out of my Hawaii assignment eighteen months early to go to Korea to head up the 1988 Olympics support, but the Naval personnel people promised me my next assignment would be back in Hawaii. The plan was to give me command of a small intelligence detachment, which was quite a vote of confidence from the folks in Washington since neither an African American nor a female had ever had an intelligence command in the navy.

During my absence, a new senior intelligence officer was assigned to the Pacific Fleet headquarters who I had never worked with, so all he knew of me was based on what he'd heard through those who had. "Mr. Ego" used this opportunity to tell him I was a mediocre intelligence officer and a moody, mean-tempered person who nobody liked working for. I found all this out because my mentor, Drew Simpson, still worked in the Naval Personnel Office and was in charge of all intelligence officer job assignments. He called me up to warn me that not only was my command assignment in Hawaii in jeopardy, but because of this situation, no other command wanted me to work for them either.

Drew asked me my side of the story and interviewed the folks who had worked for me and asked them about the charges. I'm told that when my former staff heard the charges, they went en masse to the new senior intelligence officer and told him the charges were false. My command in Korea also got involved and called to tell him I had exhibited only the most professional of behavior while in Korea. That senior intelligence guy was between a rock and hard place. I wasn't even back in Hawaii yet, and I was causing him major heartburn. In spite of the support I had, he was not inclined to have me back in Hawaii in any job, let alone a command slot. I guess I can't really blame him, but it sure made me mad at the time.

INTEGRITY, A GOOD NAME, AND RESPECT

As I walked through this situation with "Mr. Ego," I learned a major lesson about integrity and the importance of a good name. Everyone who has ever achieved anything has come under attack at some point, but this is where you really start to develop your character. When going through something like this, you have to keep to the high ground. If I had done so in dealing with

"Mr. Ego" and kept my temper under control, things might have been very different.

In the midst of my troubles with "Mr. Ego," the boss of the FOSIC resigned and was replaced by a person who didn't have a very strong operational intelligence background. My time at the Naval War College had been wonderful for my professional self-esteem, but I think my success there also caused me to sometimes get a little too full of myself. I wasn't as supportive of my new superior as I should have been and, more importantly, I didn't give him the respect he deserved. I never mouthed off at him, but my body language when he asked me to do something was very disrespectful, sort of like what teens do to their parents with the sighing and rolling of the eyes.

In truth, I was exhibiting some of the negative character traits I had disliked in "Mr. Ego." I've since learned that oftentimes when you notice a trait in someone else you dislike, you need to look in the mirror. Frequently you'll find you have that trait as well, and the reason you're reacting so strongly to that other person is because you're seeing a side of yourself you don't like.

The end result was that during the controversy in Hawaii, my boss not only didn't come to my aid, he got the job I was supposed to get. From that time onward, I went out of my way to give my total professional support to all of my bosses, even if I didn't agree with a decision or course of action. If I disagreed, I respectfully presented an alternative solution. If they rejected it, I did as General Colin Powell suggested: *I saluted smartly and then went and gave 110 percent to executing those orders as if they were my own idea.*

WE ALL LIKE HAPPY ENDINGS

I also learned that having strong spiritual support can help you walk through any negative situation and come out better on the other side. I called up Reverend Helen and told her what was going on and asked her to pray with me about it that things would be resolved in the best way possible for all involved. Seemingly out of the blue, Drew called and offered me two new career options. I'll go into more background of what he did in a later chapter, but one of the jobs was a staff position with the United States Naval Command based in London, England. The second was as a senior intelligence officer in the Navy's largest operational aviation squadron, VQ-2, in Rota, Spain. Without hesitation, I chose VQ-2, even though it wasn't a command. It was actually a much better assignment than the job I was supposed to go back to in Hawaii.

Drew told me I was the first woman as well as the first African American to hold that position. I was told my former coworkers rejoiced when they heard the news.

My time in VQ-2 turned out to be my favorite of all my jobs in the Navy. I should add here that "Mr. Ego" had a happy ending as well. I'm told he left the Navy and became a millionaire businessman. Reverend Helen and I had prayed for the best solution for all concerned, and God did indeed answer our prayers.

UNFOUNDED RUMORS CAN STILL HURT

During the last part of my career, I was somehow saddled with a wild child, drunken playgirl reputation. I still don't know how I got that one. Most of the jobs I held left me little or no time for a social life. I think part of the problem was that by the time I got promoted to captain, all of the senior naval intelligence guys who had firsthand knowledge of me had either died, retired, or where no longer in government service. The stories relating examples of the humor I so frequently used as my first line of defense in challenging situations became grossly distorted over the years, so people forgot that I usually said or did something outrageous to neutralize a potentially ugly situation.

The drunken charges were a real puzzle, however, as I seldom drink alcohol in public, and I was especially careful at official functions. My father used to tease me saying I wasn't a real sailor since my drink of choice was Diet Coke. In fact, although there were times when alcohol had me feeling pretty good, in all of my time in the Navy, I have only one drunken sailor story, but I do admit I have a laugh that could wake the dead. I can only conclude that people figured I'd have to be drunk to laugh like that.

Once I was promoted to captain, my drunken, playgirl reputation caused the naval intelligence community to pretty much wash their hands of me. Not only did I not receive any good assignments, it seemed to me that they sought out the most insignificant jobs and commands to send me to. The bottom line was I no longer had anyone in the senior leadership of naval intelligence who could vouch for my credentials, so I seriously considered retiring while I still had some semblance of dignity.

I had done a lot of groundbreaking things in my career, yet I watched with dismay as my professional accomplishments were seemingly ignored by the entire naval intelligence community. I knew there was a lot of talent around, but I hoped I'd be seriously considered for a job that I was really suited for, as had been the case for most of my naval career. I was puzzled why this was no longer the case. I decided to pray and ask God for guidance.

TAPPING INTO GOD'S PLAN

The first thing that happened was I gained clarity and insight into the root of the problem. There had indeed been a major change in the leadership of the naval intelligence community. Under the original OSIS masters, if you did well on an assignment, they made sure you got what was considered a good follow-on assignment. But most of the original OSIS masters were now retired. The new guys didn't operate like that, and I found I wasn't the only person having a hard time getting what was perceived as a good assignment. There were quite a few other senior officers who retired in frustration over the way the new leadership was making job placement decisions. I'm happy to add that as I was retiring, a former coworker from my Fleet Ocean Surveillance Information Facility (FOSIF Westpac) days was placed at the helm as director of naval intelligence. His appointment came too late for my career but was good for the naval intelligence community as a whole.

Once I realized what the real problem was, I was able to stop feeling sorry for myself and do something constructive. I remembered my father's advice about dealing with a problem. There was nothing I could do about the opinions of the new senior naval intelligence leaders, but I could conduct myself in a manner that gave no credence to the unprofessional rumors about me. I also spent a lot of time praying and reflecting over the biblical story of Joseph. I was intrigued by the many parallels between Joseph's life and my own life's journey.

Joseph was his father's favorite, so his jealous brothers kidnapped him and sold him into slavery. With the help of God, Joseph overcame all his challenges and eventually became prime minister of Egypt. When a famine devastated his homeland, his brothers came to Egypt to get food for their families. They didn't recognize Joseph at first, and when they did they were fearful and ashamed. Then comes my favorite part of the story. Joseph's insightful reply to his brothers can be found in Genesis chapter 50, verse 20: "But as for you, you meant evil against me; but God meant it for good." Joseph went on to explain that God had known there would be a great famine and had arranged for him to be in a position that would prevent his family from starving to death.

Whenever, I got depressed over my job assignments, I'd repeat to myself, "What was meant for evil, God meant it for good." I don't mean to imply that I thought I was so important that the big guys were out to do me evil. Actually, I don't think they gave me much thought at all. If they had bothered to look at my record, they would have known that an incompetent drunken playgirl couldn't have done what I did. Joseph's story encouraged me to keep watching for the good that was just waiting to be discovered in my situation. Even though I was watching for it, I still didn't see it at first.

As I waited and watched, I continued to gain strength by reflecting on Joseph's story. He had been sold into slavery and banished to Egypt. I had been banished from jobs in the Navy to jobs in the joint arena. Joseph prospered in that situation. I prospered in the Joint Commands. The end result of my joint assignments was they provided the opportunity for me to be on the ground floor and play a key role in many revolutionary concepts of intelligence support to war fighting. There was a tremendous amount of good in store for me; I just had to overcome my own negativism so I could clear my vision and truly see it.

As I continued to study the life of this amazing Bible hero, I saw more parallels reflecting what was going on in my life. At one point, Joseph was falsely accused and thrown in jail. He continued to have faith and was eventually made prime minister of the whole country. I, too, had been falsely accused and nearly court-martialed. I didn't achieve the equivalence of a prime minister, but my retirement ceremony was held at the naval intelligence headquarters, where I was surrounded by friends, family, and colleagues; that day, I was honored and treated as a queen.

UNDERSTANDING ME

I learned a tremendous amount about myself in dealing with these very trying situations. First and foremost, I realized that if you're going to forge new paths, you're going to make a few enemies along the way. Studying the lives of famous historical figures confirms the truth of this conclusion. Winston Churchill, whom I greatly admire, became a figure of ridicule throughout the country and within his own political party. He kept his head up, pressed on, and later went on to greatness as Britain's inspirational prime minister during World War II.

Second, these experiences caused me to strengthen my faith. I gained tremendous inner strength by frequently going into seclusion to pray and reflect on the condition of my own heart. This was probably the most valuable thing I did. From these quiet moments, I learned that true character and integrity come from within. Just because someone accused me of being lacking in those traits and questioned my professional capability did not mean I had to accept it as truth.

I recently gained some major insight concerning my so-called negative character traits as well. Because they are part of me, I am never going to get rid of them, so I need to make peace with them and take the good from them so they don't become destructive. I have a bad temper, but it is also that same force that gives me the drive, determination, passion, and strong desire to do the best job possible. My temper, when channeled correctly, also gives me the backbone and strength to stand up to those bullies who would try to steal success from me.

While I was still in college, my father took my brother and me to see the movie *Patton*. As you can probably tell, my dad frequently used themes from movies to teach us life lessons. After we left the movie, my father explained that from his perspective as a former enlisted man, there were two types of military leaders. One was the cultured statesman/diplomat type that was needed in peace time to fight budget wars and train the troops. Then there was the combat warrior, the old blood-and-guts kind of guy that would lead his troops into hell if that is what it took to win the war. Problem being, this type of leader was usually a disaster in peacetime because he was so hard on his troops. He needed to be put to pasture in peace and trotted out during war.

It's interesting that in the book *On Seas of Glory*, former secretary of the Navy John Lehman makes a similar comment: "In my view, naval personalities fall into three general categories. There are the daring warriors who live for glory and for battle: John Paul Jones, Stephen Decatur Jr. come immediately to mind. Such men, as once was said in a fitness report on General Patton, 'are invaluable in war but a disruptive influence in peacetime.' Then there are sailors who are equally courageous but more prudent—less dramatic leaders in both war and peace. . . . The last and largest category is made up of reluctant warriors who leave their civilian professions to go to sea in time of war. They bravely—and often brilliantly—do their duty, then return to civilian life."[3]

As I went up in rank, I always kept that conversation with my father in mind. As I struggled to know myself, I realized that I was the type of intelligence officer ideally suited to support combat and crisis operations. I thrived in those work environments and didn't do so well in peacetime situations. I hate administrative tasks and really don't like overseeing command picnics or days off at the ballpark. It's not that I don't think they are important for morale, because they are; it's just that I have a warrior mentality.

I'm sure, because I never served on a ship or was involved in hand to hand combat, some will say I don't have the credentials to be called a warrior. I know I was never able to serve on a ship, but in order to provide intelligence support to wars and crises you have to be strong mentally. You know if you don't do your job correctly someone can die. You also have to know even if you do your job correctly people will die. They might be enemies but they are living, breathing human beings with families and friends who love them. As an intelligence professional, you might not actually drop a weapon on a target but you provide the information that allows other people to do it. You have to be able to deal with the fact that you are helping someone kill people. Intelligence analysts do everything in their power to ensure that all targets are valid military targets but still you know that there are often living beings working at enemy military facilities and will likely be killed or wounded by the weapon you help put on target. That takes the mindset of what I call an intellectual warrior. For whatever reason, this is the environment I most thrived in. I want to be in the midst of supporting a combat or crisis action, not a picnic. I'm happiest with jobs that held me working on a crisis and that kept me working long hours, seven days a week.

If I had any doubts about the truth of this self-assessment, they all went away as I started to walk out of my hotel room en route to my retirement ceremony. I had been watching *Headline News*, as had been my custom all through my years of intelligence duty. I heard the newscasters announce that after the commercial break they were going to do an update on two kidnapped Christian missionaries that were being returned home. In big letters at the bottom of the screen were the words, "Wing and a Prayer." That was, of course, the title of the movie that inspired me to pursue my naval career in the first place. I already knew that was going to be the title of if not my book then one of the chapters. As for the commercial they went to, it was an advertisement saying that a certain movie would be on one of the cable channels that evening. The name of the move: *Patton*.

Takeaway: Seize the right mental attitude.

Key principles I learned from shooting myself in the foot:

1. If I maintain the right mental attitude, I can soar with the eagles. If I don't, I'll crash and burn.
2. By right mental attitude, I mean seeing the glass as half full instead of half empty, keeping my faith strong, and persevering, even if it means crawling on my hands and knees.
3. It also means getting up and dusting myself off when I stumble, no matter how embarrassed or humiliated I feel about a particular situation.
4. There is great importance in maintaining integrity and a good name.
5. Everyone who has ever achieved anything has always come under attack at some point, but now I know that is where you really start to develop your character.
6. Sometimes the reason I'm reacting so strongly to another person is because I'm seeing a side of myself I don't like.
7. Having strong spiritual support can help me walk through any negative situation and come out better on the other side.
8. Anyone who is going to forge new paths is going to make a few enemies along the way.
9. True character and integrity come from within.

NOTES

1. At www.finestquotes.com/quote_with-keyword-Knowing%20Yourself-page-0.htm.

2. Wilma Rudolph. *Never Give Up.* (Hong Kong: Great Quotations Publishing Company, 1998), p. 15.

3. John Lehman, *On Seas of Glory: Heroic Men, Great Ships, and Epic Battles of the American Navy.* (New York: Free Press, 2001), pp. 1–2.

9

The Importance of Mentors

You are the same today that you are going to be five years from now except for two things: the people with whom you associate and the books you read.

—*Charles "Tremendous" Jones*[1]

The war with Japan had been reenacted in the game rooms at the Naval War College by so many people and in so many different ways that nothing that happened during the war was a surprise—absolutely nothing except the Kamikaze tactics toward the end of the war—we had not visualized these.

—*Admiral Chester Nimitz*[2]

One of the questions I'm asked most as I talk about my Navy career is who my mentors were. To me, the traditional form of a mentor is someone who takes you under his or her wing and spends time with you teaching you what you need to know about life and/or your chosen profession. They include you in their social circle so that you can meet and be seen by the movers and shakers in your profession. Usually they are someone very highly placed in either your own organization or in your professional area, so in addition to being a teacher or advisor, they can also help you advance in your career. Air Force General Tiiu Kera did that for me during the last part of my Navy career. She was the J2 for most of the time I was stationed in Omaha, Nebraska. She made me one of her projects and knocked a lot of rough edges off I didn't even realize I had.

The Navy folks had initially sent me to a pretty insignificant job at United States Strategic Command. After observing my work ethic, General Kera created a new job for me as the deputy commander of the 500-man Joint Intelligence Center (JIC). Essentially it was a mini publishing empire responsible for creating books, magazine-style articles, and even mini documentaries on intelligence-related issues. My old boss, Evan, from my days at Naval Forces Central Command (NAVCENT), was the JIC commander. I was responsible for the day-to-day running of the JIC operations.

General Kera also went out of her way to try to put to rest the drunken playgirl rumors circulating about me by increasing my visibility to the movers and shakers in the defense world. She had me participate in a number of high-visibility protocol events, such as escorting and setting up dinners for visiting VIPs. When we got a new commander in chief toward the end of my assignment, she put me in charge of the change of command protocol stuff. From her, I learned a lot about how to successfully manage people and get everyone on board for the common good of all. I also learned a lot about navigating office politics.

She was also merciless in making sure my appearance was perfect—things like making sure my uniforms fit and my hair was immaculate. She made sure I understood that people would judge me negatively if my appearance wasn't perfect. She was transferred before my time in Omaha ended and was replaced by the general that almost court-martialed me, but I cannot thank her enough for all she did for me. I never would have been involved in leading the United States Strategic Command's (USSTRATCOM) intelligence support to combat operations if she had not created that new job for me.

However, as I look back on my life, I realize I have had many other mentors, they just didn't take the accepted and expected form. The truth is anyone who teaches you something that helps you to succeed in life is your mentor. Following that line of thinking, I've come to believe there are both positive and negative mentors. A positive mentor is someone who teaches you the tools, skills, and techniques you need to succeed in a particular endeavor. A negative mentor is someone who personifies traits you want to be sure you don't develop, for example, people who exhibit bad work habits or abusive lifestyles.

MY DAD AS MY FIRST MENTOR

As I struggled through the early part of my career, I felt that with the exception of my parents and a few close friends, there was no one who really cared about my career. On the surface, there didn't appear to be a specific person going out of his or her way to oversee or guide me. In fact, most of the time I felt no one but my dad really cared one way or the other, and I often thought I didn't have much of a future in the Navy.

Dad always told me that I'd be surprised at how often people were discussing my future and looking out for me behind the scenes. He also told me I probably had some enemies I didn't know about as well. He continually drilled into my head what he felt was a major key to ultimate success no matter what my goals in life might be. "Initially many doors may be closed to you, but if you work hard and learn everything you can about your job, when the doors do open, and they will open, you will be prepared to hit the ground running." As with most things, he was absolutely right.

Looking back, I can now see that everyone I encountered who was willing to answer a work-related question or take the time to show me some skill was mentoring me. Every boss that yelled at me when I made a mistake and urged me to perform at only the highest levels was mentoring me. The Navy chiefs in my first assignment who made sure I knew they thought I was the best junior officer in the squadron were mentoring me. The folks at my second assignment at the Fleet Ocean Surveillance Information Facility (FOSIF Westpac) who helped me learn about the various intelligence systems were powerful mentors. The Marine colonel who took the time to let me know he thought I had an exercise program that would do a Marine proud was mentoring me. The handful of people I've run into who felt one way to get ahead was to stab coworkers in the back and lie about them to superiors were also mentoring me. These dishonorable individuals were showing me what not to be and how not to behave.

CAPTAIN DREW SIMPSON

The first time I realized there were people in the naval intelligence community concerned about my career was at one of the lowest points in my life. As mentioned in an earlier chapter, I was not selected for commander the first time I came up for promotion, and though I knew I would get a second chance, statistics proved one rarely achieved promotion the second time around. For officers in the military, missing that first-round promotion often meant it was time for you to retire from military service.

I was at a loss concerning what my next step should be. I had talked career options with the Navy's equal opportunity issues advisor a few months earlier, and he had been quite helpful, so I decided to call him first concerning my current situation. I was shocked when, instead of checking with the senior naval intelligence community to find out what was going on, he told me to stop whining and get off the phone.

Realizing there was only one way I was going to get any answers, I made that call myself. One of my former bosses, Captain Drew Simpson, was now in charge of all the job assignments for officers in the naval intelligence community. Drew, a southern white male who worshipped Robert E. Lee, was fantastic. I mention his background for a purpose, as many would conclude that Drew would not have been the best person to talk to about my dilemma for a couple of obvious reasons; however, Drew personified the majority of senior officers I encountered in the Navy in that if you did a great job, you were okay with them no matter what your color, gender, or ethnic background might be. He talked to me for about an hour and told me not to give up.

I've talked about him in previous chapters but didn't mention that Drew and I had a shaky beginning. He was my department head when I arrived for instructor duty at the Navy's intelligence training school. The commanding officer wasn't sure he wanted to deal with the problems involved in having the first female instructor in the school's history. Apparently there had been a woman at the school before, but there had been so many problems that after a few shaky months she was never considered for a permanent position. It's interesting that the Air Force intelligence school, which at the time was colocated with the Navy school in Denver, had women instructors, but the Navy school did not. The job assignment folks kept telling the head of the Navy school how good I was, and the commanding officer, Captain Ford, finally reluctantly said yes. Captain Ford, who left a few months after my arrival, later told me and stated many times in public forums that accepting me on his staff was one of the best decisions he'd ever made, but I'm getting ahead of myself again.

I mention this initial reluctance on the part of the commanding officer to put into context my first meeting with then Commander Drew Simpson. When I walked into his office, and instead of the welcome I had expected, he burst out with, "I hope you're not going to be like the last woman I had

THE IMPORTANCE OF MENTORS

to work with who demanded I keep a file cabinet full of sanitary napkins." I gave him a very disgusting, smart-mouthed reply and he blanched, exhaled, and didn't speak to me for about a month. Don't ask me what I said, but I guess he figured if I had courage enough to stand up to him I deserved a shot at teaching at the school. We went from there to becoming good friends, and he became one of my greatest assets in keeping my career on track. You will hear more about him as I trace my career path for you.

OSIS MASTER TED SHEAFER

The other thing that happened was one of the very first OSIS masters, Ted Sheafer, had made admiral. I hadn't heard from him since I left Japan eight years earlier. He had apparently heard about my situation and sent me a note saying, "Gail, don't give up the ship!" I had been thinking about quitting the Navy in my despair over not making commander. Combined with the support Drew and my minister were giving me, I stuck it out and made commander the following year. Thanks to them, I also stayed on the professional fast track. Drew even told me I had the potential to make captain, which seemed totally out of my reach at the time.

Mark Victor Hansen, coauthor of the Chicken Soup for the Soul series and one of my newer mentors, says that sometimes there's a point in your life where you are unable to envision a better situation for yourself. This is the time you need a mentor, someone who can hold that better view of your future for you. Drew and Admiral Sheafer did that for me at a critical juncture in my life. Drew now sits with the angels, but for several years he was a fabulous friend and big brother protector. I miss him very much.

CAPTAIN BILL STUDEMAN

The next major professional mentoring period for me was my time on the staff of the Naval War College in Newport, Rhode Island. I was assigned to the War Gaming Department as part of the Ocean Surveillance Information System (OSIS) detachment. Our role was to play the Red Team or the enemy during the war games. Although we were located in Newport and had a Navy intelligence captain as our boss, we all actually came under an intelligence command located in Washington, DC. The person in charge of that whole organization was one of the original OSIS masters, Captain Bill Studeman.

This was a golden period in history to be at the Naval War College. Ronald Reagan had just been elected president and had appointed John Lehman, a dynamo and practical visionary, as secretary of the Navy. The Cold War was still going strong and the Soviet Union had one of the world's largest navies in the world. While the Soviet navy was expanding, ours was shrinking. Secretary Lehman states in his book *On Seas of Glory*, that, "Between 1969 and 1979 the fleet was cut from 950 ships to 479, even as the Soviets were pursuing a blue-water strategy and building their fleet toward a 1,700-ship goal."[3] Lehman also says, "The new Carter defense policy viewed offensive naval operations as a wasteful diversion of resources. Strategists reasoned that defeat of the Soviets at sea would not cripple the Soviet war effort, while an attack on Soviet naval or air facilities might threaten escalation in the early stages of a struggle. Any serious attempt at defending Norway and maintaining an aggressive defense of the northern flank of NATO was abandoned; the U.S. Navy was restricted to operations south of the Greenland–Iceland line, so that it would not be seen as threatening to the Soviets."[4] The Navy was not even supposed to use the term *maritime superiority* in any policy documents.

President Reagan gave Secretary Lehman the task of coming up with a naval strategy to counter the very impressive Soviet threat. "The first priority if the Soviets attacked," Lehman states, "would be to establish early control of the sea bridge of the North Atlantic and then carry the offensive to the vulnerable northern approaches of the Soviet Union through the Norwegian Sea. Another high priority would be to establish immediate control of the Mediterranean to defend NATO's southern flank and to carry the fight to the enemy through its southern flank. Additional critical tasks would be to insure control of the Persian Gulf and its strategic oil supplies, the Indian Ocean and its vital sea-lanes, and the strategic straits of Sunda and Malacca in Southeast Asia; assure successful defense of Japan and our allies in Southeast Asia; and to maintain control of the North Pacific, to protect Alaska, and its vital oil supply, as well as carry the fight to the Soviet Union's thinly guarded eastern flanks."[5]

As part of this new strategy, the United States and the other NATO navies started conducting offensive-themed exercises in the Norwegian Sea, while the rest of the U.S. Navy conducted similar offensive-themed exercises in the Western Pacific. This new dynamic strategy caused my time at the Naval War

College to be exceptionally exciting and valuable. Fleet commanders would test out their strategies at the Naval War College. The role of the Red Team was to provide realistic opposition by immersing ourselves in the philosophy and strategies of potential adversaries and respond accordingly as the fleet commanders moved their forces around. The quote at the beginning of this chapter comes from a letter written by Admiral Nimitz saying the success of the U.S. forces during World War II could be attributed to the fact that they had war-gamed similar scenarios prior to the war.

War gaming at the Naval War College goes back to the 1800s and is a very useful technique for testing battle plans and tactics. Prior to Pearl Harbor, the battleship had been the centerpiece of all U.S. Navy strategy, but during games conducted at the Naval War College, "the Navy's aviation community was able to develop operational concepts and procedures that were ready to implement when . . . the Japanese took away our option for battleship tactics. How did they do it? The Navy was able to use war games to cheaply, quickly, and educationally test different ideas in aviation and even ship design. For example, the circular formation used during World War II by carrier task forces was first developed during an interwar war game. Some of what they learned resulted in changes in ships already under construction."[6]

THE GLOBAL WAR GAME

During my time at the War College, the most visible war games were the Global War Game series. The first had been held during the summer of 1979 and was part of a five-year series. The second series went from 1984–1988 and was played out over a three-week period each summer. "The first game of the series, GWG '84, was a stand-alone game designed to test new gaming concepts and ensure realistic orders of battle. The 1985, 1986, and 1987 games consisted on one continuous game, with the latter games picking up where its predecessor had terminated."[7]

Bud Hay, a retired marine colonel, was director of Advanced Concepts, the center for naval warfare studies at the Naval War College. He was one of the neatest individuals I've ever met. Incredibly smart but very approachable, he had been in charge of the games since 1979. Over the years the games had become so high profile that the "Navy turned to war gaming to support their budgets. In 1988, the Marines began war gaming their POM initiatives as well."[8]

During my time there, I got to observe most of the senior Navy and Marine commanders of the time. It was pretty awesome. During one war game, all the real-world people, from the secretary of defense on down, participated, which was pretty heavy stuff for a poor girl from Newark, New Jersey. For the higher profile Global War Games, senior members of the government intelligence agencies participated and headed up the Red Team. Many of them were OSIS masters, which meant I better have my act together or the next three years would be hellish, that is if I didn't get fired first.

I NEED A MENTOR, QUICK!
When I arrived in Newport, I was overwhelmed and knew I needed help and quickly if I was going to be able to do my job with any kind of efficiency. Up to that point, my whole focus had been on tactical or operational intelligence support, which meant focusing on what happened yesterday, what's happening today, and what's going to happen tomorrow.

To do my new job, I had to learn a whole new way of thinking. If a country is going to war, how do you know? What would you see on the diplomatic front? What activity could you expect to see with their military forces? What would their economic and military strategies be? Would they use terrorism or weapons of mass destruction (WMD) and, if so, under what circumstances? Who would be their allies?

I also knew there were still a lot of people who didn't believe women belonged in military service, and now there were two of us, the first women in the history of the Naval War College, assigned to the Red Team war-gaming job. I really wanted to do a good job.

CONDOLEEZZA RICE AND DR. JOSEF KORBEL
I did have one major strong suit in that a couple of years earlier I had completed my master's degree at the Graduate School of International Studies in Denver. It was an excellent program, and while there I had one interesting mentoring experience that still sticks in my mind today. One day a young lady approached me after class and said, "I understand you're in naval intelligence. I'm working on my PhD in Soviet studies, and I can't find any information on the Soviet military. Can you help me out?"

As I recall, I sat down with her a time or two and discussed how the Soviet military was set up and gave her an unclassified book the government had put together on the Soviet military. Because I was teaching full time at the Navy's intelligence school while finishing my degree, I didn't have much time to hang out with too many of my fellow students, but there was something remarkable about this particular young lady. I remember thinking there's something special about that Condoleezza Rice.

The time I spent finishing my master's degree, plus the year I spent in Europe as an undergraduate studying European economic and political systems, gave me a good grounding in international affairs. Additionally, during my first year working on my master's degree before I joined the Navy, Dr. Josef Korbel, former secretary of state Madeleine Albright's father, was one of my academic advisors. Even though I lacked actual "sea time" experience, my earlier assignments, coupled with my educational background, had given me about 75 percent of the skill set I needed for the job. That meant I had to figure out a way to learn the remaining 25 percent and learn it quickly.

DENNIS CALLAN

I remembered once again my father's advice about the two things you can do about a problem. So I did my homework and found out that one of my new coworkers, a civilian government worker named Dennis Callan, had been part of the Red Team for about ten years. He had spent time in the military, had been trained by the OSIS masters, and had probably forgotten more than most people knew about war gaming. I asked Dennis to teach me and two other new Red Team members the ropes. We spent a few afternoons with Dennis teaching us the strategic military strategies of the bad guys and basic war-gaming techniques. What I learned from Dennis, coupled with the research I did on the Soviet Union's philosophy of war, allowed me to begin to narrow what looked like an almost impossible learning curve.

One of the biggest challenges I would face over the next three years would be convincing the U.S. admirals and generals that the Soviets *did not* operate their naval forces the way a U.S. military man would. I had to work really hard to build a good reputation, especially because they all knew I lacked the "time at sea" experience. This initially created a mindset among some of the senior officers at the Naval War College that I wasn't really fully qualified on many of the aspects of war gaming. The effects of this attitude would sometimes hit me when I least expected it.

I remember one time early in my assignment, the submarine community wanted to do a war game to test some new tactical concepts. I was the only member of the Red Team who was available to participate, and one of the senior Blue Team members had a fit, saying I wasn't qualified and there was no way I should be allowed to do it. I think all he saw was a woman who hadn't been to sea. In my mind, the only challenge I had was that the scenario of the game would be played out in the Atlantic Fleet area, while all of my operational experience had been in the Pacific Fleet. My boss felt I had the experience to do it but agreed to send Dennis along with me. I was offended, but Dennis was fast becoming one of my favorite people, and it would be good to have a friend in what might be a hostile working environment.

I did my homework, consulted with a submarine expert beforehand, and the game went reasonably well. I don't think I did an outstanding job, but I did well enough that never again did a senior Blue Team member say I wasn't qualified to participate. In fact, the Blue players started requesting me by name to participate in these games.

THE BLUE TEAM GUYS

The Blue Team guys were highly qualified in various specialties, such as submarine warfare, air warfare, amphibious warfare, and so forth. They were among the most talented and successful of their communities, and many went on to major command assignments after their time at the Naval War College. Remembering some of the more successful survival techniques I'd learned during my earlier assignments, I just went up to them and asked them to show me the ropes in their various areas of expertise.

Without exception, these guys were generous with their time and knowledge. I knew the basic capabilities of most of our operating forces, but to excel at my job I would need more in-depth details. For instance, I knew our submarines and surface ships had such submarine detection systems as sonar, but now I needed to know how they decided what tactics to use and under what circumstances? How many false contacts do these systems generate, and how do you tell the difference between a big fish and a submarine? Because I was not allowed to serve at sea, I did not know the answers to these and many other tactical questions. For more information of some of the great things these guys taught me, see the supplements at the end of this chapter. For now though, I just want to say I am so grateful for the mentoring these guys did for me at this critical point in my career.

EARNING MY PHD IN NAVAL INTELLIGENCE

I feel that my time at the Naval War College gave me the equivalent of a PhD in naval intelligence, but it took a lot of mentoring from those around me to get through that assignment successfully. There are three mentoring-related incidents during my time there, that come to mind.

During my first summer there, I participated in my first Global War Game. Senior members of the intelligence community headed up the Red Team, and I was assigned as their intelligence officer. This meant that first thing in the morning and several times during the day, I had to give these guys a briefing covering the fictional world events of the current war game. I remember sweating big time before my first briefing. I was going to have to stand up in front of the "who's who" in the intelligence community, give them an outstanding presentation, and withstand their fire if I didn't show I had a thorough grasp of the situation. These were fighting men; I knew they could be brutal and merciless.

My presentation wasn't until about 7:30 in the morning, but I came into work in the middle of the night to prepare. I managed to get through my presentation, hiding my nervousness, and at the end, they said, "Good job, Gail." But then they asked, "How about giving us a rundown of key real-world events?" I had spent so much time working on my exercise presentation; I hadn't bothered to check what was happening in the real world. I was clueless and sure my career was doomed.

In a flash, I decided to resort to humor. As I drove into work, I had been listening to the radio. I'm a big sports fan, so I had paid particularly close attention to the various game scores. Without another thought, I gave them a very accurate rundown of the latest sports statistics. To my immense relief, they laughed and let me go. I immediately went down and put together a briefing on the real-world current events. At my next scheduled presentation, I gave them an actual world event update. That incident taught me that I was an intelligence officer first and foremost, and no matter what else was going on around me, it was part of my job to know what key events were going on in the world.

BECOMING A GROUND WARFARE EXPERT

A second mentoring moment that comes to mind involved Dennis. He had been working on what was supposed to be a small ground warfare game based in the European Theater. In this particular event, the Cold War went hot and they believed there would be a major ground war fought in the European Theater. This was based on the interpretation of the Soviet view and strategy presented in NIE (National Intelligence Estimate) 11-15. "The Soviet military writings indicate that they believe a war with the West would be decisive, be global in scope, and probably escalate to a nuclear conflict. They probably expect that such a war would begin in Central Europe following a period of rising international tensions and spread to the Far East, as China enters to take advantage of Soviet involvement in Europe."[9]

The issue being looked at was how Navy and Marine forces could make an effective contribution to the ground campaign in support of the NATO air and ground forces. Originally, only a small number of Navy and Marine senior officers were going to come up to the Naval War College for four or five days and run through a few different scenarios, but in the weeks leading up to the start of the game, more and more people heard about it and wanted to participate. Soon senior army as well as NATO guys were calling up saying they were coming to play. What began as a small study had started to turn into a major event.

The games were scheduled to start on Monday. On Friday afternoon, Dennis came up to me and said, "Gail, we're getting too many people who want to participate. The War Gaming Department has decided to divide the participants into two groups. They plan on running two simultaneous games each working the same scenarios. I need you to play both the Red opposition and the Blue intelligence support for one of these groups."

I started to panic big time. I knew nothing about ground warfare, and they expected me to realistically play the Soviet European Theater commander over air, ground, and naval forces against some of the finest military minds in the world with only two days to get ready. My first thought was, "Why doesn't somebody just shoot me now and save me the humiliation I was sure I would face after the dust settled?" My second thought wasn't really productive either: "Why won't some handsome, sexy guy marry me and take me away from all this?"

When I could calm down enough to actually start thinking somewhat rationally, I realized that since Dennis had been mentoring me, he must think I'm ready to handle such an assignment. That brought some comfort. Then I realized it was not that unusual for team members to wear two hats during a war game. For most of the smaller games, we usually played the opposition as well as the intelligence support for the good guys. I know it sounds schizophrenic, but I had seen it work pretty well most of the time.

I was just starting to think maybe I could do this when he handed me the list of participants, which included some Marine and Army generals. How was I supposed to support these guys when I knew nothing about their form of warfare? I figured as soon as I opened my mouth it would be pretty apparent that I knew very little about their field and they would verbally kicked me in the butt, rip my guts out, and fire me.

As I dug deep into what experience I might have had with the Army, it dawned on me that my previous assignment at the United States Southern Command (USSOUTHCOM) had been dominated by the Army. I was by no means an expert, but I had picked up some knowledge about ground warfare that I wasn't even aware of until I had to use it. I guess you can't spend two years in an environment without learning something useful.

Then I remembered that the reserve naval intelligence unit that supported the Naval War College was going to be around that weekend, and one of the guys was an expert on ground warfare. There is no way I could have completed my game preparation without his help, which he willingly agreed to give. Seems everyone knew this was going to be a big event and wanted to be involved even in a small way. I spent the weekend totally immersed in research material at the Naval War College library and by Monday morning felt I was as ready as I would ever be to tackle this assignment.

As always, the game began with an intelligence brief. I decided to start with a discussion of how the Soviets would use their naval and air assets, which was an area I had built some expertise in during my years in operational intelligence. I would leave the part concerning the ground units until last. Doing so gave me a sense of confidence at the beginning of the briefing, which I hoped would carry me through the parts I wasn't as well informed on. I'd also learned that military commanders had a short attention span for intelligence briefings, so I only gave relevant data. I knew that if they detected any lack of confidence, that's exactly when they'd pounce. By starting with my strong suit, I was able to gain some initial credibility with them. The end result of all my efforts was I had become one of the military's experts on Soviet Army ground warfare, if only for that brief moment in time.

One important lesson I learned during that week, though, was to always follow through. For example, I received a lot of questions that I couldn't answer on the spot but promised the group I'd research it between sessions and get back to them. I was able to keep my promise all but one time. One admiral had to leave Newport early, and I hadn't been able to give him an answer before he left. So first thing the following week, I called up his office and passed the answer on to his staff. I heard a number of times in the years to come that he thought I was a great intelligence officer. It reinforced my work ethic to always get back to people with answers to their questions, even if you have to track them down to do it.

"BE SURE YOU'RE RIGHT, AND THEN GO AHEAD"

A third mentoring incident involved the Blue Team. They loved it when I was assigned as the intelligence support for the Blue side during war games, primarily because this job was the most thankless and the biggest threat to your mental stability. If the outcome of the game was not to the liking of the senior players, they usually vented their wrath on their intelligence support people.

My Blue Team coworkers thought it was a real hoot when the admirals verbally abused me during one of these evaluations. My coworkers weren't being mean; they just loved to watch my response. I would not be disrespectful to the senior men, but I would stand my ground and go toe-to-toe with them if necessary, if I really thought I was right. I constantly kept in mind, though, this quote from Davy Crockett: "Be sure you're right, and then go ahead."

The game that stands out most in my mind is one in which all of the admirals of one of the fleets were in town for a week of war game scenarios. What they expected from me as their intelligence officer was 100-percent knowledge of all enemy forces in the battle zone, all the time. This is, of course, not a realistic expectation.

I played the game, only giving out the amount of information I felt the warfighters would realistically have had at any given point in time. My years of providing operational intelligence support had given me an excellent grasp of how much information I was likely to have on hand at a given point in any given scenario. To say they were unhappy with me would be an understatement. Because of the size and scope of this game, my briefings were given in front of an auditorium full of people. My Blue Team coworkers thought it was a real hoot watching me squirm all week under the constant barrage of verbal beatings.

As always, I relied on humor to try to defuse some of the heaviest situations, like showing up with a baseball hardhat on my head and a sledgehammer in my fist, declaring I felt ready to begin my morning brief. They laughed but still proceeded to pick me apart in front of everyone. At one briefing, one of the guys started banging on the table while he screamed in my face, "A real spook would know the answer. If you were really my spook, I'd fire you!" To clarify, lest you think this was a racial slur, *spook* is the nickname used in the military for an intelligence officer. We all know, however, that it has also been used as a derogatory term for an African American.

Playing on the double entendre, I replied, "I am a real spook!" The folks in the auditorium started laughing, causing my critic to stop midsentence and ask if he'd said something funny. "No, Sir," I calmly replied, "I just said I am a real spook." He glared at me, then continued his table-banging tirade.

I thought that particular week would never end, but when it was finally over I slinked back to my desk with my tail between my legs and my head hanging down. One of my coworkers grabbed me before I could sit down and said there was an admiral waiting to see me. "Oh no," I thought, "Now they're even following me to my desk to scream at me. Either that or my Navy career is over." I figured word had gotten out regarding the outcome of the games and my career as an intelligence officer was toast.

I pulled my shoulders back and walked out to meet the admiral. He smiled and handed me a box of chocolate chip cookies (my favorite) and then turned and walked away, leaving me with my jaw hanging open. Another admiral called and invited me to have lunch with him and his staff before they left town that day. I was flabbergasted! Most of the admirals may have been frustrated with me, but I had apparently earned the professional respect of at least two of them.

THE ULTIMATE WAR GAME SCENARIO

All of this mentoring culminated for me about a year and a half into my assignment at the Naval War College when I was chosen to simulate the Soviet military commander in charge of all of the Soviet military forces in the Far

East for the annual Global War Game. It's not my intent to give a detailed overview of the 1985 Global War Game. There's an excellent study you can read written by Robert Gile entitled *Naval War College Newport Papers 20, Global War Game Second Series, 1984–1988*. What I am going to cover is how I came up with my wartime strategy for the command based on all the mentoring I had received and what I learned through participating in this very controversial game battle engagement.

During my time at the Naval War College, there were about fifty games a year, and our detachment participated in every game, which made for a pretty hectic schedule. Most of these games involved one Red Team individual doing all the game preparations, such as attending meetings and developing the order of battle with the person setting up the game scenario, then all the rest of us just showing up on game day to receive our specific assignments. Games always ended at noon on Friday so we would have the afternoon to prepare for the next week's game and not have to work through the weekend.

Global, however, was different in that all team members had major roles to play and were each responsible for game preparations for our respective areas. "The game itself might be described as 'three-sided,' with a 'Blue' team representing the United States, a 'Red' team playing the Soviet Union, and a 'Green' team for all other countries. The Blue and Red teams played on three levels: The National Command Authority (NCA) and the Supreme High Command (VGK), the Commanders in Chief (CINC) and Commanders of Theaters of Military Operations (TVD), and various corps and fleet levels on each side."[10]

During this particular war game, my opposition would be the real-world staff from the Pacific Fleet. The game was so high-profile that we all knew either the commander or his second in command would be there for all or most of the game. The Red Team senior players were usually the "who's who" of the intelligence world; many were the OSIS masters themselves. Their role was to conduct the war as realistically as possible. "Similarly, the Green team, composed mainly of retired State Department personnel, including some of ambassadorial rank, played both the respective allies of Blue and Red and all other nations as well."[11]

The Global Game also had an Intelligence Control Cell that was to make sure the Red and Blue players would only have information on their opponents force movements that they would realistically have in a given situation.

We did know, however, like the United States, the Soviet Union had a very good intelligence collection capability.

One of the major players for the Global Game as well as any of our war games was the Battle Damage Assessment (BDA) Cell. They were part of the Naval War College's War Gaming Center. These were the guys who determined the outcome of the battles. All of the BDA folks had advanced degrees in operational analysis. They had to determine if a bomb was dropped on ship A, what was the level of damage? Was the ship out of commission? If two fighter aircraft from opposing sides were shooting guns and firing missiles at each other, who would win? How many bombs would you have to drop on an enemy airfield to put it out of commission? This was an extremely technical and often controversial process. One of my favorite people, Mike Wilmore, was in charge. He spent a lot of time between games mentoring me on the effectiveness of various weapons systems in combat. We bonded over many a war game. Typically if Blue players did not like the outcome of a war game they blamed not only their intelligence support but also the BDA Cell. During game debriefs, Mike and I would often huddle together trying not to be noticed as the Blue players from the various major Navy commands berated us over game outcomes they didn't like.

A Control Cell was over the whole operation to make sure the game flowed smoothly and that all the training objectives were met. At times their task became very controversial, since many believed the game outcome could affect real-world defense budget issues. If game results showed the Soviets could defeat a particular weapon system, they feared that program could get cut out of the defense budget. Add that to the fact that most military leaders hate to lose and you've got a very volatile environment.

I was really glad I had been assigned the Soviet Union's pacific forces, since I had spent time providing intelligence support to commanders in that part of the world. Yet I knew I would have to get approval for how I used my military forces from the senior members of the Red Team, so I did my due diligence as I prepared for these games. I was very motivated to show I was up to the task at hand. I figured I had one slight advantage in that their real-world jobs were time-consuming, and I didn't think they would be able to focus much on the game until they arrived at Newport. If I came up with a well-thought-out, well-researched plan and presented it to them upon arrival, I would be a step ahead of the game and start out on the right foot.

One of the challenges was that the game time scenario would be five years in the future. Working with the entire intelligence community, I developed a list of what forces the Soviets might have by that time frame. Once I developed a force list, then I needed to decide what to do with them and load them onto the game computer.

The basis for this set of games was that World War III was about to start because it looked like Germany was reuniting and the Soviets weren't going to allow it. The Red Team was also bogged down in a conflict in Afghanistan. Blue and the People's Republic of China were helping the rebels, which put a further strain between NATO and the Warsaw Pact. At the beginning of November 1990, Red conducted a major exercise on Sakhalin Island, leaving some forces behind, making Japan nervous. On November 10, 1990, it was game time; Red forces went to increased combat readiness and started deploying ballistic missile submarines (SSBNs).[12]

Knowledge of the scenario let me know where to position my forces. I also felt that the best approach for intelligence war game players was to stick with real-world events as much as possible. As I read daily intelligence reports, I was on the lookout for incidents I could use in the game. I'd weave many of these actual incidents into my game plan. If the Blue Team argued that what I proposed could never happen, I would say it not only could but did and then give them the date and details of the real-world incident.

In keeping with my real-world approach, I decided I would stick as close as possible to actual tactics I had observed the Soviets conducting when they did their war training exercises. We may not have gone to war with them, but I had studied their training exercises very closely. Generally speaking a military will fight the way they train.

For development of my overall campaign plan strategy, I studied the latest intelligence estimates using NIE 11-15 as my main source of information. For background information on the NIE, see the supplement at the end of this chapter. According to the NIE,

Within the Soviets' overall wartime strategy . . . the primary initial tasks of the Navy remain:

- To deploy and provide protection for SSBNs in preparation for and conduct of strategic and theater nuclear strikes
- To defend the USSR and its allies from SSBNs and aircraft carriers

Accomplishment of these tasks would entail attempts to control all or portions of . . . the seas of Japan and Okhotsk and the Northwest Pacific Basin, and
to conduct sea denial operations beyond those areas to about 2,000 kilometers
from Soviet territory.[13]

It was Soviet policy to keep 75 percent of its SSBN force in an operational
status and ready to deploy within three weeks.[14] The estimate states,

> We believe that the Soviets plan to support and protect their SSBNs through an
> echeloned defense in depth. This defense would likely begin while the SSBNs
> are still in port and continue as they are dispersed and enter assigned operat-
> ing areas. Surface combatants, mine warfare ships, and antisubmarine warfare
> aircraft (ASW) probably would be used to sanitize SSBN transit routes. Gen-
> eral purpose submarines would likely escort transiting SSBNs and, along with
> aircraft, establish barrier patrols in the approaches to SSBN operating areas.
> Surface combatant task groups also would probably operate in the vicinity of
> such areas to assist in combating enemy SSNs and ASW aircraft.[15]

The NIE further states,

> The Soviets expect U.S. carrier battle groups to undertake vigorous offensive
> actions in the maritime approaches to the USSR. They believe the carrier battle
> groups would attempt to use . . . the northwestern Pacific Ocean to attack War-
> saw Pact territory, deployed naval forces including the SSBNs, and pact ground
> forces. Destruction of aircraft carriers, then, is a critical element of several
> important naval tasks. Cruise missile submarines and strike aircraft carrying
> air-to-surface missiles are the Soviets' primary anticarrier weapons. . . . To con-
> centrate their firepower, the Soviets probably would attack carrier battle groups
> with at least one regiment (twenty aircraft) and preferably two . . ."[16]

One sentence in the NIE report really jumped out at me, saying, "The Soviets would attempt to use tactical surprise and coordinated multiple strikes
on different threat axes to overwhelm battle group defenses."[17] Normally,
because of its superior capabilities, it's rare that an aircraft carrier gets successfully attacked in a war game, but just maybe I could use this information
to create a scenario no one would be suspecting.

Once the game started I was a little frustrated when the Red NCA considered
the Far East a secondary theater. They didn't want a two-front war, so most of
their efforts would be focused on the war in the central front in Europe.

Essentially, Red objectives in the Far East Theater of Military Operation (FETVD) can be summarized as follows:

- Protect the Red homeland.
- Preserve the Red strategic nuclear reserve (SSBNs).
- Neutralize Blue nuclear strike capabilities.
- Keep the People's Republic of China and Japan from actively aiding Blue combat or combat support operations.[18]

I didn't like being on the back burner but felt we were playing the scenario realistically.

I had done my research, put together my game plan, and briefed the Red NCA. They found my strategy in line with the direction they wanted to go and gave me the go ahead. My main focus was to deploy and protect my SSBNs and then wait for an opportunity to launch a massive strike on the Blue carrier battle groups.

My SSBNs carried missiles that had the range to strike targets in the United States from waters close to the Soviet Union. I deployed them in the northern Sea of Japan and the Sea of Okhotsk. I mined the approaches to their deployment areas and put one nuclear attack submarine (SSN) in close proximity to each SSBN for guard duty. The SSNs primary role was to destroy any Blue force, such as a submarine or surface ship, that would try to destroy the SSBN. It was imperative that the SSBN survive to launch its nuclear weapons. Then I mined the area surrounding their operating area and kept ASW aircraft overhead and surface ships in the area constantly on the lookout for Blue submarines. Any Blue submarine that tried to destroy my SSBNs would have to run quite a gauntlet to get anywhere near them. If they made it through the two-mine minefields and avoided detection by the surface ships and aircraft looking for them, they would still have to get by my submarine guard.

Blue kept its carrier battle groups east of the Philippines and out of range of my strike aircraft for the first part of the game. I had deployed submarines armed with cruise missiles lying in wait for them. Blue sent their submarines out to destroy them. The plan, as I understood it, was to not move the aircraft carriers closer to the Soviet Union until they had neutralized my submarine force.

Meanwhile, the air force was pounding the heck out of my land-based air defense systems. Targets included surface-to-air missiles and triple-A sites as well as radar sites. After the first part of the war, Japan wouldn't let them fly combat operations from Japanese airfields, so Blue had to fly their strikes from South Korean airfields. I was taking heavy losses of aircraft during this part of the campaign, but so was Blue.

The first week of the game was heavily in favor of Blue. I did successfully torpedo the USS *Nimitz*, though. "The *Nimitz* . . . was taken under tow for Hawaii and repair. . . . Red again attacked the *Nimitz* (three days later game time), utilizing Bear aircraft and air-to-surface missiles. One hit was obtained, and the *Nimitz* rerouted to Guam for emergency repairs before proceeding to Pearl Harbor."[19]

I had to wait until December 1990 game time before I got a shot at the carriers. As far as I knew, Blue had four or five carrier battle groups operating east of the Philippines. Blue strategy believed if you grouped several carrier battle groups together the combined air defense made them nearly invincible. By the time the scenario advanced to December 1990, Blue believed their SSNs had destroyed most of my submarines that had been lying in wait for them in the northwest Pacific and felt it was safe to move the carriers up closer to the battle.[20] What they failed to consider was I still had most of my long-range strike aircraft in tact, twelve regiments each with twenty aircraft. All of the aircraft were capable of launching cruise missiles from long distances away from the carrier and therefore could avoid the worst of its air defense. I armed my Backfire bombers with the 2,250-nautical-mile-range AS-4 air-to-surface and my Badger aircraft with the two of the 350-nautical-mile-range AS-6 air-to-surface.[21] I also had 2 Oscar Class submarines I could use in the battle; each carried 24,300-nautical-mile-range SS-N-19 cruise missiles. The submarine did not have to surface to launch its missiles, so that was a major advantage. It was a newer-class submarine and therefore was quieter and harder to detect.

I decided the key was launching all available missiles at the same time to overwhelm the Blue carrier defense. If I did not time it perfectly, I would not succeed. I knew Blue had large numbers of aircraft operating out of either the Japanese or South Korean airfields. They weren't supposed to conduct combat operations out of the Japanese airfields, but I didn't trust them to honor that commitment and so factored that into my plan. The carriers were located west of the Japanese island of Hokkaido. I decided to use a diversionary tactic to offset any aircraft coming from South Korea or Japan to the aid of the carriers. That way, the carriers would have to rely on only their own aircraft for self-defense.

I had taken some losses but still had a large number of fighter and bomber aircraft available. I cobbled together the best of what I had left and some of my older fighters for escort and launched a massive feint east over the Sea of Japan. That occupied the Japanese air defense system, which I believed was providing Blue radar information on my aircraft locations throughout the war. Blue aircraft operating from South Korea and Japanese airfields had to meet that strike.

While they were occupied, I sent out my real strike force consisting of all 12 of my strike regiments, a total of 240 aircraft. I used a tactic I'd seen in the real world in September of 1982, when Backfires launched a simulated attack against U.S. carriers operating east of the Kuril Islands. I brought my aircraft over the Sea of Okhotsk and east over the Kuril Islands, then south toward the carriers. I had the most advanced Soviet fighter aircraft at the time as escorts. Because of the ranges of the missiles the aircraft were carrying, I didn't have to fly close to the carriers. I was able to launch 480 missiles from my aircraft and 32 from my two Oscar class submarines. All of the missiles were launched within a few minutes of each other, just as I had planned.

The initial BDA results and the official ones are different. Initially, I severely damaged most of the carriers. I believe reverberations from the Blue admirals yelling can still be heard even today at Sims Hall where this Global Game was held. As I recall, the apparent success of my strategy brought the game to a temporary standstill while the Blue players argued with the BDA Cell and the Control Cell over the validity of my attack scenario. The Pacific Fleet team kept saying the outcome was wrong. They tried to say the escorting fighters didn't have the legs to stay with the strike aircraft until the launch point. I had factored refueling some of the aircraft into my plan. I also had forward deployed some aircraft with shorter legs so they didn't have to fly as far to support and protect my strike aircraft. I had early warning aircraft in place to warn the striking force of the location of the carrier aircraft as they launched to defend the carriers.

When Blue couldn't prove my plan wouldn't have worked, they tried to say I wouldn't have had enough intelligence on their position to carry out the strike. The Intelligence Control Cell sided with me, not because I was an intelligence officer but because their calculations said I did. This debate went on weeks and months even after the game ended. The Naval War College supported me as long as they could. They finally modified the game results when the Pacific Fleet staff said they would not participate in the next Global War Game if they didn't get all of the forces I had destroyed back. They won. The only thing that made me mad was I didn't get back any of the forces I'd lost in the attack. When I complained, my boss said, "Gail, the game is for Blue not Red," which shut me up pretty quickly.

Right after the game, the Central Intelligence Agency (CIA) showed up in my office and offered me a job. I gave it some thought but decided to stay in the Navy, realizing that when I bleed it comes out Navy blue. Years later, just before I retired, I ran into a high-ranking CIA official. The first words out of his mouth after hello were about that game. He looked at the guy who was with him and said, "We really thought Gail was going to get fired after that game for sinking aircraft carriers during Global, so we offered her a job." I smiled and said, "I did get passed over for commander." He blanched but I told him not to worry, it was a happy ending. I pointed to the eagles on my uniform. "See I made captain, and my next assignment was to the Pacific Fleet staff." I told him after I had been transferred, the Naval War College had invited me back to command the Far East forces again for the last Global Game of the series, but the Pacific Fleet staff refused, saying if I came back to the Global Games, I'd have to be their senior intelligence officer, which is what happened.

Looking back, I can be more objective than I was at the time and believe what should have happened was we should have rerun that part of the scenario. Blue was aware there were two Oscar-class submarines operating somewhere in the Pacific, but they did not know I also still had a significant air strike capability. I'd been protecting those assets by moving them around and camouflaging them. The game controllers could have asked the Blue team, "With better intelligence on the Red forces, how would you change things?" They didn't, or maybe they did?

THE BATTLE OF MIDWAY

Most people are aware that in the prewar years the United States war-gamed a conflict with Japan, but what many don't know is that the Japanese were into war-gaming as well. They war-gamed the attack on Pearl Harbor before they conducted the actual strike. The first game did not give them the level of success they wanted, so they modified their attack plans.

"In contrast, the Japanese war game prior to the Battle of Midway is usually cited as the best example of how *not* to war game. During the game the American side's airpower sank two Japanese carriers. Rear Admiral Ukagi Matome, commander of their carrier force for the actual operation, unilaterally reversed the umpires. With the carriers restored to the game, the Japanese side went on to capture Midway. Just weeks later, the Americans sank the same two carriers, plus two more. This time, Admiral Ukagi could not reach into the 'dead pile' and replace his ships."[22]

I believe the purpose of a war game is to provide a laboratory where we can explore different war plans or crisis response scenarios. The only casualties are to egos. War plans are complex and sometimes don't cover everything but should expose what's good and bad in a plan and allow us to modify it before we involve the lives of our military personnel.

As for my relationship with the Pacific Fleet staff, as I told the CIA guy, I don't think they would have allowed me on their staff if they didn't think highly of me. I did what any intelligence professional should do during a war game by providing a realistic opposition. I thank God that the Cold War never went hot, but I believe if it had we would have kicked Soviet butt as a result of what we learned during these war game sessions.

The end result was anyone who worked on these war games received a lot of visibility among not only the senior members of the naval intelligence community but among the rest of the intelligence community as well. Captain Studeman went on to become Vice Admiral Studeman and headed up the National Security Agency (NSA) and was even acting CIA director for a while. One of the other prominent Global Red Team members was Rich Haver. I had lots of follow-on professional contact with Rich during the rest of my Navy career. He was brilliant and merciless if you hadn't done your homework, and he felt you didn't know what you were talking about. I was thrilled when he agreed to be the keynote speaker at my retirement ceremony. It was a tremendous honor for me to end my Navy career honored by an OSIS master.

Takeaway: Mentors are important to your success.

Key principles I learned concerning the importance of mentors:

1. The truth is that anyone who teaches you something that helps you to succeed in life is your mentor.
2. I've come to believe there are both positive and negative mentors.
3. A positive mentor is someone from whom you can learn the tools, skills, and techniques you need to succeed in a particular endeavor.
4. A negative mentor is someone who personifies traits you want to be sure you don't develop, such as people who exhibit bad work habits or abusive lifestyles.

CHAPTER 9 SUPPLEMENT

What I Learned from My Mentors about SONAR

SONAR stands for sound navigation and ranging. Essentially you're using sound to find objects underwater. Objects moving under water make sound. SONAR is used to locate such objects of interest as submarines. There are two types of SONAR: active and passive. "An active SONAR sends out a signal. When a sound signal is sent into the water, part of it will be reflected back if it strikes an object or 'target.' The distance to the object can be calculated by measuring the time between when the signal is sent out and when the reflected sound, or echo, is received. For example, if four seconds elapse between the emission of the outgoing sound and the return of its echo, the sound has taken two seconds to travel to the object and two seconds to return. The average speed of sound in the water is 1,500 meters per second. So if it takes two seconds for sound to reach the object, we can assume the object is 3,000 meters away."[23] Passive SONAR listens for sound. It doesn't emit a signal, kind of like how we use our ears. If a submarine hears a signal from an active SONAR, then it knows either another submarine or surface ship is in the area.

BACKGROUND ON THE SOVIET NAVAL STRATEGY

In 1982, the CIA put out National Intelligence Estimate, or NIE, 11-15, or Soviet Naval Strategy and Programs. The purpose of an NIE was to give the government a consolidated estimate of a particular intelligence problem.

The CIA writes it and then runs it by the other intelligence organizations for input. If there is a dissenting opinion, it's footnoted in very tiny print at the bottom of the page. It was meant to be the intelligence community's best idea of what was going on. What made this particular NIE controversial was the fact that the intelligence community believed the primary mission of the Soviet Navy was defensive in nature. That initially didn't make sense to many of our warfighters. The NIE states, "Within the Soviets' overall wartime strategy, however, the primary initial tasks of the Navy remain:

- To deploy and provide protection for SSBNs in preparation for and conduct of strategic and theater nuclear strikes.
- To defend the USSR and its allies from strikes by enemy SSBNs and aircraft carriers"[24]

At the start of each major war game, one member of the Red Team would be tasked to brief this to all of the participating Navy players. The admirals and other senior U.S. military officers present found it hard to believe that a Navy as potent as the Soviet's would be used primarily in a defensive role.

At that point, whoever was the intelligence briefer would have to explain first that the Soviet military leadership was dominated by the army. Those men felt that the most important offensive arm of the Navy was the SSBNs. It was essential to protect them so in the event a conventional conflict went nuclear they could launch their weapons against targets in the United States. Second, the Soviets were well aware that the U.S. ASW capability was far superior to theirs; therefore, it was essential that a strong force be used to defend them. Once you laid out these points, the admirals usually grudgingly nodded but, there was still a large degree of skepticism you had to overcome as the game was played. This concept was nicknamed the "Bastion Theory" by intelligence types.

NOTES

1. Glenn Van Ekeren, *Speaker's Source Book II.* (New York: Prentice Hall Press, 1994), 179.

2. A quote prominently displayed at the Naval War College in Newport, Rhode Island.

3. John Lehman, *On Seas of Glory: Heroic Men, Great Ships, and Epic Battles of the American Navy.* (New York: Free Press, 2001), 345.

4. Lehman, *On Seas of Glory*, 346.

5. Lehman, *On Seas of Glory*, 362–363.

6. Matthew Caffrey, "Toward a History Based Doctrine for Wargaming." *Air&Space Journal—Chronicles Online Journal* 27 April 2000, page 14. At www .airpower.maxwell.af.mil/airchronicles/cc/caffrey.html.

7. Robert H. Gile, Naval War College Newport Papers 20, *Global War Game Second Series 1984–1988*. (Newport, Rhode Island: Naval War College Press, 2004), xiii.

8. Matthew Caffrey, "Toward a History Based Doctrine for Wargaming," 24.

9. Director Central Intelligence, *NIE 11-15-82/DSoviet Naval Strategy and Programs Through the 1990s* (Washington, DC: Director Central Intelligence, 19 October 1982), 13–14.

10. Gile, *Global War Game Second Series 1984–1988*, 3.

11. Gile, *Global War Game Second Series 1984–1988*, 3.

12. Gile, *Global War Game Second Series 1984–1988*, 35–-38.

13. Director Central Intelligence, *NIE 11-15-82*, 5.

14. Director Central Intelligence, *NIE 11-15-82*, 15.

15. Director Central Intelligence, *NIE 11-15-82*, 15–16.

16. Director Central Intelligence, *NIE 11-15-82*, 20.

17. Director Central Intelligence, *NIE 11-15-82*, 22.

18. Gile, *Global War Game Second Series 1984–1988*, 61–62.

19. Gile, *Global War Game Second Series 1984–1988*, 63.

20. Gile, *Global War Game Second Series 1984–1988*, 64.

21. Norman Polmar, *Guide to the Soviet Navy*. (Annapolis, MD: Naval Institute Press, 1991) 380–381.

22. Matthew Caffrey, "Toward a History Based Doctrine for Wargaming," 17.

23. University of Rhode Island Office of Marine Programs website at www.dosits .org/science/ssca/la.htm.

Is Being Single the Worst Thing That Can Happen to You?

It's raining men[1]

Like most people, one of my deepest dreams was that one day I would meet that special person meant just for me. To this day, I still love big, sloppy romantic movies, although the traditional idea of marriage and picket fence holds no interest for me. I just wanted to meet "him," have the world's greatest romance, marry, and then spend the rest of my life with him traveling the world, seeing the sights, and enjoying each other's company. My older relatives told me not to worry about it, just live my life, and over the course of natural events, I would meet that special person and marry. Well, he never came along, but does that mean my life has been a failure?

IS THE ONLY PATH TO HAPPINESS MARRIAGE?

For many years, I bought in to the belief that the only path to happiness was to be married. The attitude toward single people seemed to center around pity. It meant you were a sad tragic figure with coworkers whispering, "That poor dried-up old thing. Bet she lives with a bunch of cats." It seems a lot of people measure your worth by whether you're in a relationship or married with children.

I remember one night in London having dinner with my good buddy Dave and our VQ-2 commanding officer. We had just flown in from Spain to participate in an air show. We decided to distance ourselves from the junior officers and enlisted personnel so we could relax and have a quiet drink together without being under the usual scrutiny of the people who worked for us. At one point in the evening, the commanding officer, who had just a little bit too much to drink, made a derogatory comment about me, something to the effect that I was unattractive and having no dates. Dave and I started laughing hysterically, leaving him totally confused. I winked at Dave and mischievously whispered, "I'm a tramp!" Dave went along with it, "Yeah, she's a tramp." Dave knew that while I did date I wasn't a tramp and was handling what could have been an awkward moment with my trademark humor. Dave was a lifelong single and knew people had strange ideas about folks like us, so I knew this was his way of defending me.

I've learned there are many paths we walk on this thing we call life. Each one can be extremely rewarding depending on our mental attitude. Though I have had my lonely moments, I have discovered there are many advantages to being single. I've done many things in my life that I would not have been able to do if I had been married and a mother. I prayed many times for God to bring that special "him" into my life, but for whatever reason that's the only prayer He's not yet answered for me. I might not have met "him," but I have been fortunate enough to meet and enjoy the company of lots of nice "almost hims." I've also had my share of "dates from hell," but overall I'm a big fan of the male of the species.

NAVY MEN LOVE WOMEN!

Growing up I didn't give dating much thought. I just figured my elders were right and that part of my life would work itself out. My mom and a friend of hers arranged a date for my high school prom. I dated some in college, but except for the year I spent in Europe, I don't recall causing much of a stir among the male of the species. I just figured some women had "it" and some didn't. Based on my experiences, I figured I just didn't have "it" when it came to attracting men. I always thought of myself as average looking if not ugly, slightly overweight if not downright fat, but I saw a lot of average-looking women who had attracted a mate and appeared to be happily married, so I didn't worry that my lack of dates would mean I would never marry.

So it came as a complete shock when I joined the Navy and discovered I was now a sex symbol. Guys were suddenly everywhere, asking me out on dates, following me around, and calling me up. It wasn't just me, it was any Navy woman. One of my girl friends told me she had five marriage proposals before she even left Officer Candidate School (OCS). Every woman I've known in the Navy has had similar experiences. Navy men love women!

Whenever I'm trying to get this point across to people who aren't familiar with the military, I always use an incident from the movie *Top Gun* as an example. It's the scene where Tom Cruise and his buddy walk up to Kelly McGillis in an officer's club bar. They'd never seen her before, yet they start serenading her with "You've Lost That Loving Feeling" in an attempt to pick her up. I tell people that scene was very true to life and, even if she'd weighed 200 pounds, they would have still done the same thing.

I have no scientific explanation for this, but the older I get the more I realize I know very little about men when it comes to male/female romantic relationships. I suspect, though, that this Navy love of women has to do with its history of long periods of time at sea. When sailors get to a port of call, they want to make up for lost time. As a child growing up, I'd listen to my Father and his friends talk about their time in the service. They had all been in the Army, but whenever they talked about the Navy they'd laugh and say, "The fleet's in, lock up your women and children!"

THE LAW OF SUPPLY AND DEMAND

I tried not to let all this male attention go to my head. I'd taken a lot of economic courses in school and clearly understood the law of supply and demand. I figured since the male-to-female ratio was overwhelmingly in a woman's favor, it was only natural that a lot of guys would be asking me out. I kept looking in the mirror telling myself, "I'm average looking. I'm average looking." I wasn't trying to put myself down; I just didn't want to become so conceited that I would always expect men to fall all over themselves trying to impress me.

During the later years of my career, I got to hear about this situation from the male perspective. Some of my male Navy officer friends told me that they would sometimes have to tell off some of those "stuck up sisters" who had developed an unhealthy attitude about all this male attention. One guy told me that while he was stationed overseas, he'd tried to ask a couple of the female officers out on a date, but they looked down their noses at him. He said his response insinuated that they weren't really that attractive, and he wondered out loud how many dates they thought they'd have if they weren't in the Navy.

I don't blame him for being angry, but these ladies were in an environment where a woman could find it difficult not to let all that attention go to her head. I did my best not to but found out a number of years ago at a lunch with one of my old boyfriends that I hadn't done quite as well as I thought I had. He complimented me on my maturity, adding that back when we were dating I acted like a spoiled little princess. Thinking back, I replied, "It was hard not be."

I remember when I was preparing for my first trip to the Philippines how my squadron mates warned me things would be different there. They had become very protective of me and treated me like a treasured younger sister. They wanted to make sure I wasn't overly concerned if no one asked me out while I was there. They said the Philippines had some of the most beautiful women in the world, so no guy wanted to waste time on a "round eye," meaning a non-Oriental woman.

The day I arrived, I had on my shapeless oversized flight suit, my hair had frizzed up the minute I stepped off the plane into the intense humidity, and from my perspective there was nothing attractive about me, but by the time I checked into the BOQ I had a man on each arm and the phone was ringing in the room I hadn't even entered yet. I rushed to answer it, figuring it was for whomever had previously occupied that room. Instead, I heard this guy say, "You don't know me but I saw you getting off the plane and would like to take you out to dinner." This scenario has repeated over and over throughout my career.

MY STRATEGY FOR KEEPING SEXUAL TEMPTATIONS AT BAY

I was very conscious of being the first woman to hold many of my jobs and tried to be very careful with the image I was projecting. As I speak around the country, people wonder why they've never heard of me when I am introduced as the first female intelligence officer in an operational aviation squadron. I tell them it's probably because I didn't get pregnant, I didn't have an affair with my commanding officer, I'm heterosexual, and the guys accepted me as part of the team once they saw I intended to do my job without expecting any special privileges. It saddens me when it seems the only time a military woman makes the news is if there is a scandal involved.

At times, though, the male attention could be so intense it was overwhelming. For the most part, my preferred method of socializing was hanging out with a group of my friends; however, after a few unchaperoned dates, I decided I needed a strategy to keep myself under control and sexual temptation at bay when I did choose to date without the benefit of group protection. Naval men are some of the most attractive specimens in the world!

I generally lived alone so, especially during my first assignment, I was at a loss as to how to end a date gracefully. I figured I should at least invite the guy in for a cup of coffee or something, but I didn't want to give the impression I was offering anything else. A girlfriend laughingly showed me a *Playgirl*-type magazine with a centerfold that, how can I say this delicately, highlighted a part of his anatomy that resembled a fire hose. I named him "Fire Hose Eddy" and decided to keep this issue on my coffee table.

Once I put my strategy in place, I would invite him in and offer him something to drink. As I stepped into the kitchen area to get his drink, he'd casually open the magazine conspicuously left on my coffee table and look at the centerfold. Their reaction was always the same: "That's ridiculous, that's not a normal man." I'd smile innocently and say, "It isn't?" The guy would blanch, look at his watch, and say, "Gail, it's been a great evening but it's late and I have to go." Score one for the girl's team!

MY DATE FROM HELL

My date from hell actually started out well enough. He had offered to take me flying in his small plane. We flew south along the northern California coast toward Monterey and Big Sur. I made the mistake of asking if he'd ever done any aerial acrobatics with his plane. He just laughed and then proceeded to start nose-diving the plane. I told him that was real cute and asked him to stop, but he kept doing it over and over. Suddenly my stomach couldn't take it any more, and I started throwing up all over him and the airplane. He stopped diving and headed for home as quickly as possible. He only lost it once, as he was landing, when I leaned over to throw up again and accidentally put my foot on the yolk, the plane's steering wheel. He started screaming at me, and when he dropped me off at home he didn't even try to kiss me goodnight. Go figure! He also never asked me out again.

I was engaged a couple of times, but each time I was jilted before making it to the altar. I'd meet someone I thought might be "the one," then something would happen and he disappeared from my life. A scene from the TV show *Sex and the City* sort of says it all for me. While eating out with her friends, a character named Charlotte throws her hands up in the air and then puts her head on the table declaring, "I've been dating since I was fifteen and I'm exhausted. Where is he?!" I could relate to her plight.

I'M OVER-THE-HILL

I kept thinking as I got older, guys would stop asking me out. I had bought into the belief system that once a woman was passed thirty she was over-the-hill, but even in my 40s guys were still making passes at me. I remember once when my second aviation squadron deployed with a detachment of aircraft and aircrew to Greece. There were no base living quarters for us, so we had to stay at a beautiful hotel; the sacrifices I've had to make for my country. Anyway, one afternoon I was sitting on my hotel balcony, reading a romance novel. It was a gorgeous day, my balcony overlooked the bay, and I was enjoying some much-needed peace and quiet.

My reverie was interrupted by voices from the balcony above me. I thought they were from my squadron but didn't recognize any of their voices. They obviously couldn't see me from their vantage point, as I heard one guy say, "I sure would like to spend some private time with Commander Harris." One of his buddies reminded him I was old enough to be his mother, but he replied, "I don't care, she's hot!" I had a big grin on my face for the rest of the day.

DEALING WITH FOREIGN MEN

I found that foreign men, particularly those in Europe and the Middle East, were fascinated by American women. The first time I went to the Middle East was during the Gulf War. I didn't have much advance notice, so I didn't have time to shop for conservative civilian clothes. The best I could come up with was a small wardrobe of extremely baggy clothes. Besides I was forty-two years old—old by American dating standards. I never in my wildest dreams thought that the sight of an old, middle-aged me dressed in baggy Western clothes would appear sexually provocative or offensive to any man, anywhere.

My squadron commanding officer dropped me off at my hotel. I checked in and got on the elevator to ride up to my room. Inside the elevator was a lone Arab man who looked at me with what appeared to be a lustful stare. Then he passionately declared his love for American women and proceeded to started kissing and touching me all over. I knew he only had two hands, but it felt more like four. I pushed him away and with as much dignity as I could muster said, "American women are not tramps." He chuckled and left me alone for the rest of the short ride to my floor.

I dumped my suitcase off in my room and headed for the hotel dining room, checking to make sure my earlier assailant was not on the elevator. After dinner, I decided that after my long flight from Spain, I'd just go back to my room and crash. There was a man standing next to me that I assumed was waiting for the elevator. I was exhausted from my long flight and didn't pay any attention to him. Suddenly I realized he was talking out loud, saying something like, "I love American woman, $1,000 dollars." Thinking he was a little crazy, I tried to ignore him, but he kept repeating it, getting louder and louder. I thought to myself, "Why does this man want me to give him $1,000?" I didn't really get it until I got back to my room. Remember, I did say I was tired from my long flight.

When I first told that story to Reverend Helen, she couldn't stop laughing. "Only an American woman would not have realized what the guy was really asking," she laughed. My incredulous response was, "But I'm a middle-aged woman! Who would have thought?" She was hysterical by then and told me to get off the phone so she could call all her friends.

MEN MAKE GREAT FRIENDS

The relationships I treasured the most with guys, however, were the friendships I made all along the way. Men actually make really great friends. They're nurturing, supportive, and very protective. I found they always offered to fix breaks either in my home or my car and were there for me when another guy broke my heart. They would volunteer to beat the fool up or, if I wanted a more restrained reaction, they'd give me the male perspective on the situation. Two guys I originally met while stationed in Japan particularly stand out as I write this chapter. Jack Shankles and Barry Flynn, along with their wives, have always been there for me through career challenges or men issues. Their support has been consistent and has meant the world to me. Thanks, guys!

I've got to admit, though, that my male friends spoiled me outrageously over the years. When I was stationed in Panama, one of my best friends was a fellow intelligence officer named Jim. We worked shift work, so we were not always off from work at the same time, but if he was off, he'd hang out his window and watch for me to come home. He knew I was a huge Frank Sinatra fan and loved New York City. When he saw my car approaching, he would turn his stereo up real loud and play Frank Sinatra, singing, "New York, New York!" He'd lean out his window and yell, "Hey Gail, come on up for a drink."

DATING RULES FOR SENIOR OFFICERS

As I got older and more senior in rank, dating became increasingly more problematic. In the military, if you're a single senior officer, your dating options within military circles are very limited. You are forbidden by military law to date enlisted people. Because the majority of people in the military are enlisted, that's eliminating a large pool of potential dates. You can date other officers, but if they are junior in rank that's generally frowned upon as well.

I also found that as I got more senior in years, most of the people in my work environment were married. The dating issue would have still been manageable if I had been stationed in the United States, where I could mingle with nonmilitary people, but as I was stationed overseas a good portion of the time, it became more and more difficult. In Europe, it wasn't too hard to meet and date people who lived or worked in that country, but in the Orient or Middle East, it was really challenging to meet nice people from that culture to interact with. Clubs and bars often catered to Americans, but I don't believe that's an ideal situation in which to meet the kind of people I'd want to be in any kind of real relationship with.

Thankfully, most of the jobs I had overseas as a senior officer were very time-consuming. I loved the work, so the long hours were okay with me. I will admit there were times I'd get depressed if I wasn't dating someone interesting. At times I'd let those thoughts get the better of me and begin to feel like a real loser, thinking something must be really wrong with me. How could it be that with all of these men around I couldn't find the "him" placed on this earth just for me?

During those down times, I'd spend a lot of time listening to my Frank Sinatra and Luther Vandross records and dreaming of that special "him" that I was going to meet some day. Then I'd try a new strategy to put me in the right place at the right time to find the right "him." Sometimes I would stop dating for a year or two. I would pray and ask God to send "him" to me. I would attend church, join the singles group, and pursue outside interests I really enjoyed, like hiking and biking. I had been told that you're most attractive when you're pursuing things that bring you joy. I even tried the Internet dating thing, but nothing seemed to work.

The turning point came in what would be my final conversation with my dad before he died. Knowing he wasn't long for this world, I had taken to calling him once a day. On that last call, out of the blue, he said, "Gail, I know you're depressed because you've never married. You have to play the hand you're dealt. Enjoy your life just as it is." Those words blew away all those thoughts that had caused me so much unhappiness over the years. I felt like a weight had been lifted off of my shoulders. From that moment on, I have rejoiced in my singleness and realized I have much to be thankful for. I've traveled the world and done lots of things I would have never been able to do if I had followed the traditional path of marriage and family.

HALLELUIAH! IT'S RAINING MEN

During my last years in the Navy, I cut way down on dating. Demands of the job really didn't allow much time for it, plus, as a senior officer, I was particularly careful to always consider professional decorum. The more senior you are in rank, the more prominent your job; therefore, you are expected to conduct yourself both professionally and personally above reproach. I had an even bigger challenge than most since I was saddled with the wild child, playgirl reputation. I managed to conduct myself professionally most of the time, but every now and then I'd slip, just a little.

In Nebraska, I had 500 people working for me and was under a lot of scrutiny. The command was at Offutt Air Force Base, and we were sponsoring a big air show. One of the fringe benefits of being in the military is the participants show up early and practice a day before the actual event. If you're stationed on base, you get to see the show a day early and avoid the huge crowds the events normally garner. This was going to be a big one that would include the Navy's Blue Angels.

The day before the big event, one of the participating Army Airborne units was practicing their 400-man parachute jump. When I saw those 400 men jumping from planes, I couldn't help myself. I started jumping around and singing the song by the Weather Girls, "It's Raining Men! Hallelujah!" I only had a few months before I transferred, so I didn't get into any trouble, although they teased me about it during my farewell award ceremony.

TODAY'S DEPARTMENT OF DEFENSE

I don't have any statistics to back it up, but I've noticed that most women in the military now marry pretty early in their careers. Usually it's to someone they've met during their initial training or during their first job assignment. When I joined the Navy, women could be married, but if you had children, even step children, you had to retire. Thankfully, that policy has changed due to a Supreme Court decision.

Shortly before I retired from the Navy, I was at a ceremony for a woman being promoted to captain. She had a small baby on her arm and was in the advanced stages of pregnancy with a second. I think I was the only person in the room that recognized the historical significance of that. You've got to hand it to the military, though. Once the Supreme Court decision was made, they jumped into the parenthood thing with both feet. The Department of Defense is now the largest child day care provider in the world. When I say that, I know it conjures up images of hundreds of babies crawling around in formation in military diapers, but my married friends tell me these are first-class facilities.

I'M FAST APPROACHING 60!

I've talked about dating in my 20s, 30s, and 40s. As I'm writing this, I'm in my 50s and fast approaching 60, so you're probably wondering, how's the dating thing now? I'm reminded of the movie *The Lion in Winter*, the version starring Peter O'Toole and Katherine Hepburn. The story line tells of the turbulent relationship between King Henry II of England and his estranged wife, the fiery Queen Eleanor of Aquitaine. Theirs had been a unique marriage in that he had imprisoned her because she kept plotting to overthrow him. Throughout the movie, Eleanor kept taunting Henry about his numerous infidelities, when at one point Henry challenged her about her lifestyle, to which Eleanor replied, "At my age, I don't get much traffic anymore."

I've not lived a promiscuous lifestyle but, like Eleanor, I don't get as much traffic as I used to; however, this season of my life has been one of the happiest. I'm more comfortable in my skin and with the course of my life than at any other period in my life. I still have the occasional wild experience, like at a gas station in New Mexico where an attractive Hispanic man drove by, honked his horn, and waved. I smiled and waved back, not giving the incident much thought. The next thing I knew, he turned his truck around, walked right up to me, gave me a passionate kiss, and then asked me out. It's tough being an "old maid," but someone has to do it.

I've had many marriage proposals over the years but none from someone I thought I could go the distance with. My last three proposals went like this:

Guy number one: "I've been in therapy and think I could handle being married to a fat woman."

Guy number two: "You're getting old; I'm probably your last chance, so you'd better marry me."

Guy number three: "Have you gone through menopause yet? I want you to be the mother of my children."

I share these proposals not to garner pity but only to show why I believe I could not go the distance with any of these three guys. My dad always told me the right man would think of all the women in the world and decide I was the greatest and the one he'd want to spend his life with. I refuse to settle for less. God has given me many blessings and, when the time is right, He'll take care of that as well.

If for some reason it's not in my destiny to marry, I'll continue to lead a life of fun, joy, and travel and, even though when I'm older and grayer it may only be a drizzle, it will still be raining men.

Takeaway: Just because you're single doesn't mean your life will suck.

Key principles I learned about being single:

1. There are many paths on this thing we call life.
2. The right man would think of all the women in the world and decide I was the greatest and the one he'd want to spend his life with.
3. I refuse to settle for less.
4. God has given me many blessings and, when the time is right, He'll take care of that as well.
5. If for some reason it's not in my destiny to marry, I'll continue to lead a life of fun, joy, and travel.

NOTE

1. Paul Jubara and Paul Shaffer. *It's Raining Men*. The Weather Girls, 1982, Columbia Records.

Bloom Where You're Planted, or How I Became an Iraqi Expert

You need to overcome the tug of people against you as you reach for high goals.

—*George S. Patton*[1]

You have enemies? Good. That means you've stood up for something sometime in your life.

—*Winston Churchill*[2]

In the late 1980s, I was assigned to the Navy's Pacific Fleet command in Hawaii. As mentioned in earlier chapters, while there I came up for promotion to commander but was passed over. The worst part was I had been told I was a shoo-in for this promotion and that my next job assignment had already been selected. I called my mentor, Drew Simpson, who was in charge of job assignments. Drew was great and very supportive. The competition for promotion was fierce, and it didn't take much to put you out of the running. I told Drew I thought it was because of my on-going battle with weight and that maybe it was time for me to resign. He told me to hang in there and let him do some checking around.

In spite of the support from Drew and my former boss, Ted Sheafer, who was now an admiral, I was still bummed out, so I made an appointment with Reverend Helen. Upbeat and forceful, she let me cry for a while, and then we got down to business. "Gail, remember who you are. You are made in the image of our Creator. You are a child of God who loves you, and if you pray and ask believing for the promotion, it's yours. Your words will not return to you void."

She spent several minutes praying for me, and I felt like the weight of despair had been lifted off of me. I actually started to feel good again. She then asked, "Of course you could wait and get your promotion next year, but why not sooner?"

"No, the way the Navy works," I explained, "I won't be up for promotion again until the board meets next year."

She got a thoughtful look on her face and asked, "So what are you going to do for the next year?"

"My boss says he will let me keep my job as head of the Soviet navy analysis shop." It was considered one of the best and most prestigious jobs on the staff. It actually wouldn't be too bad staying here, except that in my eyes I was ready for and had earned a promotion.

Reverend Helen wasn't done with her line of questioning, though. "You've told me what you're going to do at work, but what about your personal life?"

I hadn't really thought much about it, but as she said that, a weird idea popped in my head. "I think I'll focus on having fun. I haven't had any for a long time."

Reverend Helen got a mischievous look on her face and asked, "Do you have to wear your uniform every day to work?"

Wondering what was going on in her mind, I nodded, yes.

"Do they tell you what kind of underwear to have on?" I shook my head no, totally puzzled by her line of questioning.

"Here's what you're going to do. When you leave here, don't go back to work. Go to the mall and go into the Frederick's of Hollywood store and buy some of the wildest underwear you can find. Wear that under your uniform. I guarantee you'll be walking around all day with a big grin on your face, and everyone will be wondering what's going on."

I did go shopping, but I didn't ever wear it. Just buying it and the thought of wearing it under my conservative uniform made me walk around work with a big smile on my face.

That's one way to cope with what I had perceived as an unfair situation in my life. On a more serious note, Reverend Helen also advised me to focus on Mark 11:24 any time I started to get discouraged over my promotion prospects: "Whatever things soever ye desire, when ye pray, believe that ye receive them, and ye shall have them." What everyone was really trying to get me to see was that if I would bloom where I was planted right now, do the best at whatever I put my hand to, I could overcome any obstacle that came my way and get the exact promotion God had in place for me and at the right time.

THE LETTER

Well, I did just that and, for the most part, handled things pretty well. I worked hard, strove to be the best at whatever I put my hand to, and had fun along the way. Shortly before the promotion board was scheduled to meet, I woke up in the middle of the night and had a strong urge to write a letter to them. I got out of bed and started rapidly scribbling down the words as they came to me. It was almost as if I were being dictated to by someone bigger and smarter than me. After I finished, I knew without a doubt in my deepest being I would be promoted this time around, no matter what the odds.

Admiral Sheafer was so impressed with the letter that he later told me I needed to write an article in the Navy-themed magazine *Proceedings* telling people how to write an effective letter to a promotion board. I never wrote the article, but I've shared my formula with many people over the years. About four years ago, I got a phone call from one of my favorite people, Sarah, who had successfully followed my advice after she had been passed over.

After the normal catch-up conversation, she began a rather long-winded discussion about a young man who had been passed over and made an appointment with her to talk about his options. She had asked him if he had considered writing a letter to the promotion board, and he said he had. A friend had given him a copy of a letter he had used as a model for writing the promotion board after he had been passed over for promotion. When he showed her the letter, it was my letter still circulating around the Navy after all this time.

The letter followed a pretty straightforward concept consisting of four parts. In part 1, I explained why I was writing the letter. Part 2 consisted of what I considered the highlights of my career, where I mentioned my series of "firsts." Part 3 is where I addressed anything I thought could be considered as negative on my record. I openly addressed my weight issues, mentioning that it was a medical problem but also pointing out I had always passed the actual fitness part of the test. The last part of the letter is designed to reach the heart of the board members. In this section, I explained why I joined the Navy in the first place. Whenever I explain how to write this part of the letter, I say it has to come from your heart and soul. This will not overcome a record of poor performance but will cause the board members to look at your record more closely.

When screening a record for promotion, the board normally only spends two or three minutes a record. They have to screen large numbers of records, so they seldom see your entire record in detail. A summary of your grades and the jobs you've held is displayed on a large screen. A member of your job specialty stands up in front of the board and gives them a brief summary of your record, pointing out what's good and what's bad. When you write a letter, it has to be read to the promotion board. Sometimes this is all that is needed to get you over the hump and let the board members notice something you've done that shows you deserve to be promoted. I always caution people not to whine. No one wants to hear that your boss didn't like you. To the best of my knowledge, everyone who followed this advice was promoted on the second try.

AN OPPORTUNITY TO SHOWCASE MY TALENTS

Meanwhile, Drew was doing everything he could to make sure I was in a good position to make captain. He pulled me out of Hawaii eighteen months early and sent me to Korea to head up the intelligence support for the upcoming 1988 Olympics. He felt my strength lay in the area of warning and providing operational intelligence support in crisis situations. In lay terms, that means figuring out if the bad guy was going to attack and warning the decision makers ahead of time so they can counter it.

Pulling me out of Hawaii early and sending me to that job required the approval of the secretary of defense. I would be working with the U.S. and South Korean military, intelligence agencies, and police organizations. Drew couldn't force the Navy to promote me, but what he could do is make sure I had jobs that showcased my best talents. If I didn't do well, I wouldn't get promoted for sure; but if I did well in that job, at least I had a fighting chance.

After a year in Korea, the plan was to return and head up a small Navy intelligence command in Hawaii.

As I explained in a previous chapter, going back to Hawaii after my time in Korea turned out not to be an option. Drew never gave up on me, though. "Gail, let me talk to Admiral Sheafer and see what we can come up with. Don't do anything until you hear from me." I promised Drew I wouldn't do anything until I heard back from him. I was glad he was quick, though.

I figured it would be at least a month or so before I heard back, but he called a couple of hours later and told me, "We have two choices for you. You can be assigned with the Naval Forces Europe, which is headquartered in London, England, or join VQ-2, the Navy's largest aviation squadron, headquartered in Rota, Spain." The choice was easy for me, and that is how I ended up with VQ-2 in Spain. I was over the moon about my new assignment. Since the federal law that restricted the assignment of women to ships that might go into combat was still in effect, this was the only job with an operational mission open to me as a commander.

The VQ aircraft were land-based. The squadron flew the EP-3 and EA-3 aircraft, the Navy's only land-based signals intelligence (SIGINT) reconnaissance aircraft. These aircraft specialized in collecting information on radars and communications of countries that might be a threat to U.S. forces. The value-added service they provided was real-time tactical intelligence to U.S. military forces. The press has given them the nickname spy planes. In addition to flying missions out of Spain, the squadron also routinely flew missions from Italy and Greece. Because of the demands of my job, I would be required to spend a significant amount of time in those countries as well. I was so glad I had patiently waited until the right assignment came along. Little did I know just how perfect this assignment was for my career.

BEST ASSIGNMENT EVER

When I arrived in Spain, I made it a point to be on my best behavior. I didn't want them to be sorry that they'd agreed to take me. One day I was quietly going about my work when there was a knock on my office door. There stood the commanding officer and the number two guy, the executive officer (XO). Thereby followed a dialogue I will never forget.

"Hi Gail, we just wanted to see if you were settling in okay."

I stood up at attention. "Yes, Sir, everything is fine."

"Well, the XO and I wanted to say we're a little bit disappointed with you."

I started to panic. What had I done wrong? "Sir, I don't understand?"

The commanding officer smiled, and said, "We had heard you were a lot of fun and had a lot of spirit. You've been acting very reserved and quiet since you arrived."

I started to relax and leaned against my desk. "I didn't want you to think the ugly things some folks said about me were true, so I've been doing my best not to cause any problems."

They laughed and then the executive officer spoke up, "We want the wild woman we've heard about. You're with the aviation community now, be yourself."

I was elated! But then he added, "What's with the black shoes?"

When wearing khakis, naval aviators are authorized to wear brown shoes, which distinguishes them from the other warfare specialties. Since I was in the intelligence community I'd always worn black shoes.

"I didn't know I was authorized to wear them but I will see what I can do. The uniform shop here doesn't have many items for women."

They chuckled and left. I felt really good about the dialogue, realizing they were making a statement that if they had believed what was being said about me, they never would have agreed to have me on their team. I decided to relax and not worry about behaving a certain way anymore. I could tell that I was really going to enjoy this assignment.

The next day was our All Officers meeting. I decided to introduce the squadron to the real Gail, so I walked into the meeting late and in my bare feet. "Captain, I apologize for being late, but per your request I was looking for some brown shoes to wear. I couldn't find the shoes, but my feet are brown. Will that do?" Everyone fell out laughing, and I settled down and began to enjoy the best assignment I'd ever had.

Beyond a doubt, that bunch was the greatest group of people I've ever been assigned with, and there was an unexpected bonus in this assignment for me as well. When the first Gulf War started about a year or so into the assignment, it put me in a combat unit. If I had gone back to Hawaii as planned, I would not have been involved in the war and probably would not have been promoted to captain.

UNPLANNED AND UNEXPECTED

My involvement in the Iraq crisis as an intelligence analyst was unplanned and totally unexpected. Once the war started, my job was to ensure that the aviators in the squadron had the best intelligence possible to do their job and to enable them to survive in a war environment. That meant my folks and I had to keep track of anything the enemy had that could harm our aircraft, which involved screening thousands of intelligence reports and providing key data to the flight crews both before and during their flights.

Before being assigned to the squadron, I knew very little about the Middle East or Persian Gulf region. For most of my Navy career, my jobs had caused me to focus on Soviet military forces in the Far East. Even during my assignment at the Naval War College, I focused on the Far East; however, I wasn't totally lost once I had to focus on Iraq. They had a lot of Soviet military equipment, which I was already very familiar with. I knew how far and how high their surface-to-air missiles could go and what distance their aircraft could fly before running out of gas. The only shift I had to make in my thinking was learning which military bases they were operating out of.

At the beginning of the crisis, we had a big presentation scheduled to bring all the flight crews up to speed on the Iraqi threat. I decided I would do the first briefing. As I was preparing, my senior enlisted analyst requested a meeting with me and asked why I was doing the briefing. I realized I was now senior management and had to learn how to delegate. I turned the briefing back over to him. I knew I was going to have my hands full becoming the Iraqi expert I would need to be to do the job I was there to do.

BACKGROUND ON THE IRAQI WAR

Before I go into my involvement in the Iraqi situation, I need to give you some background on what was going on at this volatile time in history. Bear with me on this, there is a point to all that I am going to share with you here and in the next two chapters.

In December of 1998, the United States Central Command (USCENTCOM), under orders from the Clinton administration, launched Operation Desert Fox, a four-day operation as stated in that organization's official history, "aimed at installations associated with development of weapons of mass destruction, units providing security to such programs, and Iraq's national command and control network. Additional targets included selected Republican Guard facilities, airfields, and the Basrah oil refinery that was involved in production of illegal gas and oil exports."[3] On just the first day of operations, 280 cruise missiles were launched and, as stated in a December 28, 1998, *Time* magazine article, that total was almost as many as was used during the entire first Gulf War.[4]

Desert Fox was only one of a series of intense military operations conducted during a period referred to as the "Forgotten War," the time period between when the first Gulf War ended in March of 1991, and the second began in March of 2003. As stated in USCENTCOM's official history, on January 13 and 18, 1993, strikes were conducted against selected air defense targets. On January 17, 1993, the Navy launched forty-four TLAM cruise missile strikes against the Zaafaraniyah nuclear-related facility because of Iraq's refusal to comply with United Nations (UN) nuclear inspection requirements. On June 27, 1993, another Navy strike was launched against the headquarters of the Iraqi Intelligence service "in response to the discovery of Iraqi plans to assassinate former President Bush during his visit to Kuwait."[5]

In October 1994, "in response to a clear threat of Iraqi aggression against Kuwaiti and associated troop movements in southern Iraq," USCENTCOM, under what was called Operation Vigilant Warrior, deployed more than 28,000 troops and 200 additional aircraft to the Gulf region. In September 1996, as part of Operation Desert Strike, the command launched twelve cruise missiles against surface-to-air missile sites and command and control facilities in southern Iraq.[6]

What if these combined attacks, coupled with vigorous enforcement of UN sanctions, not only destroyed a large number of suspected weapons of mass destruction (WMD) stocks that had not been uncovered by the UN inspectors but also so severely damaged Iraq's military/industrial infrastructure that it prevented that country from having the capability to significantly rebuild their weapons program? If, and I say if, this was the case, it would not have been an easy thing to know for sure given the challenge of the intelligence gathering in the aftermath of Iraq's refusal to allow UN inspectors in country at the end of 1998.

A December 17, 1998, article in the *New York Times* quoted senior U.S. officials discussing Desert Fox as stating that the "air strikes would significantly hamper Iraq's programs to make poison gas and nuclear weapons, and they readily acknowledged that the weapons programs would continue. . . . Without the UN inspection program . . . the Clinton administration would have only a limited ability to determine whether Iraq is manufacturing and stockpiling weapons of massed destruction."[7] The same article quoted Pentagon officials as saying, "It's a very unpalatable scenario. . . . We can keep track of some of what's going on on the ground with satellites and surveillance planes. But that's not the same as having inspectors on the ground, poking around or at least trying to poke around Iraqi installations."[8]

The nature of intelligence is that you will seldom have the luxury of enough information to present a case that will stand up in court. I've always thought that the real key question that should have been asked before we began this most recent Iraq War was, Had our Iraq policies during the Forgotten War neutralized Saddam and his capability to reconstitute his WMD force? I don't know because I was retired by 2003, but I wondered if the Bush administration was familiar with and really understood what had been done in Iraq during the Clinton administration. I wonder if the new guys just dismissed out of hand what had been done before they took office. I was sitting on the sidelines, but it appeared to me they had, along with many in the media as well. I've been interviewed many times mostly by radio talk show hosts. Without exception, they were not familiar with the events of the Forgotten War. My attitude is you need to be careful with your criticisms if you don't know the whole story.

BECOMING AN IRAQI EXPERT

The part of the Iraqi conflict that I was personally involved with during the first Gulf War focused on supplying the VQ2 flight crews with enough data to support coalition forces conducting bombing raids on Iraqi targets. Our guys would be flying in with the attacking aircraft providing real time on the scene intelligence reports. Research showed me that USCENTCOM had identified twelve types of targets we would go after: "leadership command facilities; electricity production facilities; telecommunications and C3 nodes; air defense systems; military depots and storage facilities; nuclear, biological, and chemical weapons research, production, and storage facilities; air forces and airfields; railroads and bridges; Scud missile launchers and production and storage facilities; oil refineries and distribution facilities; naval forces and port facilities; and ground forces, especially the Republican Guard."[9]

My team had to become experts on these targets, and to do that, we had to determine where to obtain the best and most up-to-date information available. I spent a lot of time on the phone asking around to find who put out the best information on Iraq. Once I did that, I had to figure out how to get the information sent to us in Spain as we were gearing up but also to our flight crews and intelligence personnel operating at various detachments in the war zone. I found all the intelligence agencies I coordinated with were more than willing to give us everything we asked for.

I've got to blow the horn of my naval intelligence community. It was generally acknowledged that they produced the best and most comprehensive intelligence on the Iraqi air force and air defense system. They had an organization called Spear that was headed up by a naval aviator with a staff consisting of a mix of flyers and intelligence types. An intelligence analyst with no flying background is handicapped when it comes to fully understanding the technical capabilities of aircraft, but when you put him or her with an aviator and have them study together how the bad guys use their aircraft; you come up with some awesome analysis. We were concerned that our aircraft, particularly the EP-3, would be especially vulnerable to antiaircraft artillery (AAA) and surface-to-air missiles (SAMs). We wanted to be sure we did everything in our power to give them the information they needed to stay alive and do their mission. We pored over and memorized the Spear intelligence reports. We found that Saddam had a very sophisticated system in place that we would have to figure out and quickly.

"Air Force officials would later claim it was far more imposing than that developed by Soviets in Eastern Europe at the height of the Cold War. Saddam's layered system used a mix of Soviet and Western equipment, including advanced radars, interceptor aircraft, surface-to-air missiles, and antiaircraft artillery. Saddam's forces boasted some 7,000 radar and optically guided antiaircraft guns and 16,000 radar and infrared guided surface-to-air missiles. . . . The antiaircraft artillery was most dangerous below 15,000 feet, while the surface-to-air missiles provided overlapping coverage from near ground level to about 40,000 feet."[10]

I was really challenged trying to become knowledgeable on some technical parts of the target set USCENTCOM came up with. I had been a liberal arts major, and the only science course I'd taken in college was botany. On day one of the flight, crew commanders came in for some help with mission planning. "Hey Gail, do the Iraqis have any microwave towers? If so do you know where they are?" I wondered, what in the world is he talking about? I had a microwave oven in my office, did those things have towers associated with them? Why would we want to destroy Iraqi microwave ovens? I didn't want to appear brain-dead stupid, so I told him I'd research it and get back to him.

I hit the phones to bug the rest of the intelligence community. I'm of the mindset that I'd rather ask a stupid question than make a stupid mistake. I found out that "oftentimes, communications are transmitted partly by satellite and partly via microwave towers. In other cases—particularly in the case of telephone calls within a country, as in Canada—microwave towers serve as the entire means of transmission and reception."[11] Who knew!

THE BEST OF THE BEST

The men and women that worked for me did an outstanding job. They were among the best and most innovative intelligence professionals I have ever worked with. They worked long hours learning everything they needed to know to support the flight crews with little or no time off under very difficult conditions and never once complained about it. Our job was made significantly easier by the fact that the VQ flight crew members were essentially flying intelligence professionals. That meant we didn't have to spend much time going over the intelligence information and explaining the significance of what we were providing. In fact, they were the sharpest intelligence types I've ever encountered.

My folks did all the really hard intelligence stuff. All I had to do was provide top cover for them and make sure everyone had the intelligence information, computers, and communications equipment needed to do their job. Before the flight crews went out on their mission, my folks gave them detailed information on enemy positions. When the flight crews returned from their mission, they had to send out a report of what happened. Since the information was classified, it had to be sent over special communications circuits. Most of the intelligence information my folks needed to support these flights came in over these circuits as well. I began to realize this was going to be a problem.

TRAILBLAZING

I started to see a pattern developing in the progression of the types of job assignments I had experienced up to this point. It seems I always had to figure out how to operate in situations and parts of the world few people had any experience in. When I had to set up intelligence support for the Olympics, there was no plan in place. I had to make it up as I went along. I was in the same situation now with this command. The information technology revolution was changing how society and the intelligence community did business, but there were still a lot of interoperability problems. I found that many of the organizations had radios and computers that couldn't talk to each other. Often our squadron flight crews and supporting personnel would be operating out of new locations that weren't set up to provide us with the logistics and operational support we needed to do our job. I would have to figure out how to support my squadron and the intelligence folks who worked for me in this new war environment.

At the beginning of the war, there were some locations we had to operate out of that did not have the communications architecture we needed to send and receive intelligence traffic. I contacted the Central Intelligence Agency (CIA) folks in the war zone and asked for help. At first, they were kind enough to let my people read the intelligence traffic and send messages over circuits from their work spaces, but they got sick of us after awhile, so I had to come up with another solution. One of my guys spent about two days on the phone calling up every intelligence organization we could think of looking for help with "no joy," as the aviators say when stumped.

One morning I came in, and he had good news for me. "Ma'am, I talked to a man who is the number two guy in the Intelligence Systems Department in ONI [Office of Naval Intelligence]. His name is Brent and says he's one of your former students from the Intel School. He wants you to give him a call." I remembered Brent well. He had been one of my best students. I called him and found out he had left active duty and taken a job as a civilian in the intelligence community.

After updating each other on our individual lives, we shifted into business mode. "Gail, your assistant told me about your requirements. I think we have a solution for you using some off-the-shelf commercial technology we have here. We have a system that plugs into any commercial phone line and will allow you to send and receive classified data automatically, encrypting the information going in and decrypting it at the receiving end."

Brent and his folks put the equipment together for us and came out and installed it at all of our operating sites. We could send and receive intelligence traffic with a system that worked so well that after the war it was later used at many naval commands.

A MIXED BLESSING

This turned out to be a mixed blessing for me, though. My commanding officer felt my real value was working with the intelligence community to make sure we continued to get all the computer and other communications equipment we needed to conduct our wartime mission. He wouldn't let me go to the war front saying he needed me to remain behind in Spain to coordinate everything.

Our aircraft were operating out of three locations to support the war. We flew out of Greece in support of the aircraft flying out of Turkey to smack Iraq. We flew out of a Saudi Arabian base on the Red Sea in support of aircraft carriers striking Iraq from those locations. In support of forces operating from the Persian Gulf, we were flying our aircraft out of Bahrain. When I first arrived in VQ-2, part of our operational missions flew out of Athens. After I'd been there a few months, the Greeks kicked us out of Athens and told us we would have to operate out of Souda Bay, Crete.

To do this we had to build a new building to operate out of, and somehow yours truly was designated the project manager. It's pretty typical in the Navy in that when you're doing a good job you get rewarded with more work. I would have a Seabee Detachment to handle the construction, but my commanding officer wanted me to keep track of everything and make sure it met the specifications of a classified facility. Sounds easy enough, but every time we got a Seabee Detachment working on it, they'd get pulled to help set up facilities somewhere else for the war.

I knew I was toast when one day a newly arrived Seabee Detachment commander called me up saying that the concrete slab the last detachment put in was a foot smaller than the prefab building they were supposed to put up on it. It took a number of phone calls to find out that the Air Force had decided to add some more sound attenuation materials to the wall, which made the walls thicker than specified in the original plans, without letting me know. I called the Seabee guy back, explaining what I had learned. He was pretty upbeat and positive, saying he thought they could compensate for it but not to let anyone put heavy file cabinets along the outside walls.

I had many similar situations to deal with, hence the reason my commanding officer didn't want me to leave Spain and go off to the war. All my life I'd been preparing for a war, and now I wasn't going to be allowed to go to the front because of my smooth-talking phone skills. I came up with a solution, though, telling my boss I needed to go inspect the equipment and building facilities our flight crews were operating out of, because if something was wrong I could go to jail. The Navy security gurus will throw you in jail if you make mistakes protecting classified equipment and material.

My folks operating in the war zones were responsible for finding work spaces and then making them secure and compliant with government regulations. Not just any space or building can be turned into an intelligence facility. I stayed in constant phone contact with my folks, making sure all the paperwork documenting that it was within required military standards was sent to the Navy security folks. By the time all the necessary paperwork was done, it was as thick as a phone book. In the course of overseeing all of this, I did manage to go to Bahrain shortly before the ground war started, but that was as close to combat as I ever came. My dad always teased me that my only frontline experience was staying in a hotel with room service and cable television. We had several Scud alerts during my time in the zone, but thankfully none ever landed near the location I worked or stayed in.

READY FOR A NEW PLACE TO BLOOM

After the war, I thought my career was in great shape. In my performance report, my commanding officer said I was the perfect wartime intelligence officer. I thought I would have no problem getting a good follow-on assignment. When I called the detailer who had replaced Drew to discuss follow-on job assignments, I mentioned that I had been five pounds overweight during the war but had since corrected the problem. We were always told to keep the job assignments people informed of any potential personal or professional problems. This new detailer acted like I had committed a major crime. I was puzzled by his reaction and didn't think it was any big deal since I had lost the weight and it wasn't mentioned in my performance report.

Remembering how things like this had escalated in the past, I decided to check with my commanding officer, who seemed genuinely surprised by my questions. He said he was on his way to Washington and would personally ask the detailer to keep me in my current position for at least six more months until we could determine where my next assignment would be. In fact, he said he was so happy with me he would really like to keep me an extra year. When I called to follow up with the detailer after my commanding officer's visit, he said I was a troublemaker and that he wasn't going to extend me where I was and he had no follow-on assignments for me.

I finally sent him a letter detailing not only what I had done in my current job but throughout my career. The senior Navy intelligence guy in Rota, Spain, at the time was my beloved mentor Drew Simpson, who went to see this guy to speak on my behalf. He was there when my letter arrived and said it literally punched the guy in the nose. He refused to extend me but stopped trying to force me to resign.

At the time, this situation didn't raise any red flags, and I didn't take his treatment too personally since he was equally nasty to many of the other Navy intelligence officers stationed in Rota. We all kept comparing notes on the guy and considered him an aberration. So once again, I was determined to bloom where I was planted, happy I wasn't being forced to resign.

UNDER INVESTIGATION

After the war ended, I discovered one of the issues that could be putting a delay on securing my next assignment. My folks who were working out of our location in Greece couldn't account for five classified floppy disks. Turns out they had given them to another Navy organization that had run out of them and forgotten to annotate that information in our paperwork.

As soon as I learned what had happened, I called up the Navy security folks in Washington. Based on the results from my preliminary investigation of the incident, they assured me they did not plan on taking any negative action against me. Apparently during the war, there had been many security violations because of some of the conditions people had to work under. They just asked us to send out the final investigation results so they could use the results they were compiling to help modify regulations to make sure things like this wouldn't happen again.

I thought that was the end of it, but the people in charge of the Mediterranean Navy units wanted to look into it further. The Naval Criminal Investigative Service (NCIS) conducted the investigation, and I was exonerated after they concluded that I had adequate security procedures in place and the lost disks were the result of operating under difficult war conditions. Even though the NCIS report said I had done nothing wrong, Navy leadership in the Mediterranean conducted two additional JAG investigations, and I was exonerated in both. I really thought this whole thing was behind me until I was called into my commanding officer's office. He nervously handed me a letter from the senior admiral in the Mediterranean command. It was something called a nonpunitive counseling letter, which doesn't go into your official record but is considered a punch in the mouth.

Almost choked by my rising anger, I crumbled the letter and threw it on the floor. My commanding officer remained calm as he let me vent my anger and then offered to do what he could to straighten this out. When he said he was surprised he didn't get one as well, I calmed down, realizing whatever I did would reflect on him. He and the other commanding officers I had worked for in the squadron had treated me better and fairer than anyone else during my entire time in the Navy. I did not want to get him into trouble, so I thanked him, left his office, and decided to call my dad.

As usual, Dad was the all-knowing voice of reason. "When are you going to learn to see these things coming? It's obvious someone is jealous of the success you're having in your job and is trying to discredit you. Didn't you say the letter doesn't go in your record?"

I reluctantly answered, "Yes."

"Then suck it up," he advised. "The admiral probably doesn't know the full story. I'm sure whoever is out to get you didn't tell him about the investigation results. If you file a complaint against him you'll win, but you're going to embarrass him, making a very powerful enemy, and then you'll really have some problems. If you want to stay in the Navy, let it go. But for future reference, you've got to learn how to protect yourself better."

I went back to my commanding officer's office and told him I was going to let it go. He looked very relieved. The assignments guy finally gave me what he thought was an insignificant assignment to the small Naval Forces Central Command (NAVCENT) planning staff in Tampa, Florida. I was glad I finally had my orders and decided I was going to make the best of it at my new assignment.

Takeaway: Believe in yourself, even when no one else does.

Key principles I learned about blooming where I am planted.

1. If I would bloom where I was planted right now and do the best at whatever I put my hand to, I could overcome any obstacle that came my way and get the exact promotion God had in place for me.

2. I was so glad I had patiently waited until the right assignment came along.

3. I'd rather ask a stupid question than make a stupid mistake.

NOTES

1. At www.best-quotes-poems.com/George-Patton.html.

2. At www.brainyquote.com/words/st/stood224441.html.

3. Jay E. Hines, "History of the Persian Gulf War, and Subsequent Actions of the U.S. Central Command." Available at www.daveross.com/centcom.html, p. 13.

4. Johanna McGeary, Jaime FlorCruz, Scott MacLeod, Barry Hillenbrand, Paul Quinn-Judge, William Dowell, J. F. O. McAllister, and Mark Thompson, "What Good Did It Do?" *Time* 152, no. 26 (December 28, 1998), p. 2. Available at www.time.com/time/printout/0,8816,989920,00.html.

5. Hines, "History of the Persian Gulf War, and Subsequent Actions of the U.S. Central Command," p. 5.

6. Hines, "History of the Persian Gulf War, and Subsequent Actions of the U.S. Central Command," p. 9.

7. At www.nytimes.com/1998/12/17/world/attack-on-iraq-the-strategy-strikes-aimed-at-crippling-factories-for-weapons.html?scp=23&sq=December%201998%20Iraq%20articles&st=cse.

8. At www.nytimes.com/1998/12/17/world/attack-on-iraq-the-strategy-strikes-aimed-at-crippling-factories-for-weapons.html?scp=23&sq=December%201998%20Iraq%20articles&st=cse.

9. Edward J. Marolda and Robert J. Schneller Jr., *Shield and Sword: The United States Navy and the Persian Gulf War.* (Annapolis, MD: United States Naval Institute Press, 2001), p. 168.

10. Marolda and Schneller Jr., *Sword and Shield*, p. 172.

11. Jeffrey T. Richelson, *The U.S. Intelligence Community.* 5th ed. (Boulder, CO: Westview Press, 2008), p. 183.

The Forgotten Iraq War, 1991–2003

Prepare for the unknown by studying how others in the past have coped with the unforeseeable and the unpredictable.

—George S. Patton[1]

Lead, follow, or get out of the way.

—Thomas Paine[2]

It was a hot, humid day in April of 1992, when I reported for duty at the Naval Forces Central Command (NAVCENT) in Tampa, Florida.[3] I stepped out of my air-conditioned car and immediately felt my clothes starting to stick to my body and my hair starting to frizz. I looked at the nondescript one-story building in front of me that was apparently the temporary location of the naval component of the United States Central Command (CENTCOM). I had been told by well-meaning friends that NAVCENT was a dead-end assignment. Looking at this unimpressive building I was beginning to think they might be right. I thought I was in the wrong place until I saw someone in a Navy uniform enter the building. Hoping it was more impressive on the inside, I plunked my hat down on top of my frizzing hair and walked toward my future.

As I looked around for a chief to check in with, I checked out what would be my classroom to learn what George S. Patton meant when he said, "Prepare for the unknown by studying how others in the past have coped with the unforeseeable and the unpredictable." At the time, though, all I could see was a lot of desks crammed into one small open area with a few unimposing offices positioned off to one side of the room. There weren't even many people around. To say I was unimpressed is an understatement.

WELCOME TO NAVCENT

I walked up to the first chief I saw and introduced myself. Giving me a warm handshake and a wide, friendly smile, he replied, "Welcome aboard ma'am. We've been expecting you. Most of the staff is over at CENTCOM for the morning briefings, but I think someone from the intel shop is around to assist you with your paperwork." I entered one of the small offices, and the weight of the world dropped off my shoulders as I was greeted by one of my favorite people in the whole world—Steve. He and I had last been stationed together in Hawaii.

Steve shook my hand and asked, "What happened? We expected to see you a few weeks ago while you were here on your house-hunting trip."

I explained how I had the flu right after finding a house and had spent the next couple of weeks at my parent's house in Houston recuperating. I apologized for not connecting with him sooner and told him I hoped I hadn't offended my new boss.

Steve smiled and said, "We figured something must have happened. I had hoped to be able to give you a heads up on what you'd be walking into. Everyone here is running around with their hair on fire."

We had some time before the rest of the staff returned from the CENTCOM meetings, so I sat down as Steve hit me with a blast of information on the new Iraq situation. He explained that most intelligence analysts were surprised that not only was Saddam still around, he was definitely becoming more and more defiant. It had become obvious to everyone involved that Saddam was not going to abide by the terms agreed upon at the end of the first Iraq war. CENTCOM was given a directive to set up a military organization to enforce United Nations (UN) sanctions against Iraq. To accomplish this mission, CENTCOM was currently setting up a multinational organization called the Joint Task Force Southwest Asia (JTF-SWA) to manage the effort known as Operation Southern Watch that would operate out of Saudi Arabia.

As I listened to this barrage of information, I began to wonder if I was up to the task. Except for my experience with the first Gulf War, my knowledge of the region was very limited. One of my favorite books was T. E. Lawrence's *Seven Pillars of Wisdom*, but I didn't think a book about an experience there during World War I would be relevant now. Obviously I had a lot of catching up to do with Persian Gulf current events.

Once my squadron's part in the Gulf War had concluded, I had paid very little attention to what was or was not happening in Iraq. As an intelligence officer, I had been trained to focus only on the current events that affected or impacted U.S. interests and/or military operations in my specific geographic region of responsibility. My squadron was subordinate to the United States European Command (EUCOM), so that had been my sole geographic focus during my last assignment. I knew my first order of business was to quickly get caught up on all of the current Iraq issues.

CATCH UP TIME

My head hadn't totally been in the sand on Iraq, so I did a quick mental inventory of what I did know about the current situation there. Although I didn't know all the details, I did know Iraq had not been cooperating with the UN weapons inspection teams. I was familiar with UN Resolution 687, which gave UN inspectors the authority to locate and remove all of Iraq's nuclear, biological, and chemical weapons and equipment. Initially Saddam had agreed, but there had been a brief incident in July of 1991, where Saddam had refused to provide the UN inspectors with previously agreed upon details on his weapons program. Saddam relented only after the United States threatened to resume bombing Iraq. This particular incident stood out in my mind because it revealed he was only one year away from having a nuclear weapon capability, while previous intelligence information had estimated he was still ten years away from it.

I dragged my mind back to the task at hand, realizing Iraq wouldn't be my only concern. I would have to become knowledgeable about all of the countries and geopolitical concerns in this region. CENTCOM's geographic area of responsibility was huge. During my time at NAVCENT, it included something like 25 countries with a physical area stretching more than 3,100 miles east to west and 3,600 miles north to south. NAVCENT was in charge of all naval operations throughout CENTCOM's area of responsibility. (Today, some of the countries that used to be in their area of responsibility have been taken over by the new African Command but CENTCOM's responsibility still remains significant. CENTCOM is in charge of the military units in Iraq and Afghanistan.)

As my indoctrination continued, I learned that Iran was also a potential hot spot. Every six months, the Navy replaced its units deployed in the Persian Gulf entering through the Hormuz Strait, which took them past Iran. Stories in the Iranian press and reports on their radio station while this was happening stated we were really coming into the Gulf to attack them, not Iraq. Each time that happened, Iran would increase its defensive posture and step up its military activity. It made for tension there, even as we dealt with the rapidly escalating conflict in Iraq.

ONE SLIGHT GLITCH, AGAIN

As I began to settle into my new position, I found there was one slight glitch that might prevent me from actually participating in the ongoing Iraqi crisis. My official job description led my superiors to assign me the position of intelligence planner, while the Bahrain navy intelligence staff got all the real action. Apparently the consensus of NAVCENT's Bahrain staff was that they did all the real work with rarely a day off, while their Tampa counterparts played golf every day. I was used to having to prove myself, so that attitude didn't bother me too much, at first.

When I officially took over my new job, I was told my responsibilities included briefing the naval and Marine units deploying to the Persian Gulf area. I knew our team was also responsible for being part of CENTCOM's long-range war planning effort. Saddam's actions were keeping us busy detailing plans of what we would do if we had to go to war with Iraq again. I had been studying my favorite book on international relations, *Politics among Nations: The Struggle for Power and Peace*, by Hans J. Morgenthau, and underlined what seemed relevant to the issues of the day. "The military leader must think in absolute terms. He lives in the present and in the immediate future. The sole question before him is how to win victories as cheaply and quickly as possible and how to avoid defeat."[4]

CENTCOM was also responsible for conducting the yearly war games. These war games included all the key staff members from the various service components, including Army, Navy, Air Force, Marines, and special operations. With most of the NAVCENT staff in Bahrain, it usually fell on the Tampa staff to represent the Navy at these games. Since I had spent three years doing this at the Naval War College, I didn't have a learning curve. I would be the acting N2 (senior naval intelligence officer) during these high-visibility games. My responsibilities involved providing the intelligence support for all the Navy and Marine units participating in the simulated conflict. We would test the effectiveness of our plans and then use the lessons learned to fine-tune our crisis and war strategies. These yearly games generally lasted from one to two weeks.

From this you would think I had plenty to do, but I soon discovered that, except when I was participating in war games, I really had nothing else to do. The CENTCOM intelligence personnel did a great job on the intelligence portion of the war plans; I only had to read through them and make sure they covered topics relevant to the Navy. Steve was already doing an outstanding job briefing the Navy and Marine units deploying to the Persian Gulf.

As you might recall from previous chapters, my attitude tanks with nothing to do; I was soon feeling useless and becoming restless. It didn't help any that many of the NAVCENT Tampa staff were taking part in real-world planning while I was stuck working futuristic "what if" scenarios. It seemed a waste of time for me to sit around discussing what we should do if we had to go to war again when there was a real-life crisis going on in Iraq. Every day, U.S. Navy forces conducted operations designed to keep Saddam from attacking his neighbors, coalition forces, or UN inspectors, and I was being forced to sit on the sidelines because of some glitch in my job description. The theme song from *Twilight Zone* kept playing over and over in my head.

LEFT BEHIND

Feeling left out and of little value to my command, I made a couple of trips to Bahrain to introduce myself to the staff and look for ways I could assist them, even though I was stationed in Tampa. Even though they were overseeing multiple operations, they rightfully wondered what help I could be to them sitting in my Tampa office. Still, I learned what I could and was determined to stay abreast of all that was going on. I found that their operations included a mine countermeasures program to protect the global oil shipments transited through the Persian Gulf. By the time I'd arrived in Tampa in early 1992, "naval forces had destroyed over half of the 1,288 mines found in the gulf."[5]

The Bahrain staff was also busy conducting maritime interdiction, "which had begun in August 1990 during the initial stage of Desert Shield, enforced UN sanctions, and were conducted by Australia, Britain, France, and the United States. When the Iraqi port of Umm Qasr opened in July 1993, interception operations were reinstituted in the northern gulf. By that time, more than 19,150 ships had been challenged and more than 8,250 had been boarded and inspected."[6] I found out that by the time the second Gulf War started, the U.S. Navy alone had searched more than 12,000 ships.

I filed all this information away, feeling I was going to need every bit of background data to accomplish what I would eventually be called upon to do. I continued to gather information and stayed up-to-date on current events as well. From the warfare specialists I worked with in Tampa, I learned our naval forces were planning on playing a major role in the JTF-SWA operations. My excitement gained momentum when I found out that the admiral I worked for was going to be the second in command. My bubble burst the day I was informed I would remain behind in Tampa. Rumor had it that the Saudi defense minister had informed CENTCOM they would not allow U.S. military women to enter their Ministry of Defense. I decided against asking the admiral if that was the reason I was being left behind.

Instead, I called my dad and proceeded with my "poor me, stuck in a nothing job, being left behind again" monologue. He let me go on for a couple of minutes, then in a stern voice with no vestige of sympathy in it snapped, "Stop whining and get your act together." I listened in shocked silence wondering where the sympathy was I thought I deserved.

As if he read my mind, Dad continued, "I'm sick of you calling me up with arrows sticking out of your back and complaining about your job. You think no one knows of all the good things you've done in the Navy, but I say you're wrong. You'd be surprised at how often your bosses and coworkers are talking about you behind your back, for good or for bad, depending on how well you're performing at your job. No matter how insignificant you think your job is, do the absolute best job you can possibly do. You make sure you show up on time with your shoes shined and uniform in great shape. If they choose not to use you, don't let it be because you weren't there and available. And another thing, get a grip on your temper because you're shooting yourself in the foot, and one of these days you're going to end up in big trouble."

Stunned, all I could say was, "OK, Daddy, I'll do my best."

After hanging up, I spent the rest of the evening praying and thinking about how I could make myself useful at work. I decided it was vitally important to keep my heart and intentions pure. I didn't want to be involved for personal glory or gain, but I did want to help and make a difference. In the middle of the night, my attitude began to change, my intuition kicked in, and I started gaining some new perspectives. I'm a firm believer that praying is talking to God, and intuitive flashes or hunches are God talking back to you when you place yourself in a position to hear. I have found that God seldom participates in our little pity parties.

STUDY THE PAST TO COPE WITH THE FUTURE

Remember I began this chapter stating this little one-room, unimpressive facility would be where I would come to understand what George S. Patton meant when he said, "Prepare for the unknown by studying how others in the past have coped with the unforeseeable and the unpredictable." I realized I had a wealth of information available due to my experience during the Cold War. I also realized that our defense posture had not caught up to current military events and was still structured to fight a Cold War threat. It became crystal clear to me that my assignment for now was to determine what relevance this revelation had in connection with my position here at NAVCENT.

I began to organize my thoughts starting with the Cold War military plans already in place designed to support almost any crisis scenario imaginable. I realized there were already agreements in place giving us operating bases around the world should we need to move our forces in to deal with a specific crisis location. There was also an intricate communications infrastructure already set up so we could get information to and from these deployed forces. Our alert status during the Cold War had mandated we know what types of weapons and military forces would be needed to meet any enemy aggression. By no means am I saying every thing was perfect, but we had done it for so long and so often that we did not have a huge learning curve in the conduct of operations should a major crisis arise.

From this point, I evaluated what I had learned from participating in the first Gulf War. I knew for a fact that we needed to constantly develop new techniques in intelligence to meet the demands of new potential threats. We must begin to develop new ways to collect and screen data, new ways to disseminate it to the warfighters, and new ways of looking at and identifying potential threats. As I processed what I already knew, I thought about the relevance of all this in connection with the current situation with Iraq. Patton had said we needed to prepare for the unknown by studying the past. To me that meant I had to do something with all of the information I had accumulated.

CENTCOM and its components had a major crisis going on, and I knew their intelligence staff was barely more than a hundred at the time, leaving them extremely shorthanded in this department. I also knew that the NAVCENT intelligence staff in Bahrain was so shorthanded they had to go through the personnel system and pull people from other organizations and commands to augment them. In comparison, I found that the Pacific and Atlantic commanders both had huge intelligence staffs. A plan began to take shape in my mind.

APPARENTLY DC IS CLUELESS

As I tried to present my plan to the powers that be, I realized we had another major problem. Many in the Washington, DC, naval intelligence crowd were clueless regarding the issues and effects of this crisis on the intelligence support system. I uncovered this alarming information when Evan, the senior Navy intelligence officer in Bahrain, told me he had not been invited to the annual naval intelligence conference. As I pursued it further, I was told he wasn't invited because NAVCENT was not considered a major command.

I was flabbergasted! We had the hottest show in town, but apparently Evan's job was not considered high up enough in the intelligence command structure to warrant an invitation to the conference. Without his presence, there would be no one representing naval intelligence issues in the Persian Gulf. My former boss from my Japan days, Admiral Sheafer, was now head of naval intelligence. There's no doubt in my mind he was current on what was going on—the man was brilliant—but I figured I'd better not call him unless all else failed. If I did, I would make enemies of some members of his staff. He was overseeing a multitude of issues and depended on his staff to take care of things like these conferences without his having to micromanage. I took a deep breath and patiently explained to one of his people in charge of the conference what was going on in our operations area and finally secured an invitation for Evan. I still got the feeling my contact still didn't seem to understand the importance of having a NAVCENT representative there. It dawned on me that if the DC folks were that clueless, I needed to intensely watch for opportunities to rectify the situation. It's amazing what you can discover when you place yourself on full alert.

For example, everyone was elated when NAVCENT finally moved into offices on base right across the parking lot from CENTCOM headquarters. The move meant even more to me, however, as I discovered that the Operation Southern Watch planning sessions that JTF-SWA would oversee once it was stood up were being held there without NAVCENT intelligence participation. My research confirmed that many of the problems in intelligence support and coordination between CENTCOM and the Navy and Marine units during the Gulf War had never been successfully resolved. It just made sense to me that having a NAVCENT intelligence person participating in these meetings would help improve Navy/Marine coordination. Exuding as much confidence as I could muster, I decided to present my thoughts to my admiral.

I knocked on his door and entered his office to find his chief of staff there as well. I asked for a few minutes of their time, and the admiral asked me what was on my mind.

"I've been giving the Iraq crisis a lot of thought. It occurred to me that there are a lot of intelligence issues that might come into play, and since the staff in Bahrain hasn't been able to send anyone to participate in the planning here, do you mind if I attend some of the planning sessions over at CENTCOM? I would be sure to coordinate everything I do with the intelligence folks in Bahrain."

His smile widened in approval as he surprised me by saying, "Excellent idea, should have thought of it myself. Let me know if you need my help."

I walked out of his office with a spring in my step. Mentally, I paraphrased a line from one of my favorite Broadway plays, *Applause*, thinking, "Hey CENTCOM, fasten your seatbelts. It's going to be a bumpy flight."

SEEKING HIGHER HELP

It turned out that I was the second most senior Navy intelligence officer in Tampa, which gave me some clout. I did my homework and found that the most senior officer was a captain on the CENTCOM staff. I called him up and asked for his help in smoothing the way with the CENTCOM staff so I could attend their "secret" meetings. He was great and let me know where and when the intelligence planning meetings were being held and then made sure no one threw me out once I got there.

As a subordinate, here's a word to the wise that will make your life a whole lot easier. Make sure you keep your supervising and oversight "bosses" in the loop, and they'll become a powerful ally 90 percent of the time. Neglect to keep them informed and you're likely to create an enemy who thinks you're stabbing them in the back. I followed this sound advice, and before I went to my first meeting, I contacted Evan and told him what I'd like to do. I told him I had done my research and greased the skids at CENTCOM so there would be no problem with my attending meetings if he thought that would be useful to him. He readily agreed. He also called up the CENTCOM J2, an Army general, and told him I would be participating. I attended so many meetings at CENTCOM that many of them actually thought I was part of their staff.

In retrospect, I'd also like to share the advantage I found from this experience in seeking "higher help" for life issues. Once I stopped wallowing in self-pity and began to seek divine help, I found that my so-called "hunches" were most likely divinely inspired. As I stepped out in faith, I witnessed obstacles falling away, doors suddenly opening, and assistance coming from some of the most unexpected sources. I realize now that God was making a river for me in the desert, and I was beginning to thrive in what had first seemed a desolate, unfruitful, dead-end assignment.

ON A ROLL

Evan really appreciated my offer to attend the CENTCOM planning meetings, since he had his hands full with his other duties and responsibilities. He also shared with me that he was so shorthanded he couldn't spare anyone to take part in setting up what would become the JTF-SWA. Since I was on a roll, I offered to take this on along with coordinating the intelligence portion of the command's move ashore from the command ship USS *LaSalle*. We both knew this would help improve the intelligence communication circuits between Tampa and Bahrain.

Evan is one of the most knowledgeable people I've ever known, especially when it came to intel on the Middle East and the Persian Gulf. He had done his graduate work on the Middle East at John Hopkins University. Professionally speaking, I was an unknown to him, but Evan gave me the benefit of the doubt and a chance to prove myself in spite of my poor reputation among some in the naval intelligence community. I was determined to make sure it wasn't a decision he would ever live to regret. I was off to the races.

I decided to start in the area of intelligence coordination, since it was critical that NAVCENT Bahrain be able to not only communicate with both the CENTCOM and JTF-SWA staff but do it in near real time. There had been a serious lack of interoperability between the Navy and CENTCOM's intelligence systems during the first Gulf War. Intelligence analysts put a lot of time and effort into deciding what targets to attack after pouring over annotated imagery and confirming they were valid military targets. The dissemination of target imagery from CENTCOM to the carrier battle groups during the first Gulf War had proved to be a major problem. Navy ships had a system for electronically sending and receiving photographs, but it was not compatible with the system CENTCOM was using. This meant that photos of potential targets had to be flown to the carrier, which put the intelligence personnel on the carrier behind the power curve as they planned for air strikes against Iraqi targets. I found that the talented CENTCOM personnel had solved the technical end of this problem, but now it was my job to ensure that the Navy and Marine units deploying to the Persian Gulf had the right equipment.

T.E.A.M.
Striving to accomplish all that I had offered to do taught me very quickly the value of team building and establishing working relationships with people from different organizations. My mentor and good friend Mark Victor Hansen, coauthor of the Chicken Soup for the Soul series, told me TEAM is an acronym for, "Together Everyone Accomplishes Miracles." After I overcame my first challenge of getting invited to the CENTCOM planning sessions, I found I still had many more hurdles to surmount.

At the time, many on the CENTCOM staff really had no idea what the Navy was bringing to the table in the area of intelligence capabilities and systems. As a result, I was continually asking how they planned to keep the Navy and Marine units in the Persian Gulf informed. At first, they thought I was needlessly complicating things, but after I said I would take care of coordinating this, all was well, for the moment any way.

During one such meeting, the topic of airborne intelligence collection assets came up. They were only planning to use the Air Force RC-135s to support air operations. I knew the Air Force didn't have enough RC-135s to handle the magnitude of this operation, so I naively suggested using some of the Navy's assets. I knew from my experience with the EP-3s and the P-3s that they had significant intelligence collection capability; the EP-3s capability in particular was similar to the RC-135. Both the EP-3 and the regular P-3 had performed magnificently in the Gulf War. One senior Air Force representative went ballistic at the suggestion, causing the meeting facilitator to intervene and table the discussion.

Confused, I returned to my office and talked to the NAVCENT air missions planning guys about my encounter. They rolled their eyes and laughed as they explained military politics to me. It seems that because of budget discussions going on in Congress, some in the Air Force wanted this to be an all-Air Force show to avoid having any of their programs cut. A light bulb came on as I remembered that while I was in VQ-2 I had assisted my commanding officer in briefing congressional staffers and had fielded questions on why there was a need for both Air Force and Navy airborne intelligence-collection aircraft.

It turned out that one of my former commanding officers was now in charge of the VQ program in DC, so I called him and let him know what was going on. He arranged to have knowledgeable VQ personnel flown to Tampa to brief the CENTCOM people on Navy aircraft capabilities. At the same time, I coordinated with my former boss to ensure a VQ liaison officer was included in the JTF staff. Teamwork resulted in a win-win for all concerned.

SHIP-TO-SHORE COMMUNICATIONS

The next major hurdle I faced involved collecting and then communicating the correct information to the naval aircraft carriers. Intelligence support to warfighters involves collecting and evaluating mountains of information so the type of information actually needed is communicated in a timely and efficient manner. Asking the right questions was essential in obtaining the right information. For example, I knew that during the first Gulf War, two Navy ships struck Iraqi mines. Consequently, I had to make sure that data on Iraqi mine-laying capabilities was included in CENTCOM's official request to the intelligence community. Step one was obtaining pertinent intelligence information. I had learned that if you don't ask for the information, you might not get it.

Once intelligence is collected, it has to be processed, analyzed, and then disseminated efficiently and in a timely manner. Dissemination of information has been a major problem for the Navy, especially since the intelligence community collects enough information in just three hours to fill the Library of Congress. Because naval carriers operate offshore, we had to figure out how to get only the pertinent data to ships at sea and accomplish it as quickly as possible. The communications pipelines to a ship are typically smaller than those to land-based commands, so the challenge seemed almost insurmountable.

That's where TEAM came into play again. Since I had never been allowed to serve on a carrier, I was definitely not an expert on the technical intelligence communication requirements needed to support our ships at sea, so I connected with the Navy intelligence folks at Naval Operations in Washington, DC. When I explained what was happening, they assembled a group of experts that came in several times to help with the technical side of the intelligence planning.

Next on my agenda was to make sure the proposed plans reached the intelligence officers deploying with the carrier battle groups. The CENTCOM intelligence staff didn't understand the importance of supplying the Navy intelligence officers with the game plan ahead of time, so they refused to share this vital information with me. Experience had shown me that without this information, intelligence officers preparing for deployment would not know the right support materials and information to bring with them. At the time it was a challenge to get large amounts of intelligence publications and support material to ships at sea, so informing these officers ahead of time was essential to the success of the operation. Now, of course, it can be done electronically, but at the time I needed a way to accomplish this quickly and efficiently.

To solve this problem, I got in good with the J3 side of the CENTCOM staff, the actual warfighters themselves. These were the guys making the decisions on what military forces were needed in the Persian Gulf as well as what strategies would be needed to hold Saddam's feet to the fire. As variations of the plans were worked and reworked, they briefed all the senior officers, admirals, and generals on the CENTCOM staff. Upon receiving the approval of this team, the plan was then sent on to the Washington, DC, crowd for their approval. The officers briefing the proposed plans happily shared the contents with me and I, in turn, sent them off to senior naval intelligence officers in the fleets as well as to those who would be going to the Persian Gulf onboard the carriers.

SOMETIMES IT'S WHO YOU KNOW

I made what was nearly a destructive choice when I decided not to ask for official permission to do this. I was solving a major communication problem, so I chose instead to follow Rear Admiral Grace Hopper's famous advice: "It's easier to ask forgiveness than it is to get permission."[7] I had been putting in some horrendously long hours, so when a CENTCOM buddy offered to finish faxing out the latest reports, I jumped at the chance to call it a night. Unfortunately, he was extremely busy himself and forgot to take the materials off the machine once he finished sending them. An air force colonel discovered the plans, traced them back to me, and called me at home screaming and yelling that he would see that I was court-martialed.

I was saved by my Navy intelligence captain guardian angel, who somehow defused the situation, though I still had to go before the CENTCOM senior intelligence officer to explain my actions. When I explained the situation to him and why I had done it, he agreed that it was the right thing to do but asked that I limit sharing the plans to the actual intelligence officers who would be deploying to the Persian Gulf. That problem out of the way, I decided to use the moment to hit him with what I saw as another potential issue where the intelligence community was concerned.

I had been able to handle a lot of the issues myself using what I had learned from previous experiences, but I knew the CENTCOM intelligence people were in the midst of deciding what the intelligence staff at JTF-SWA headquartered in Saudi Arabia would look like. Try as I might, they refused to let me participate, apparently not planning on having any Navy intelligence people as part of the JTF staff. I explained to the general what I knew of the size of the naval force that would be involved and what I had heard it would consist of. I explained because of the size of the naval force expected to be deployed, it was crucial that the JTF staff understand naval intelligence requirements. He was surprised no one on his staff had told him the extent of the Navy involvement in this operation and quickly arranged for me to be part of the JTF-SWA staff planning team. Sometimes it's who you know as well as what you know that gets the job done.

I managed to get four Navy intelligence officer staff positions secured on the JTF team. I immediately connected with the naval intelligence personnel folks in Washington, explained the deal, and asked them to be sure they sent superstars to fill these four positions. For the remainder of my time at NAVCENT, the CENTCOM J2 considered me his lead action officer on all naval intelligence matters.

This turned out to be an unexpected blessing for me. The position of the CENTCOM senior intelligence officer (J2, as he was called) was very prestigious and was held by a general. The first J2 I worked closely with was Lieutenant General Pat Hughes. General Hughes was a visionary and used telecommunications advances to take intelligence community coordination to a level I'd never seen before. Using a secure video communications link, he would meet with all of the senior members of the Washington and military intelligence community. He would give them an update on Iraq and then let them know what intelligence assets and personnel he needed to do the job. I was allowed to stay in the room as these meetings were conducted. I might have been sitting in the cheap seats, but I was there.

In my opinion, this was a brilliant strategy. Every military command's J2 thought his needs and requirements were most important. Only a finite amount of intelligence assets were available, so there was no way everyone was going to get everything they wanted. By throwing everything on the table, this gave everyone a feeling they were part of a solution. Whenever I hear media reports saying the intelligence community doesn't work together, I laugh. There's a lot of coordination, especially when there is a crisis going on, sometimes too much. Watching General Hughes and his successor, Lieutenant General James King, work was a tremendous educational experience for me in how to coordinate with key intelligence players. I was much honored that they considered me their Navy action officer.

This proved to be a valuable asset for me when, later on in my career, my integrity over the scope of the work I did at NAVCENT was challenged. My boss at the time didn't believe I had done such extensive work at so high a level while assigned to NAVCENT. As God would have it, one of my former CENTCOM J2s just happened to be visiting this command as this crisis came to a head. When I saw him, I shook his hand and referred to my time with him at NAVCENT. He turned to my boss and said, "She says she worked for

NAVCENT, but she really worked for me!" I turned to my boss and smirked. I couldn't help myself. I guess it is who you know.

THREATS OF WAR

In July of 1992, while in the midst of all this crisis planning, another war with Iraq was beginning to look like a real possibility. For three weeks, Saddam had been playing a dangerous game of chicken by refusing to let the UN inspectors enter his Agriculture Ministry. The UN believed there were missile-related documents inside the building and was authorized by the cease-fire agreement to collect all such information. The UN inspectors sat outside the ministry building while crowds of Iraqis threw things at them, slashed their vehicle's tires, and generally threatened to cause them bodily harm.

On July 18, 1992, the *New York Times* reported, "the standoff at the Agriculture Ministry is one of a number of confrontations between the United Nations and Iraq. Iraq has broken off talks on the Security Council's plan to allow limited oil sales and has boycotted the United Nations Commission fixing a new boundary with Kuwait. It is also balking at renewing a humanitarian aid agreement with the United Nations, which allows the organization to station guards around the country, and it has refused to provide names of foreign companies that sold it sophisticated technology and equipment."[8]

The United States and its allies rattled their swords, and Saddam backed down for the moment. He did, however, gain some powerful concessions, including limiting the UN inspection team to include personnel only from countries that had not fought against Iraq during the first Gulf War. By the time the inspectors finally got into the Agriculture Ministry complex, they didn't find anything. Many felt Saddam had removed the documents they were looking for sometime during the stand off. As all this was playing out, those of us at CENTCOM and NAVCENT were frantically putting the finishing touches on JTF-SWA while simultaneously preparing to kick Saddam's butt, if necessary.

To give you an idea of the activity level in our offices at this time, I had to leave my desk one day to deal with a crisis concerning my new housing. Heavy rains had caused some very serious leakage that took me about two and a half hours to resolve. When I returned to work, one of my coworkers looked up from his desk and told me I had received a total of forty-two messages in the short time I was away from my desk.

On August 26, 1992, shortly after the Agriculture Ministry complex crisis ended, JTF-SWA became fully operational. "The command and control unit for United Nations coalition forces deployed in the Persian Gulf region. Its mission is to monitor and control air space south of the 33rd parallel in Iraq, in support of Operation Southern Watch. . . . Coalition forces in the region monitor Iraq's compliance with United Nations security resolutions."[9] The bottom line on this was that Iraq was no longer able to fly aircraft south of the 32nd parallel, which became known as the "no-fly zone." Coalition forces were recruited to fly combat and reconnaissance aircraft to ensure Iraqi compliance with this resolution. To say we were busy is definitely an understatement.

ENDLESS WAR

After we got that up and running, I sat in my office in a daze. I realized I'd only been on the job for about four months, with two and half years left on this assignment. There was a hit song playing on the radio called, "Endless Love." Because Saddam was continuing his pattern of noncompliance, I realized I was looking at what could be entitled "The Endless War." On the bright side, I knew there was no way I would be forced to take up golf because of having nothing else to do. Call me masochistic, but I wouldn't have had it any other way.

Now that JTF-SWA was up and running, I began to concentrate all my efforts on helping the folks in Bahrain with their move ashore. I found I had a huge task before me with no budget to accomplish it. Once again fate smiled on me as I discovered one of my former students from my days at the Navy's intelligence training school, Brent, who had helped me out tremendously during the first Gulf War, was still the number two person working on intelligence communication and computer system issues for the Navy. I called him up only to discover he was coming to Orlando with his family to visit Disney World. He took a break from his vacation and came by my Tampa office, where I told him the mission of NAVCENT and the requirements I felt were needed to accomplish it. He took all the information and said he'd see what he could do.

He called me at home later that evening, saying he had fully briefed Admiral Sheafer, who was still the head of naval intelligence. His response was, "Give her what she wants." As a result, the Office of Naval Intelligence took care of all of the mission requirements, including building an intelligence communications center; setting up a video teleconferencing system; and even providing a new building for the NAVCENT intelligence staff in Bahrain, all at no cost to my command. Even as I enjoyed this victory, another battle awaited me just around the next corner.

I found out after the fury of activity calmed down that while I was spending time in Bahrain working hard to accomplish all of these tasks, a rumor had started back in Tampa that I was only able to coordinate all this because I was having an affair with someone in Washington. The women of my command were outraged, and when I returned to Tampa, a couple of them took me aside advising me to bring the guy who they believed had originated the rumors up on charges and offering to back me up if need be. Not only was I dealing with the Iraqi situation and constantly battling for the intelligence community, but now it seemed I was again fighting for my professional reputation. I shook my head and even managed a mischievous smile as I responded. "Frankly, as much as I'm being hassled about my weight, I'm flattered that someone thinks an affair is conceivable. Guess even though I'm fat, I'm hot."

They laughed as I added that the person or persons who believed that about me needed to get a life or better yet find something useful to do with their time. My friends supported me as I decided not to add another battlefront to the multiple endless wars I was already directly involved in. I had my hands full supporting the warfighters and didn't want the additional stress I knew would be involved in filing a discrimination complaint. I made sure, though, that all I was doing was reflected in my performance reports. Whenever you receive one of those things, your boss has to talk to you about it face to face before sending it off to Washington, DC. That's your opportunity to complain if you want to, and thankfully the work I was doing was always reflected on these performance reports. That was one battle I didn't have to fight.

I decided that it was better to have a good record speak for me rather than go for personal vengeance over what was spoken as a lie. It seemed I was destined to be warring on several battlefronts all at the same time. My father had instilled in me the wisdom of carefully choosing which battles I really wanted to invest my time and energy into.

ONE CRISIS AFTER ANOTHER

On the Iraqi front, it seemed like there was one crisis after another. Saddam continued to hassle the UN weapons inspectors and in December of 1992, decided to challenge the "no-fly" restrictions by sending in a MiG 25. The MiG locked on to a U.S. F-16 with its radar, usually perceived as a prelude to launching some form of attack, so the F-16 shot it down. If that wasn't enough, Saddam also secretly moved surface-to-air missiles (SAMS) into the "no-fly zone," which I'm proud to say the intelligence analysts quickly detected. Saddam ignored UN requests to remove them, which resulted in coalition forces moving into the area to directly deal with the problem.

"On January 13 and 18, Southern Watch aircraft conducted strikes against selected Iraqi air defense targets threatening coalition forces. Meanwhile, on January 17, the U.S. Navy conducted a Tomahawk Land Attack Missile (TLAM) strike against the Zaafaraniyah Nuclear Fabrication Facility because of Iraq's refusal to comply with UN nuclear inspection requirements. Four surface vessels fired a total of forty-four TLAM cruise missiles against the facility, rendering it unusable."[10] I have to stop here and give credit where credit is due. Obviously Saddam never announced his intentions or explained his actions. Every single day intelligence analysts had to check on his military forces to make sure they weren't in violation of UN sanctions. This is a lengthy and complex process involving scanning Iraqi landscape pictures, checking the status of all Saddam's known military garrisons and storage facilities, and making sure all equipment is accounted for and operating in acceptable locations. Saddam frequently moved the SAMS around to avoid detection and kept artillery units nearby to protect them. Successful attacks against these threats took a lot of hard prep work and coordination, as I was soon to personally find out.

OUCH, MORE REORGANIZATION

My time continued to be hectic but productive as far as the war was concerned, but there was some difficult office politics I was soon forced to deal with. By far the worst period during this assignment happened when NAVCENT headquarters in Bahrain decided to reorganize the Tampa office and broke up my intelligence team by assigning us all to different departments. Apparently there were still those who felt the Tampa side of the staff wasn't contributing much to their efforts. Evan told me he had tried to prevent this reorganization but had been unsuccessful in all of his attempts to keep us intact.

Since I was no longer officially part of the NAVCENT intelligence department, I was informed I could no longer communicate with the intelligence personnel in Bahrain. I had gotten new bosses in Tampa who also tried to move me out of the specially designed workspace that housed the remains of the intelligence shop in Tampa, commonly referred to as being behind the Green Door. I refused to move out of the office, informing them I still needed to be in a classified workspace because of the nature of my job. They didn't like it, but fortunately there wasn't much they could do about it.

The other "ex"-intelligence folks and I continued to act as a team. We had our own communications circuits and continued to send and receive intelligence information keeping up with what was happening with Iraq. Maybe I couldn't officially work on the Iraqi problem directly, but we all knew if we just hung in there we'd either get a new boss or get reassigned. Apparently the CENTCOM intelligence folks knew of my situation yet kept inviting me to their staff meetings to show their support and help me to keep up with intelligence issues. Seems as though I had been there and done this several times before! *Hadn't I already passed this test?*

Once again, except for attending meetings at CENTCOM, I found myself with nothing to do. And once again, I sought counsel from my father, who advised me to make sure I showed up for work on time and left on time. He assured me that if my command refused to give me any work it wasn't my problem but theirs. I followed his wise advice and at the same time intensified my prayer life. Years earlier, my first spiritual mentor, Reverend Helen, had told me that many problems could be solved if I focused on God instead of the problem. My mantra came from an old spiritual song title: "I don't believe you brought me this far to just leave me."

Once again, with the encouragement of my father and this song, I gutted it out even though I was given absolutely no official duties. At one point, I was even told I could no longer talk to the CENTCOM intelligence staff either, but I decided as long as I was invited to CENTCOM staff meetings, I would continue to go. Interestingly enough I was not allowed to attend NAVCENT Tampa staff meetings either. A Thomas Paine quote continually surfaced in my thinking at this time: "Lead, follow, or get out of the way." I just needed to figure out what that meant for me at this period in my life. As you will see, I would walk into my next life passage with new challenges.

Takeaway: "Lead, follow, or get out of the way."

Key principles I learned about the Forgotten War:

1. "Prepare for the unknown by studying how others in the past have coped with the unforeseeable and the unpredictable." To me that meant I had to do something with all of the information I had accumulated.
2. I learned to make sure to keep my supervising and oversight "bosses" in the loop and have them become powerful allies instead of enemies who thought I was trying to stab them in the back.
3. Once I stopped wallowing in self-pity and began to seek divine help, I found that my so-called "hunches" were most likely divinely inspired. As I stepped out in faith, I witnessed obstacles falling away, doors suddenly opening, and assistance coming from some of the most unexpected sources. I realize now that God was making a river for me in the desert, and I was beginning to thrive in what had first seemed a desolate, unfruitful, dead-end assignment.
4. Striving to accomplish all that I had offered to do taught me very quickly the value of team building and establishing working relationships with people from different organizations.
5. My father had instilled in me the wisdom of carefully choosing which battles I really wanted to invest my time and energy into.
6. Many problems could be solved if I focused on God instead of the problem.

NOTES

1. From www.brainyquote.com/quotes/authors/g/george_s_patton.html.

2. From www.brainyquote.com/quotes/authors/t/thomas_paine.html.

3. The following is a brief background on NAVCENT. During the Persian Gulf War, the powers that be in the Defense Department decided to use the 7th Fleet as the core of their wartime naval command under CENTCOM instead of the former NAVCENT located at Pearl Harbor. A portion of the Pearl Harbor staff did go to the Persian Gulf during the war, but once the conflict ended, the Navy moved the remnants of the Pearl Harbor staff of about forty or so people to Tampa, Florida. CENTCOM wanted NAVCENT colocated with their headquarters there for better

liaison and planning purposes. Coordination between their staff and the Navy had been a major problem during the war.

The Navy decided to keep the main part of its NAVCENT staff in Bahrain, building this new command around the remnants of what had been known as Commander Middle East Forces. This relatively small command had been operating in some form since January 1, 1949. At the beginning of the first Gulf War this command was absorbed into NAVCENT and was located on the USS *LaSalle* with plans to move its staff ashore as part of its new command role in Bahrain. This is basically where things stood when I came on staff at NAVCENT, Tampa, Florida.

4. Hans J. Morgenthau, *Politics among Nations: The Struggle for Power and Peace.* (New York: Alfred A. Knopf, 1966), 546.

5. Dr. Edward J. Marolda, "The United States Navy and the Persian Gulf." Available at www.history.navy.mil/wars/dstorm/sword-shield.htm, page 19.

6. Jay E. Hines, "From Desert One to Southern Watch: The Evolution of U.S. Central Command." *Joint Forces Quarterly* (Spring 2000), 46.

7. Diane Hamblen, "Only the Limits of Our Imagination: An Exclusive Interview with Rear Admiral Grace M. Hopper." *Chips Ahoy* 6, no. 16 (July 1986): 3.

8. Available at www.nytimes.com/1992/07/18/world/un-aide-tells-iraq-it-risks -attack-for-truce-defiance.html?scp=1&sq=July%2018,%201992%20Iraq%20article s&st=cse.

9. Global Secrity.org, "Joint Task Force-Southwest Asia." Available at www .globalsecurity.org/military/agency/dod/jtf-swa.htm.

10. Jay E. Hines, "History of the Persian Gulf War, and Subsequent Actions of the U.S. Central Command." Available at www.daveross.com/centcom.html, p. 13.

13

Rivers in the Desert

For I, the Lord your God, will hold your right hand, saying to you, 'Fear not, I will help you.'

—*Isaiah 41:13*[1]

Once again, except for attending meetings at CENTCOM, I found myself with nothing to do. I was focusing a lot of my spare time on God instead of the fact that someone had a problem with me and I seemed to be running on a treadmill, going nowhere fast. My thoughts often went to an old spiritual song that said God hadn't brought me this far to just leave me. Knowing He was in charge of my future, I followed my dad's advice and showed up at work every day on time and with my shoes polished.

BETTER WATCH YOUR BACK

I was walking past the NAVCENT Tampa administrative spaces one afternoon, when one of the chiefs called out and asked if I had a few minutes to talk. He was one of my favorite staff members and had house-sat for me a few times during my frequent trips to Bahrain. "Sure Chief, always. What's up?" He suggested we go outside and get some fresh air. I certainly had nothing better to do and figured some fresh air sounded good to me as well. We headed out toward a small patio outside our building.

Once outside, the chief seemed a little uncomfortable, took a deep breath, and got right to the point. "Ma'am, a fellow chief and good friend of mine works at another major command here at MacDill Air Force Base. Apparently the general in charge heard NAVCENT wasn't using you and tried to get them to let you come work for him. He remembered you from Korea, saying you were one of the best intelligence officers he's ever seen and if NAVCENT didn't want you he did." Noting the look of surprise on my face, he smiled. "See, you never told me you'd been in Korea, so hopefully that'll prove I'm not lying to you."

"Chief, thanks for telling me. I wonder why no one has said anything to me about it."

"Probably because NAVCENT turned him down. Maybe they don't want you to know, afraid you might bring discrimination charges or something."

I was puzzled and getting a little angry. "This doesn't make sense to me. This command obviously is not interested in my services, why wouldn't they let me go or better yet send me to help out NAVCENT Bahrain?" The chief shook his head as he started to head back inside, saying, "Don't know the answer to that, but you'd better watch your back."

I stayed outside and pondered my situation. I have many job skills, but understanding office politics is not one of them. My dad always told me my biggest problem was I didn't understand that not everyone thought like me. I believed if you gave 110 percent on the job, kept your heart and intentions pure, and focused on the mission, you would get rewarded with good performance reports and challenging follow-on assignments. I didn't understand people who tried to get ahead by stabbing coworkers in the back or taking credit for work done by others.

ON THE POSITIVE SIDE

On the positive side, my intelligence office environment was one of the best I've ever had. In addition to Steve, a longtime friend from my Japan days, retired Navy Chief Barry Flynn, had joined the staff as a civilian intelligence worker. There were four other people in the office that I'd never worked with before, but they were incredibly gifted workers and all possessed a great sense of humor. We spent a good part of the day laughing and telling jokes and sea stories. In retrospect, I don't think I would have survived this part of my assignment if not for them. They were my safe haven in the midst of a hostile workplace.

Evan, the senior intelligence officer for NAVCENT (N2), and his wife Nancy had become good friends, but he operated out of Bahrain and was due to be transferred soon. I hoped I would be able to get along with his replacement. The CENTCOM folks kept inviting me to meetings, so I at least had those to look forward to. The admiral in charge of the Tampa staff was a good man, but I didn't feel I could go to him with my concerns. I figured he had enough on his plate dealing with the Iraq situation and shouldn't be burdened with "office politics" unless something illegal was going on. There was nothing illegal about someone not liking me. My dad kept telling me not to take it personally. He said anytime you stepped out of the box in the workplace and tried to do things that had never been done before or institute new procedures, you were going to make enemies and come under a lot of criticism. His advice to me was if I couldn't stand the heat, get a job as a janitor.

I decided to keep praying and putting my faith in God. In addition, the quote that begins this chapter, Isaiah 43:19, resonated with me and kept me looking for those rivers in the desert.

> Do not remember the former things,
> Nor consider the things of old.
> Behold, I will do a new thing,
> Now it shall spring forth;
> Shall you not know it?
> I will even make a road in the wilderness
> And rivers in the desert.[2]

HANDPICKED

One day I was sitting in a meeting over at CENTCOM when someone came into the room and whispered in my ear that I had a call from DC. It was from the job assignments guy, so I rushed out thinking it must be important for him to track me down like this. He was new in the job, replacing the guy who had tried to force me to retire. "Gail, sorry to pull you out of your meeting, but I've got a problem and hopefully you can help me. I need someone to go to Egypt for a few months and fill in as Acting Naval Attaché. The current guy in the job is unexpectedly retiring. We're shortening his replacement's training, but there will still be a four-month gap. I need somebody to leave tomorrow. Do you want to go fill in for a few months?" It was a no-brainer for me, but I just had to ask, "Will my command let me go?" I wondered if I should tell him what the chief had told me.

Before I got the chance, he answered, "It's already been cleared with the big boss in Bahrain. The director of naval intelligence (my old boss, Admiral Sheafer) told him they needed someone who was a quick study and could do the job without any training. Based on your previous achievements, he thought you were the best one for the job. You've been hand selected out of everyone in the Navy." I felt my ego start to puff up.

"There is one problem, though. When we presented your name to the embassy, they turned you down, saying a woman had never been a military attaché to the Middle East before and they didn't think the military guys in that part of the world would deal with you." My ego started to deflate, but I decided to keep my mouth shut and keep listening. "The director told the embassy either they took you or they wouldn't get anybody."

Shouting a mental, hooray, I said, "Thanks sir, I won't let you down."

"I know you won't, now get going! Let me know if you need my help with anything."

As I walked back to my office, I realized what a tremendous vote of confidence this was for me. It also showed I had some powerful allies on the NAVCENT Bahrain staff. I've never asked Evan about it, though I'm sure he had a hand in it some how as well.

MY EGYPT ASSIGNMENT

My Egypt assignment worked out really well. On my first day there, I was taken over to the Egyptian Ministry of Defense. A colonel came up to me and said, "You don't know it, but today you are the most famous woman in Cairo." I later told my girlfriends that my time in Egypt was the closest a mortal could come to being treated like a goddess. I had to constantly put that thought out of my mind and remind myself it wasn't me, it was the position I held, or my ego would be out of control.

I will say that never in my entire career have I been treated with such respect and professional courtesy. As I mentioned, initially the embassy turned down my temporary appointment, saying that military people from the

Middle East would not deal with a woman. Happily, the embassy was wrong, as every foreign military attaché I dealt with, including those from Saudi Arabia and Jordan, couldn't have been more respectful. I was the talk of Cairo when the Saudi military attaché invited me into his home. He and his wife were the most polite and graceful people I've ever met.

But even while I was assigned in Egypt, I became involved in a Saddam-related crisis. I was involved in so many crises with Iraq that I honestly don't remember which incident it was, but I believe it was the time we received intelligence that showed Saddam had sponsored an assassination attempt on former President Bush during a 1992 visit to Kuwait. In preparation for this particular crisis, NAVCENT decided they wanted to beef up their naval forces in the Persian Gulf. They had one aircraft carrier positioned there and decided they wanted a second. The nearest available aircraft carrier was the USS *Theodore Roosevelt*, which was operating in the Mediterranean and would have to go through the Suez Canal to reach its new assignment.

Part of my job as acting naval attaché in Egypt was to arrange for the transit of naval units through the Suez Canal. No one had given me a heads up on this chain of events, so I found out about it watching the news. I was livid and immediately called the captain who was head of operations for NAVCENT.

"Captain, why didn't you guys give me a heads up; I had to find out about this from CNN! The *Theodore Roosevelt* is a nuke, and the Egyptian government requires thirty-days notice to handle the diplomatic stuff for a nuke Suez transit, plus we need the personal approval of President Mubarek. For the next few days my access to him will be slim to none because he's hosting a conference with all the leaders of Africa. Last night, the ambassador gave President Mubarek a classified "heads up briefing" on this operation. If you guys had let me know about the Suez transit requirement we could have gotten this taken care of last night."

This captain was notoriously short-fused, but he chuckled and in a very patient tone replied, "Calm down, Gail. I didn't find out about it either, and I'll be the guy running things. Just do the best you can and let me know if you need any help from us." I was finally able to see the humor in the situation and laughed with him, agreeing to keep him posted.

HELP FROM ABOVE

I hung up and said a silent prayer. If ever I needed help from above this was it. Dealing with the Egyptian diplomatic service was very complicated. The senior U.S. defense attaché, an army colonel, and the U.S. ambassador were extremely helpful. They called in a few markers and gave me the names of the people I needed to talk to. I made official visits and countless calls to help speed the request through diplomatic channels while being as charming as I knew how to be. It was tense at times, but I managed to get the approval in three days. I was subsequently told by a person in the know that this is what got me promoted to captain.

The tensest moment for me during this whole situation turned out to be my favorite Egyptian assignment story. The USS *Theodore Roosevelt* had started transiting toward the Suez Canal as soon as they received their orders. I was showering in my hotel in preparation for an official dinner function when the phone in my bathroom rang. The *Theodore Roosevelt* was letting me know they were a few miles away from the Suez Canal entrance. I panicked. "Wow, guys, I don't have diplomatic approval yet. I expect it sometime tomorrow. Whatever you do don't get close enough to the Egyptian shore so that you can be seen from land."

I explained that the reason we have this restriction in the first place is apparently President Mubarek was at a vacation home overlooking the Suez Canal and saw a nuclear aircraft carrier transiting through without having been previously informed. After that, from what I'd been told, he said he had to personally approve all nuclear transits. The *Theodore Roosevelt* guys knew what I'd been through in the last couple of days, so they were patient with me and said, "No problem. Let us know when we can approach the canal." After I hung up, I realized I had just conducted a major military meeting in the nude.

THE IRAQI CRISIS ACTION CELL

When I returned to Tampa after my few months in Egypt, I had a new department head who had come over to the NAVCENT Tampa staff from a CENT-COM job. He took me aside and said he had no problem with me working on intelligence issues with the senior CENTCOM and NAVCENT intelligence officers, he just wanted me to keep him in the loop. I hadn't had time to tell him of my problems, so I'm guessing that the people on the CENTCOM staff must have known what was going on with me and didn't like the way I was being treated.

A really neat and talented intelligence officer, Bill had replaced Evan. He and his deputy, Keith, were both super to work with. For the rest of my time on the NAVCENT staff, whenever there was a crisis, I'd work with the CENTCOM intelligence folks making sure the Navy intelligence requirements were understood and appropriately handled and then I'd head over to Bahrain and run the Iraqi Crisis Action Cell and the Intelligence Watch until the crisis was over. In civilian terms, I ran the newsroom. On one occasion, I even filled in as the acting senior intelligence officer for Bill while he took a well-deserved vacation. It happened to coincide with the period when Saddam's two son-in-laws and two of his daughters defected. Sometimes I felt like a crisis magnet.

I do remember one incident that gave everyone a chuckle. One of the tasks of the intelligence support to the Navy was to identify ships that were in violation of the sanctions. This was no easy task and sometimes made for a tense environment. One ship violated the sanctions, evaded Navy forces, and arrived in the port of a Persian Gulf country. During this particular incident, I happened to be in Bahrain filling in as the acting senior intelligence officer (N2). The NAVCENT commander, a three-star admiral, said, "Gail, I have to go visit this government along with some U.S. State Department folks. I need proof that this ship has violated the sanctions or we won't be able to confiscate the cargo. What have you got for me?"

The captain of this merchant ship was pretty slick, so the only thing I had was a photo of that ship in an Iraqi port that was of such poor quality; it looked like one of those inkblot things they use in psychological testing. The admiral laughed and said he could really see himself going up to a senior foreign government official waving that fuzzy ink dot picture as proof!

UNITED STATES STRATEGIC COMMAND

After I was promoted to captain, I fully expected to be given a good follow-on assignment. I had learned to make sure all of my achievements were documented in my record and felt I was up for a good follow-on job this time. Instead, I saw a repetition of what had happened to me when it was time for me to leave Spain. The detailer who had sent me to Egypt had moved on to another job, and Admiral Sheafer was no longer in charge of naval intelligence. The people currently in that job had no firsthand knowledge of my capabilities and, according to my sources in DC, thought I was a drunken tramp. I wrote a letter to the new head of naval intelligence telling him that wasn't true, but he never bothered to answer it.

As a result, I was given orders to report to the United States Strategic Command (STRATCOM), a position most thought was one of those not so good jobs, but before I jumped head-on into that black hole of depression again, I decided to open up a letter I'd received from my future boss. Turns out it was a woman general, and her letter was insightful and inspirational. I had never worked for a woman before, but I thought, this is somebody I would like to work for. I sensed that General Tiiu Kera would be a great role model, and she was.

At first I felt the job was not very challenging, but I decided to once again try to bloom where I was planted. After I had been there a few months, my new boss was so impressed she created a position for me as the number two person in the 500-man Joint Intelligence Center (JIC). In civilian terms, a JIC is a combination of a daily newspaper and a weekly magazine. We also developed stories for the military intelligence TV news network. I was blooming away!

OPERATION DESERT FOX

My expertise in joint warfare continued to serve me well as things started heating up again with Saddam. A good friend, Captain Hal Neal, who was now stationed with CENTCOM, called me up out of the blue. He was in the midst of preparing for what was to become Operation Desert Fox, but because of the intense pace of operations already in place, all of his folks were fully engaged.

CENTCOM and its components were fully engaged in enforcement of the UN sanctions and the northern and southern no-fly zones. The pace and intensity of military operations in the region never really slowed down after the first Gulf War. I had just been watching the secretary of defense testify to Congress as the current crisis was heating up, and he mentioned that up to that point there had been more than 2,000 incidents. I was very familiar with what was going on in that part of the world.

Hal explained that to support Desert Fox, he felt he needed to augment his staff. Rather than physically send people to the Persian Gulf or CENTCOM headquarters in Tampa, Hal figured he could take advantage of technological breakthroughs and provide real-time tactical support to military operations from other intelligence organizations in the United States. He asked me, "Do you want to play?" I replied, "Sure, but let me run it by my boss." She was totally in favor of it.

We ended up assisting in the intelligence support for the cruise missile attacks in which more than 415 cruise missiles were used. This concept worked so well STRATCOM was asked to do the same thing for the conflict in Kosovo. We ended up providing the intelligence support for more than 300 targets, plus we took over the intelligence support for the forces supporting the northern Iraqi no-fly zone.

This experience taught me that there is no such thing as an unimportant job. I remembered the advice I heard given in a speech by Dr. Martin Luther King Jr.: "If you are a street sweeper, sweep the streets as if you were Michelangelo painting the Sistine Chapel." My time at NAVCENT turned out to be a tremendous opportunity for me. I ultimately ended up having far more responsibility than many of my professional peers did, even though they were in what most considered great career-enhancing assignments. Blooming where I was planted, I learned to look for the rivers in the desert. I learned a tremendous amount concerning what type of intelligence support was needed for conducting successful military operations and how to survive even the most radical life changes.

Takeaway: You can survive radical life changes.

Key principles I learned about looking for those rivers in the desert:

1. There is no such thing as an unimportant job.
2. Blooming where I was planted, I learned to look for the rivers in the desert.
3. I learned a tremendous amount concerning what type of intelligence support was needed for conducting successful military operations.
4. Anytime you step out of the box in the workplace and try to do things that have never been done before or institute new procedures, you are going to

make enemies and come under a lot of criticism. Dad's advice to me was if I couldn't stand the heat, get a job as a janitor.

5 Don't be hampered by your job description. It could be out of date.

NOTES

1. Robert H. Schuller and Paul Dunn, *The New Possibility Thinkers Bible*. (Nashville: Thomas Nelson, 1996), 823.

2. Schuller et al., *The New Possibility Thinkers Bible*, 826.

Cyber Warfare: A New Form of Terror

How I Became Semi-Computer Literate

Your Destiny is not determined by your critics.

—*Joel Osteen*[1]

As I approached my last assignment in the Navy, I was exhausted and my soul weary. I was afraid I had reached my limit and couldn't take anymore. I was still reeling from almost being court-martialed over lies told about me during my time at United States Strategic Command (STRATCOM). I couldn't get over the injustice of being accused of lying about something and then trying to cover it up.

I was also having a hard time getting over the negative reaction of the Director of Naval Intelligence to the innovations I had made with the concept of federated intelligence support while at STRATCOM. At the request of the STRATCOM J2, I had attended a conference of all the senior naval intelligence officers. I was proudly giving a presentation on the groundbreaking work we were doing in Kosovo and Iraq when the Director of Naval Intelligence proceeded to eviscerate me in front of my peers, declaring I had no authority to do the work I had been doing. I stood my ground during his verbal beating, the worst and most personal I'd ever experienced.

It seemed that no matter how hard I worked to do the best job possible, my achievements continued to be ignored or disparaged while the military apparently hoped I would just go away. I was really having a pity party, once again falling into my negative habit of whining and feeling sorry for myself when it appeared that things weren't going my way. While I continued in this destructive, negative state of mind, bad things kept happening. I was pretty well convinced it was time to retire from the Navy. It seemed obvious my time there was coming to an end.

SPACECOM

Holly, one of my oldest and best friends, was now in charge of job assignments for naval intelligence officers. Knowing that I had planned to retire in Colorado, she talked the powers that be into assigning me to United States Space Command, nicknamed SPACECOM, located in Colorado Springs. When she called to tell me, I was so shocked I was speechless. She jokes that that was the only time in all the time she's known me that she's seen me speechless. I decided to postpone my retirement for a little while longer.

As it came time for me to transfer, however, I became increasingly concerned that something was wrong. Traditionally, your new command assigns you a sponsor to help you with the transition and be your primary point of contact. Your sponsor provides you such information as how to find temporary housing while you're looking for what would be your permanent residence during your assignment. They also send you information about your new command and keep you posted on what your new job will be.

I was assigned a sponsor, but he never answered my calls or sent me any information. It got so bad I didn't even know what building I was supposed to report to when I arrived. A friend I had been assigned with at STRATCOM had been transferred to SPACECOM a few months before me. Finally I called him and asked for help, and he was able to find out where I was supposed to show up the first day of work. That was just a precursor of things to come. On my first day of work, I found out my new command hadn't assigned me an office, a desk, a phone, or even a job. Even my normally optimistic mom said she had never seen any of my previous commands treat me so poorly. I kept asking Holly if she was sure the command wanted me.

I found out later that the guy who was slated to be the new J2, senior intelligence officer for the command, Mike, had apparently heard a lot of negative things about me and wasn't sure he wanted a troublemaker like me on his staff. Holly kept telling him the stories weren't true and asked him to take a chance on me and promised him if it didn't work out she would fix the situation. I'm glad

I didn't know about this when I first arrived; it might have been the straw that broke the camel's back.

CYBER WARFARE

The outgoing J2 finally called me into his office for a welcome aboard chat. He explained that SPACECOM had been given the task of developing policy and procedures for a new form of warfare for all of the Department of Defense called Computer Network Operations, known in the public domain as "cyber warfare." There was a great concern among national security specialists that because of the dependence of the United States on technology, we were extremely vulnerable in that area. At the time I arrived at the command, 90 percent of all military communications went over commercial circuits at some point in the course of their transmissions. Because the commercial circuits weren't fully protected, there was a potential that someone could hack into and disrupt military communications. It was felt that the bad guys knew how dependent we were and could cause a great deal of damage to our ability to conduct military operations by simply attacking our computer networks.

As I was writing this chapter, I came across an article in the March 2008, *Armed Forces Journal* saying the Pentagon reported "more than 79,000 intrusions in 2005 . . . about 1,300 of the attacks supposedly were successful, including the penetration of computers linked to the Army's 101st Airborne and 82nd Airborne."[2]

Even my old command, the Naval War College, was not immune. An article in the *Washington Times* reported that in November of 2006, "Chinese computer hackers penetrated the Naval War College network . . . forcing security authorities to shut down all e-mail and official computer networks."[3] Obviously, they were right in assuming this could become a major problem if not dealt with quickly.

As I'm writing this, U.S. Strategic Command is now the Department of Defense lead on cyber warfare. In 2007, the organization's commander, General James E. Cartwright, told Congress "America is under widespread attack in cyberspace."[4] "During the fiscal year 2007, the Department of Homeland Security received 37,000 reports of attempted breaches on government and private systems, which included 12,986 direct assaults on federal agencies and more than 80,000 attempted attacks on Department of Defense computer network systems.[5]

The J2 said he wanted me to be in charge of developing the intelligence piece, but since it was so new, he couldn't tell me what to do or how to do it. On top of that, he apparently hadn't bothered to tell anyone else I was assigned that task, so whenever I tried to research background on cyber warfare through other organizations, they blew me off. Even the people within SPACECOM who were working on the problem didn't want to be bothered with me. Baffled and frustrated, I just kept plugging away, spending most of my workday reading books on computers and studying the ins and outs of Internet and military communications.

I filled the rest of my time working out in the gym or day dreaming about Wesley Snipes. I had seen him in the movie *Blade* and developed a major crush on his movie character. My boredom came to a head one day, so I called Holly. I could tell by her tight-voiced, businesslike phone manner that she was probably juggling several crises and didn't have time to play the "Ain't It Awful Game" with me. I took perverse pleasure, however, in saying, "I know you don't have time to talk, but I just wanted to tell you, I don't know when or where but one day I'm going to have a wild, hot date with Wesley Snipes!" She tried to suppress a giggle as her sense of humor kicked in and replied, "You're delusional," and then hung up on me.

FINALLY, A BREAK?
Finally, I got a break. Mike, the new J2, called me into his office and gave me some guidance. The command had set up a cyber warfare working group headed by another Navy captain, Joe Smith (not his real name). Mike told me to report to Joe and that I would be responsible for working the intelligence piece of the strategy. My spirits picked up, thinking maybe things were changing for the better.

The next day I excitedly reported to Joe in his office, which was located on the other side of the base from the headquarters building. My thoughts were positive and upbeat as I walked to my first meeting with my new boss; however, any hopes I had for being part of the team ended quickly when, although I had a desk, I had no direction, no tasks, and absolutely nothing to do. I wasn't even invited to his staff meetings.

One day, while they were all in meetings, I looked around trying to figure out how to make myself useful. I noticed Joe was having problems securing the paperwork he needed to get his working space approved at classified security levels. Apparently they had been working the issue for months and had not been able to make any progress. Because I had done a lot of work in the area, I thought that if I helped them out, maybe they would see I had some value and allow me into their inner circle.

I looked over the required paperwork, made a couple of phone calls, and was able to solve the problem in a couple of days. If you understand security and intelligence issues, it's not hard to get things done. In addition to filling out lots of paperwork for your requests, you call up the person in charge and tell them what you need and why you need it. To get a "yes" you have to give them a compelling reason for it, which I am quite good at. From experience, I also knew that the intelligence department didn't have a rigid chain of command structure like the rest of the military or government, so a great deal of my success came because I wasn't afraid to pick up the phone and call anyone in the intelligence community regardless of their rank or position to get the job done.

Joe called me into his office, gave me a thoughtful look, and quietly said, "I'm glad you're here. I don't know what I would have done without your help." I walked out of his office, glad I had done the extra value-added service and feeling pretty good about what I thought was a now good working relationship with my new supervisor.

The very next day I happened to be over at headquarters and saw Joe coming out of the J2's office. When he saw me, he looked away, muttered a quick hello, and walked out of the office. I felt a hard knot forming in my stomach. I shrugged the feeling off and told myself to stop being paranoid. This is a major organization with lots of problems to solve every day, so everything was not about me. Just as I finished giving myself this internal pep talk, Mike came out of his office, saw me, and said he needed to talk to me. He looked uncomfortable, and my unease returned. "Joe said he would like me to replace you."

Struggling to hide my confusion, I replied in my most professional tone, "Did he say why? I helped him out with a security issue, and he told me he was glad I was working for him."

His face clouded with uneasiness, "He said you were too senior and he'd like me to send someone more junior to work for him."

My temper flared. "From the day I arrived, I've been treated like a redheaded stepchild. I am a captain in the United States Navy, and whether that bothers some people or not is irrelevant. I was sent here to do a job, and as long as I remain in the Navy, I will be treated with the dignity and respect I have earned. I don't ask to be treated special. I just ask to be accorded the same degree of respect that my peers are receiving. As far as I can tell, I am the only person on the staff of my rank who is being treated this way. All the others have jobs, desks, phones, etc."

Mike seemed genuinely surprised and started to get the drift of where I was going with this. "Gail, I don't think this has anything to do with your race or your sex."

Still working on my breathing, I looked Mike in the eye and said, "You don't know me very well, but I'm not oversensitive or given to imagine these things. I was the first woman or first black to be assigned to all of my jobs. I can't begin to tell you all the crap I've had to endure, but not once did I bring charges against anyone. I've prided myself on handling biased situations like this myself, but what Joe is doing is not right."

Looking at me thoughtfully, Mike leaned forward and said, "As a white male, I can't begin to totally understand what you've been through, but I promise you this, I'll look into this further, and if race or sex is an issue, I'll fix it."

Suddenly exhausted, I leaned back in my chair and ran my hands through my hair. "Tell you what, I'm going on vacation in a couple of days. When I get back, if this situation has not been fixed, for the first time in my career I'm going to file a discrimination complaint."

Mike replied, "I said, I will look into it and get back to you."

Praying hard to keep my temper at bay and maintain a professional attitude, I replied, "All that I ask is that I be allowed to work the task assigned to me, which as I understand is developing intelligence policy for the Department of Defense in cyber warfare. I've been doing a lot of research and feel if we don't move fast to get on top of this, we could have a cyber Pearl Harbor incident on our hands." As I rose to leave his office, I thought I saw a look of admiration pass over Mike's face.

I got into my car, turned on the engine, and just sat there for a couple of minutes as I realized I had no place to go. Going "home" gave me no sense of peace. I was having a house built, so I was staying in a basement apartment in a high-crime area until my house was ready. Since I never really had a sponsor, I didn't know what areas to avoid. I knew it was temporary, so I didn't wander around after dark, kept my door locked, and had a .38 in my nightstand in case some jerk broke into my apartment. I'd managed to fill the place with a few personal items, but it was still not my idea of a good living environment. I spent the evening drinking cheap wine and listening to Frank Sinatra sing of lonely hearts and broken dreams.

NEVER LET THEM SEE YOU SWEAT

The next day I went over to clean out my desk, eternally glad Joe was no where around, because I wasn't really sure I would have been able to hold my temper if I'd seen him. I reminded myself of the negative things that had happened to me in the past when I lost my temper, so I took a couple of deep breaths and remembered the line from that old deodorant commercial, "Never let them see you sweat." I felt embarrassed and humiliated but went over to my desk head held high. It didn't take me very long to pack up my stuff, and thankfully the other people in the office avoided speaking to or looking at me.

As I was getting ready to leave, I got a call from Mike's secretary asking me to go talk to a black air force colonel who had just been selected for general. I suspected Mike hoped this colonel, soon to be general, could diffuse the discrimination situation. When I arrived, I was told to go right in, and he got right to the point. "Mike asked me to talk to you. He says you have some concerns that I may be able to help you with and maybe give you a better perspective on what's going on here." He paused, asked me to sit down, looked me right in the eye, and asked, "Why would you want to work in an environment where you are obviously not wanted?"

I felt my stomach churning with frustration, but I lifted my chin, looked him straight in the eye, and said with as much dignity as I could muster, "Whether I'm wanted or not is irrelevant. If Joe has a problem with me because I'm black, a female, or a Dallas Cowboys fan, that is his problem. I was sent here to do a job, I was given the task of working on the cyber warfare project, and that's what I'm going to do."

The colonel shrugged and changed the subject. "Understand you're going on leave tomorrow. That's good. Maybe you'll have time to put your situation in the proper perspective before you get back."

Feeling I was being dismissed, I rose, stuck out my hand, and said, "Perhaps, and by the way, congratulations on your promotion to general." As I walked out the door, I was thinking what a waste of time that had been. I wondered why anyone thought my talking to him would make me back down from wanting to be treated with the respect I thought I was due.

WHERE I AM MEANT TO BE

That evening as I packed for my trip in my dingy apartment, I felt drained, hollow, and listless. Had all of my efforts to follow my dream been for naught? I didn't really want to file an equal opportunity complaint. What would be the point? I would just be labeled a troublemaker again, so maybe I should just go ahead and retire. I felt very much alone and overcome by feelings of despair and hopelessness. Thoughts of death seemed very appealing, and as I got my gun out of my nightstand, I started thinking how easy it would be to end it right then and there. What was the point in going on?

Somehow a glimmer of light broke through my dark thoughts. I made myself put the gun back in the nightstand and started going through my collection of personal theme songs. As you have probably already learned, music and movie themes always seem to ease my troubled mind. I suddenly remembered when my mom had bullied me into taking some younger relatives to the Walt Disney cartoon movie *Hercules* and how unexpectedly mesmerized I was by the film. In the Disney version, an evil guy had arranged for Hercules, the son of a god, to be cast upon the earth when he was a baby, leaving him with no knowledge of his true heritage. He had loving adopted parents but was a ridiculed misfit in society. He decided to leave home and seek his destiny, knowing there was something better for him and something he was meant to do.

I identified with young Hercules' quest to discover his true place in the world where he would fit in and be appreciated. I played the song on my portable stereo over and over as I finished packing. The opening words of the song gave me the stamina to keep going one more day.

> I have often dreamed of a far off place
> Where a great warm welcome will be waiting for me.
> Where the crowds will cheer when they see my face
> And a voice keeps saying, this is where I'm meant to be.
> I will find my way, I can go the distance
> I'll be there someday, if I can just be strong.
> I know every mile will be worth my while,
> I would go most any where to feel like I belong![6]

A SPIRITUAL RECHARGING

As I drove out to the airport the next day, I realized I couldn't have chosen a better time to go on a vacation. I resolved to shake off my depression and do my best to enjoy myself. I had discovered this tour of Brazil a few months earlier while reading *Essence* magazine. I had been to Brazil on a brief one-day trip while stationed in Panama in the mid-1980s, which was enough to whet my appetite to return someday. I saw the ad in the magazine and signed up, not really knowing what I was getting into.

When I signed on for the trip, the only thing I noticed was the destination. I didn't pay much attention to anything else, like who our guides and escorts would be. When I arrived in Brazil, I discovered just what a powerful group of people I would be traveling with. Susan Taylor, the then editor of *Essence*, led the trip. Gentle, wise, and beautiful inside and out, Susan radiated a serene spirituality. Also part of the group was best-selling author and motivational speaker Iyanla Vanzant and medical doctor and ordained minister Dr. Thurman Munson. Another well-known minister was also part of the group, Reverend Dr. Barbara King, founder and minister of the Hillside Chapel and Truth Center in Atlanta. Both Dr. Munson and Dr. King had written best-selling motivational books, and my love for reading sparked my interest to try and spend some time with them.

There were only about eighty of us on this trip, so you had plenty of opportunity to talk to and mingle with these folks. Every one of these celebrities was friendly and approachable. Just being in the presence of these exceptional individuals gave me a powerful spiritual boost. I felt my soul beginning to heal while all thoughts of suicide lost ground.

We spent several days in the Bahia province of Brazil and a couple of days in Rio de Janeiro. Brazil was hot and humid, my least favorite weather, but it was such a beautiful country I happily put up with it. With the presence of all the ministers and motivational speakers, each day we would have a church service of some sort. As the days flew by, I found I was getting spiritually recharged and feeling stronger and stronger.

On one of our last days in the Salvador Bahia province, we were scheduled to visit a school for the poor run by an order of black Catholic nuns. Prior to going on the trip, Susan had sent us a letter asking us to bring school supplies so that we could donate them to the school. As I boarded the bus that would take us over to the school, I noticed an empty seat next to the Reverend Dr.

King. I asked her if anyone was sitting there, and she said with a twinkle in her eye, "Yes, you are." I immediately felt at ease. As we rode over to the school she asked, "Do you know the background of the school?" I replied that I really only knew what was in the letter we received from Susan prior to the trip.

She got a distant look in her eyes and said, "About a year ago, the head of the order visited my church. Their organization has a fascinating history. They are an old order of black Catholic nuns who, back in the nineteenth century, bought the freedom of elderly black female slaves and took care of them until they passed on. They wanted to ensure that although the women might have lived their lives as slaves, they would die free. During the service at my church," she continued, "I asked my members to donate some money to the order. I believe we collected something like $5,000, which was good but no big deal for my congregation. We had donated similar amounts of money before to various other churches and charities. Several months later, I received a thank-you note and update from the nuns. It seems they took that money and were able to build a whole new church!"

I was silent, taking the story in and seriously wondering what kind of church they could build for $5,000. I figured it had to be a dump. When we arrived at the school, the nuns greeted us with big smiles and hugs. They said they were having a special church service for us, but first they would give us a tour of the school and church and then provide a lunch. I wandered along with the group, making appropriate noises at the appropriate times, but my mind was back in Colorado and the sorry state of my Navy career. When my mind did focus back to my immediate surroundings, it was only to wonder what we were having for lunch. I was beginning to wish this tour was over.

I AM A CHILD OF GOD

We finally left the school and headed over to the church. My first sight of the church left me awestruck. It was small but one of the most beautiful churches I had ever seen. The walls of the church were painted a simple white, but it seemed to me those were the whitest walls I'd ever seen, especially in contrast to the deep, dark wood of the pews and ceiling beams. I felt goose bumps breaking out all over my body and waves like electrical currents going up and down my spine. I somehow sensed the presence and spirit of the nun's spirituality, self-sacrifice, and dedication. I felt I was picking up vibes not just from the nuns living today but from all the nuns from time past. As I entered the church, I felt I was standing on holy ground. There was a hushed atmosphere, and I noticed that my fellow tour members were speaking in quiet tones as if they too felt something special in this sacred environment.

Suddenly a scene from the movie *Hercules* flashed through my mind. Young Hercules had traveled a long distance and ended up in a temple. Suddenly his true father, Zeus, appeared and told him who he really was. Standing there in that church I had another flash; I was the child of the one true God. That meant I was a powerful being capable of just about anything and that I was not alone as I journeyed through life. As long as my goals were pure and just, my heavenly father was on my side. With God all things were possible, and I suddenly knew without a shadow of a doubt that I had all the necessary tools to achieve my God-given destiny.

THE RIGHT PERSPECTIVE

This trip did indeed help me put my work situation in proper perspective. First of all, in the grand scheme of things, it really wasn't all that important. Second, I was not the only person in history who had been treated badly by coworkers. I realized that all the lessons of life I had learned up to that point were things that you didn't learn just once. I realized I had to stay ever vigilant so that each and every day I would stay the course. As for my Navy career, the mental picture I got was that I was in the fifteenth round of a championship fight. I may have been knocked down a few times, maybe even more than my share, but if I kept getting back up and stayed prayed up, I could still win the fight.

I recommitted to the long-ago vow I had made as an ensign on my very first assignment. I didn't care how many people thought I was stupid, a nonentity, or a poor excuse for a naval officer; I was going to do everything in my power to be one of the best naval intelligence officers in history. I didn't know how or why I had become such a lightning rod, but I knew that with God on my side I would be victorious.

I also knew it was the lot of most intelligence professionals to labor in silence. Most would never know what we did unless, of course, something went wrong. We were in the profession because we were called and believed in the importance of what we were doing, not for the glory.

REFLECTIONS

Each night in Brazil, before I went to sleep, I reflected on the many lessons I had learned on my Navy career journey.

- "Never, never quit."—Winston Churchill[7]
- "Most people never run far enough on their first wind to find out they've got a second. Give your dreams all you've got and you'll be amazed at the energy that comes out of you."—William James[8]
- "Don't wish it were easier, wish you were better. Don't wish for fewer problems, wish for more skills. Don't wish for less challenges, wish for more wisdom." —Earl Shoaf[9]
- "It takes courage and stamina, when unsure and embarrassed by humiliating disaster, to seek in the ruins the elements of success. Yet this is the true mark of achievement . . ."—Dennis Kimbro[10]

While writing this chapter, I was reading Joel Osteen's excellent book, *Your Best Life Now*. The chapter where he talks about the purpose of trials really resonated with me. "The trial is a test of your faith, character, and endurance. Don't give up. Don't quit. Don't whine and complain . . . instead, stand strong and fight the good fight of faith . . . it is the struggle that gives us the strength. Without opposition or resistance, there is no potential for progress. Without the resistance of air, an eagle can't soar."[11]

I CAN GO THE DISTANCE
I shared some of my trials and tribulations with my fellow travelers, and during our last prayer service, Susan and the others had prayed for me. I was grateful and humbled by the experience and returned to Colorado with my spiritual armor on. On the return flight, I kept repeating the words young Hercules sang after he realized he was the son of a god.

> I will beat the odds, I can go the distance
> I will face the world, fearless, proud, and strong
> I will please the gods, I can go the distance
> Till I find my hero's welcome, right where I belong![12]

When I returned to work, my situation started to improve. I knew it was God's hand at work in my life and on my behalf. Mike told me he had worked out a compromise. John, an air force lieutenant colonel, would be sent over to work with the command Computer Network Operations team and would keep me in the loop. I would still be the intelligence lead for that job but would answer to Mike, not Joe Smith. John was a talented man of integrity who willingly shared information with me as he worked on the project.

Joe Smith, the Navy captain in charge of the team, invited me to lunch and apologized for his earlier treatment of me. During the rest of my time there, however, he continued to do everything in his power to make my life a professional hell, even complaining about me to the higher-ups. No one seemed to believe his lies, though, and I often wondered why no one ever took that guy to task. I tried to ignore the situation as best I could. One day, Captain Smith's boss, a three-star air force general, stopped me in the hall, shook my hand, and personally apologized for Captain Smith's behavior. It happened to be my birthday. It was one of the best presents I've ever received. I did what I was called to do, and God took care of the rest.

After that, no matter how bad my situation got, and at times it was pretty bad, I was determined to stay the course and focus on the job at hand. Mike told me they were hiring an employee from one of the local defense companies to help me out. My morale got another super boost when one of my favorite people in the whole world, Bud, stuck his head in my office and told me he had been hired to help me out. I also got assigned a kick-ass Marine and another employee from Bud's company to round out my team. I began to see the light at the end of the tunnel.

CHIEF OF INTELLIGENCE PLANS AND POLICY

Mike also decided to give me a job as head of one of the intelligence departments that came under him. My official title was now chief of Intelligence Plans and Policy. It was a department of 23 people, nothing like the 500 I had managed at STRATCOM, but it gave me some credibility with the SPACECOM staff. The people in that department had given me an office when I got kicked off of the command's Computer Network Operations team and had gone out of their way to be kind to me. Once I was named their new boss, for some unknown reason, they couldn't stand me.

I still don't know where the hostility came from, but I dealt with the situation as best I could. I went out of my way to listen to their input and gave them good professional evaluations and time off when they needed it, but it didn't seem to make any difference. I finally just shrugged it off and pressed on. There was a handful of the workers that were very supportive, so it wasn't a totally hostile environment.

Just before I retired, one of the workers, a very sharp air force lieutenant colonel, came in and said she had been wrong about me and that she wasn't the only one in the department that had finally developed a good opinion of me. I smiled and accepted the compliment in the spirit it was given. In any event, now I was ready to tackle my last project in the Navy. I was determined to go out on a positive note and give it my very best effort.

MY LAST PROJECT

I decided to tackle cyber warfare or computer network operations, as we say in the military, in chunks. I was handicapped at the beginning by my lack of computer smarts, having been dragged into the computer age kicking and screaming. I didn't like computers and felt they were evil. In my new role, I was often asked to speak at numerous conferences and inevitably started out my talks trashing computers by yelling, "Remember the Terminator movies! One day those things are going to rise up and take over the world!"

As I prepared to take on my last project in the Navy, my first impression was these computers took an awful lot of extra work. They were moody and a mystery making me wondered why they couldn't be like my stereo or TV; I'd press the "on" button and they'd come on. With a computer, however, there seemed to be no guarantee that when you pressed the "on" button they would just come on. Sometimes they wouldn't, and it was a total hassle trying to figure out why. Even if they did come right on, they might or might not do what you asked them to do with no discernable reason for the unrelated operation they chose to do. Seems I always ended up spending a lot of time cursing at the thing and on the phone with the Help Desk. I wish I had a dollar for every time I'd call them with a problem and they'd say something like, "It's not supposed to do that" or "I've never heard of computers doing that before."

One thing became painfully apparent to me if I had any hope of accomplishing my task in this area of cyber warfare. I needed a computer mentor and quickly. Holly came to my rescue, putting me in touch with Commander Bob Gourley, who was assigned as the senior intelligence officer at a command called the Joint Task Force Computer Network Operations, or JTF-CNO. Bob was a computer genius and super to work with. He took me under his wing and gave me all kinds of background material to work with, and I became somewhat literate on the subject of cyber warfare.

Holly also told me to touch base with a mutual good friend, Captain Terry Roberts, who was in charge of the Systems Department at the Office of Naval Intelligence. Terry was leading a multiservice and multiorganization working group in the DC area. They were making revolutionary changes in the way the Navy and other organizations were doing business with computers. Terry had the unique gift of being able to take complex technical subjects and break them down for me into an understandable language. She really educated me on a lot of technical stuff like virtual conferencing and the importance of efficient use of computer databases.

In spite of the improvements in my situation, I began to realize I was still standing in front of an oncoming tidal wave. The news was full of stories of the effects of hacking and malicious viruses on our computer infrastructure. Shortly after I arrived at SPACECOM, the command hosted a conference on Computer Network Operations. Representatives from various Department of Defense commands and intelligence organizations were concerned about the lack of policies and procedures to combat this new form of war. I used the conference as an opportunity to introduce myself to the intelligence types so I could actually visit a number of these commands and gain a firsthand understanding of the issues they were facing and problems that needed to be solved.

Mike said he would give me the budget to travel to wherever I needed to go to get the job done; however, my visit requests were often met with indifference or barely concealed hostility. Looking down their nose at me like I smelled bad, they'd say stuff like, "Who are you again? Why should we talk to you?" Mike told me he spent a lot of time on the phone confirming to various organizations that I was indeed the lead for the project. I put my ego aside and persisted with follow-up phone calls and e-mails until the various organizations agreed to let me visit. Once I arrived, they usually pawned me off on one of their underlings, but at least I was making some progress.

Gradually I gained insights into the challenges of cyber warfare, or as we called it Computer Network Operations (CNO). The military had divided CNO into two subareas: Computer Network Defense (CND) and Computer Network Attack (CNA). One discipline was protecting our networks from those that wanted to do us harm, and the second involved actually using computer techniques as a weapon. For instance, rather than bombing the bad guy's electric grid, we could use some form of computer attack to knock it out but not necessarily destroy it. That way after the conflict was over you didn't have to rebuild it, just take out whatever computer bug you had put in it.

Many in the intelligence community didn't think intelligence had a role in this area, feeling it was a telecommunication specialist's responsibility. As I went about visiting various organizations, I came to believe that just as the intelligence community had tracked the capability of bad guys to use bombs and cruise missiles against us, we needed to track an enemy's use of computer network operations against us as well. As always, the role of intelligence would be support but not just in our traditional role of working with the warfighters. It would now include supporting the people responsible for our communications networks.

HOW DO YOU EAT AN ELEPHANT?

I decided the problem was so huge that the best tactic was to approach it like the old joke, "How do you eat an elephant? Answer: One bite at a time." The problem was immense, and I knew I couldn't fix it all but at least we could take some very crucial beginning steps. After my informal survey of the concerns of various commands and organizations, I identified three problem areas that work should have begun on months ago.

The first was determining what type of information the intelligence community should collect to determine bad guy capabilities. There is a whole discipline in intelligence called collection management that focused on what information to tell the sensors and/or people to collect.

The second area involved databases or where the information on CNO was stored. Each organization keeps records of attempts made to attack their networks. Ideally everyone within the Department of Defense needed to use the same or interoperable databases so that information could be easily shared, monitored, and/or retrieved.

For example, I'm at United States Central Command (CENTCOM) headquarters in Tampa, Florida. My people come in and tell me someone attempted to hack into the command computers. My first question would be, Has any other military organization been hit recently or is it just us? If every command or government organization is recording hacking attempts and using the same database to record the attempts, I can do a Google type search and get the answer quickly; however, if each organization is using a separate database, then being an outside organization, I would not be able to access the data and would have to call each organization and ask them individually, which would be extremely time consuming. As an intelligence professional, you need to be able to ascertain whether this is an isolated incident or if we are under attack.

Many of the organizations had put a lot of time and money into their telecommunications and computer systems, but they often weren't compatible with those of other organizations. Some organizations thought they had the best system and didn't want to change or didn't want to be compatible with any other organizations.

The third area that needed policy development was reporting. When and how would intelligence reports be sent out on computer incidents? Would all incidents be reported immediately or only those caused by bad guys from foreign countries or terrorists? Under what circumstances would intelligence reports be sent out? Who would get them? Who would send them? Should it be a command's communications specialist or operations specialist or the Intelligence Watch? Would you send out a report immediately or just a daily or weekly summary report? The communications departments of organizations also sent out reports on computer hacking activity. Should intelligence send out separate reports or merge their information in the communications reports?

Once I had identified the three main problems, my next step was to figure out how to solve them. A Defense Intelligence Agency (DIA) employee named Steve who was assigned to SPACECOM came up with the perfect solution. Why not convene a conference and ask the organizations to attend and help solve the identified problems? The conference attendees would be organized into working groups, one for each of the three areas we needed to develop. Each group would be chaired by someone other than a SPACECOM person to get buy-in from the participants. Knowing that many people throughout the Department of Defense were concerned that SPACECOM was going to dictate a solution without consulting them, if I involved other commands and organizations in the process, I knew I could eventually get everyone's help and more effectively solve the problems.

Even though I thought it was a great idea, for it to work I needed the support of SPACECOM. I knew the command's CNO group, led by my nemesis Joe, would not help me, but Mike proved to be my ace in the hole. He loved the idea and promised to support it. I made it a point to get to know Tom, an air force colonel, my counterpart in the J3 (Operations Department), who had been friendly to me at various staff meetings. He also agreed to support the conference. All that was missing was support from the staff's J6, Communications Department. Initially they said they would participate, but they failed to show up when the conference started and didn't even bother to tell me they would not be attending. Oh, well, two out of three isn't bad considering all the obstacles that needed to be overcome.

Tom and Mike both agreed to give opening talks at the conference. Mike also arranged to have SPACECOM's second in command, a Navy admiral, open the conference. This gave the conference the validity it needed in the eyes of potential attendees. The admiral also signed the invitation to attend the conference I sent out. If the invite had come from me, most organizations would have blown the conference off; but when the number two man at SPACECOM sent out the invite, it would have been impolite not to participate.

Mike also agreed to come over each day's end and have the working group chairmen brief him on their progress. The working groups were charged with coming up with solutions that everyone had agreed on. This along with Mike's participation was the key to the ultimate success of the conference. My hope was that knowing that they would have to brief Mike every day, conference attendees would come up with solutions instead of spending the day complaining and calling each other names, like I'd observed at other CNO conferences.

For the last day of the conference, putting to use what I had learned from my CENTCOM days, I also set up a video teleconference with all the senior members of the intelligence community. The working group chairmen would have to brief these guys as well. I was hoping that professional pride would cause them to focus on solutions and not professional infighting.

In the days leading up to the conference, there were a lot of naysayers and critics, saying I would never get the intelligence community's various organizations to work together as a team. Apparently for the last two years no one had been able to make progress in the area of computer policy. My small team and I refused to listen to their negativity and set about organizing the conference, finding a location to hold it, and working out all the details to actually pull this off.

I also got people to volunteer to head up the working groups. Terry and Bob would cochair the database working groups. DIA volunteered to head up both the collection management working group and the reporting working group. For the latter, they chose a remarkable man named Don Lewis. Don was one of those quietly efficient, modest guys that I later found out had been awarded one of the highest awards for bravery while in Vietnam, the Bronze Star. Don never talked about it, I just happened to see it in his official biography.

I knew it was very important that I set the tone from day one of the conference. I had really been seeking a unique way to open to ensure this conference was not a repeat of what had happened the previous two years. In the middle of the night, a few days prior to the start of the conference, I had one of those moments I believe came by divine inspiration. I knew I had to get conference attendees to focus on solutions, not problems or organizational turf battles. I had read a story in Chicken Soup for the Soul that had really moved me and decided to use it at the start of the conference to motivate the attendees to work together. I decided to keep that fact to myself, figuring no matter how supportive Mike was, he probably would have a problem with me doing a motivational talk to an audience of hardened military professionals.

A few days before the conference, I took the proposed schedule of events in to Mike for his approval. Looking up from his desk, he looked at me and mischievously said, "Just got off the phone with Holly. She says you keep calling her at work saying you're going to have a wild, hot date with Wesley Snipes."

"I am, just don't know how or when," I threw back at him. "Meanwhile I've been practicing. Want to hear about my weekend date?"

Putting his hands over his ears, Mike started laughing, "No, I don't want to know, don't tell me."

"Okay, then here's the final conference agenda. Pretty much what we've talked about, except for I'd like to have fifteen minutes at the beginning before you, Tom, and the admiral do your welcome talks."

Tilting his head, eyebrows raised inquiringly, Mike asked, "What do you want to talk about?"

"Oh, just some administrative stuff like where the restrooms are located and stuff like that."

SPACECOM was a paranoid organization, so if you were going to give a talk you had to float the PowerPoint presentation up the chain of command.

Usually it was a tedious process, with people arguing with you over the color of the slide's background or some other petty detail. I really hoped I wasn't going to have to go that route, especially with what I believed I was supposed to do in that opening fifteen minutes.

Shrugging Mike said, "That sounds fine, we'll need to kill some time anyway since the admiral's assistant said he couldn't get him over until about 8:30. Tom and I don't want to give our talks until after the big guy speaks."

"Do I have to run the couple of slides I plan on using up the chain of command?"

Mike waved me out of his office saying everything looked good. As I left, I did a mental victory dance and thanked God for intervening. I knew I was home free at least on this part.

THE DAY OF THE CONFERENCE

When I awoke early on the day of the conference, I did what had been my routine since returning from Brazil—I spent about an hour in prayer before leaving for work. The prayer plus my living environment started my day off right. I had finally moved into the house I had built. I had incorporated my favorite features from every home I had ever lived in, like tall ceilings, plenty of windows, and a built-in sound system. I wanted my home to be a place of refuge where I could restore my soul at the end of every workday.

Between the good vibes I got from my new home and the spiritual high I got from my prayer routine, I felt unstoppable. I asked for God's assistance in making the conference successful and having everyone work together as a team to solve the three problems I had identified. As I left my house, there was no doubt in my mind that the conference was going to be a success. Failure was not an option.

The conference was being held in a large auditorium at a facility located in a building owned by one of the defense companies. I expected attendees from 30 different Department of Defense commands and intelligence organizations as well as folks from local Defense companies that had asked to attend the open sessions. There were three large work spaces that would house our individual working groups.

I timed my arrival at the site just as the conference was scheduled to start, doing my best not to be noticed. I wanted most folk's initial impression of me to begin when they saw me on stage at the start of the conference. My people had done a great job with the set up, and the attendees all seemed to be in a good mood as they wandered around renewing friendships; drinking coffee; and eating bagels, donuts, and fruit. I had paid for the breakfast spread out of my own pocket instead of charging the normal conference fee for munchies.

I motioned for my people to start moving our guests into the auditorium. As folks filed in, I stood at the edge of the stage. Once everyone was seated, I swaggered over to the center of the stage like the Navy captain that I was, purposely decked out with all of my military medals and awards. Looking out over the audience, I smiled, "First off, I'd like to thank you all for taking time from your busy schedules to come to this conference. As a way of showing my appreciation, breakfast this morning was on me. I can afford to pay for it because I'm single and rich." I heard a few chuckles. So far, so good.

"Our purpose this week is to come up with a solution to three critical problems in CNO: collection management, computer data bases, and reporting." I showed slides with the names of the people who would be leading the working groups. "You'll note that the working groups are not all led by SPACECOM personnel because this is to be a group effort. If some of you are skeptical of that fact and believe I will try to dictate a solution, let me ease your mind. I am not smart enough to do this myself, in fact I hate computers, they're evil. I refuse to have one in my home, I have Web TV." I paused as more laughter came from the audience. "You laugh but in all of the news reports on computer hacking, I have never heard of anyone hacking into Web TV." More laughter.

"Let me give you Gail's rules for operating this week. Rules 1 through 10, if you come up with a problem you also have to come up with a proposed solution in the same breath. We will not spend the week wringing our hands and whining about problems. This week is about solutions. I figure if you're smart enough to know something's a problem, you should be smart enough to come up with a fix." Scanning the audience, I stuck my hand out pointing, "Anyone who breaks that rule will lose their bathroom privileges, and I have a kick-ass Marine who will enforce it." More laughter.

GOODBYE STANDARD MILITARY CONFERENCE PROTOCOL
I paused, looked as solemn as I could to indicate a change in direction, and asked, "How many of you have children?" Most of the audience raised their

hands. I took a deep breath and silently said goodbye to standard military conference protocol. "I'm going to tell you a true story and then explain the significance of what it means to our work this week." I slowly walked from one end of the stage to the other maintaining audience eye contact.

"In 1988, there was an earthquake in Armenia that was 8.2 on the Richter scale. In the first few minutes after the quake, 40,000 people were killed. One man looked around at the damage and saw his home had been destroyed. He took his wife over to his neighbor's house, asking his neighbor to watch out for her while he went to look for his nine-year-old son who had been at school at the time of the quake. His neighbor tried to talk him out of it, saying he should let the professionals handle it."

"The man looked his neighbor in the eye and replied, 'You don't understand. I've told my son that no matter what happened to him in this life I would always be there for him.' When this father arrived at the school, he saw that it had been flattened like a pancake, and many other parents were standing around crying and wringing their hands. He looked at them and said: 'Are you going to help me?' The other parents asked him what he thought he could do, and he said he was going to start looking for his son. The other parents told him to look at the damage and to realize no one could have survived the destruction that had taken place."

"Ignoring their defeated attitudes, he headed for the basic location of his son's classroom and started digging. Local firemen, militia, and others tried to stop him instead of helping him. Each time, rather than arguing with them, he simply asked, 'Are you going to help me?' When they said no, he would go back to digging."

I suddenly thought of my own father who had always told my brother, my sister, and me that he would be there for us regardless of the circumstances. As I remembered how he worked two jobs to help pay for my college and how often he'd picked me up and encouraged me to go on when life got tough, I felt the tears coming. My dad was now in heaven, but on that day I felt his presence with me there on that stage. My voice started to crack, but I pressed on.

"Twelve hours passed, then 18 hours, and then 24 hours went by as this father determinedly searched for his son. Finally, after 37 hours of digging, he came to an air pocket and yelled down into the hole. Upon hearing his son's voice, he asked, 'Armand, how are you?' His son replied, 'Dad, out of my 33 classmates, 14 of us are still alive. We're tired, scared, thirsty, and hungry, but I kept telling everyone that if my dad survived this he would come and get me.' His father said, 'Son, give me your hand.' But his son replied, 'No Dad, let the others go first because I know you will be there for me.'"[13] As I looked out at that audience of hardened warriors, I noticed many seemed to be deeply affected by the story.

"The relevance of that story in regards to what we are here to do this week," I explained, "is that we need to realize that the Information Technology Revolution has caused an earthquake in the way we do business, but buried beneath the rubble is the warfighter. I don't care what you keep hearing about operational successes and intelligence failures, the intelligence community has been there for the warfighter since the dawn of time. Today and this whole week I'm going to start digging. Are you going to help me?"

The guys and gals started cheering, the Marines and the Army guys did that grunting thing they do, and that week we made history. We worked as one team and solved all of those issues. The working group chairmen did an incredible job keeping everyone on track. On that first day, though, there was an awful lot of dissension and problems in Don's group, making us all wonder if they would be able to accomplish anything. Don worked long into the night and came back the second day, reined everyone in, and got them all on the same page. The working group chairmen's jobs didn't stop at conference's end. They kept each group together and worked to solve each new issue that came up during the next two years.

I could write a whole book on the subject but will give you just one example of the complex scope of the problem. One issue was in the area of intelligence oversight. Contrary to what you see in many Hollywood movies and TV shows, the U.S. intelligence community does not normally spy on U.S. citizens because it is against the law. The Global War on Terrorism has caused a few of these rules to change, but that was not the case for my time on active duty. If there was a computer incident and it seemed to originate in the United States, the Federal Bureau of Investigation (FBI) and local law enforcement agencies could not share the information with the intelligence community. The intelligence community was only informed if the incident originated from a foreign source. Any teenage hacker can tell you that an incident might look like it's originating from a U.S. source, but it can actually be coming from a computer located any where in the world.

The result was that the intelligence community was being informed of about only 40 percent of the computer incidents. The reporting working group from the conference asked the Department of Defense legal types for a ruling on this problem, stating that a computer host Internet protocol address was not in itself considered a U.S. citizen; therefore, the oversight rules would not reply. It took the legal community a year, but they finally made the ruling.

The Department of Defense eventually moved the mission from SPACECOM to STRATCOM. JTF-CNO is now called JTF-GNO (Global Network Operations). Don said every once in a while he's asked to get up and tell the story of how it all began and that people never cease to be amazed at all that was accomplished by so many different organizations working together as one team during that first conference.

We continued to work the solutions developed at that first conference. Surrounded by super people like Bob; Terry; Don; my small staff; and many dedicated, talented people from more than thirty various government organizations, my last task was one of the most rewarding of my Navy career.

COUNTDOWN TO RETIREMENT

The various working groups I'd been overseeing developed long-range plans of what hardware and software we would need to improve computer network defense within the Department of Defense. My friend, Captain Terry Roberts, had been assigned a new job in the office that oversaw portions of the intelligence budget. I called and asked her if there would be any money allocated to support cyber warfare. Terry told me to gather information from all of the more than thirty commands I had been working with and determine exactly how much money it would take to speed up the hardware and software changes. I also put together an argument as to why the program was important.

In the meantime, Terry did her research on what current intelligence budget proposals looked like. She was working in her office in the Pentagon, waiting for me to join her so we could meet with the senior person in charge of allocating these funds and see if we could have it designated specifically toward the intelligence portion of cyber warfare, on September 11, 2001. Fortunately she was not injured in the attack on the Pentagon. The meeting, of course, was cancelled, but now I felt an urgency to get this information to those who make the decisions concerning cyber warfare.

After 9/11, I knew the government would be increasing the intelligence budget and wanted to make sure the importance of intelligence participation in cyber warfare would not be overlooked. Unfortunately, just a few days before 9/11, the J2 at SPACECOM who had been so supportive was replaced by another guy also named Mike. I spent an afternoon briefing the new J2 on our efforts of the preceding two years and the importance of aggressively pursuing the part the intelligence community should play in the area of cyber warfare. At the end of it, he told me he hadn't understood a word I'd said and declared that cyber warfare wasn't an intelligence issue and the budget money should be spent on other programs. I was totally floored by this attitude.

Then the under secretary of defense who was overseeing the cyber warfare program wanted me to continue working as SPACECOM's representative to him, but the new J2 said if the under secretary wanted me to work on the program he would have to pay for it out of his budget. His whole mindset seemed to be that what I was doing was not in any way related to intelligence. This was the final straw for me that clearly revealed that my time in the Navy was to come to an end. It was time for me to move into retirement and begin the next phase of my life's journey.

MOVING INTO RETIREMENT

A couple of years earlier, while still assigned at STRATCOM, I was returning from a vacation and had met Mark Victor Hansen, coauthor of the Chicken Soup for the Soul books at the Omaha airport. We struck up a conversation and, after hearing some of my story, he invited me to come to hear him speak. I went to several of his conferences after that, and he became one of my mentors. He encouraged me to leave the Navy and pursue a career in speaking and writing.

A few months before my disappointing briefing with my new J2 and before 9/11, I had received a call from Stu, an old friend of mine, saying, "Hey Gail, I'm your relief." Surprised, since I had only served two of the three years of this assignment, I called Holly and she laughingly told me I was only obligated to do two of the three years. She knew I wanted to retire, so she had done some research and was making sure a good guy replaced me. I knew Stu and his wife wanted to move to Colorado to be close to their families, so I felt comfortable that I could retire in peace. I felt troubled leaving while the nation was at war but figured with one friend in charge of job assignments and another the new Director of Naval Intelligence and the Navy was not asking me not to retire I obviously wasn't wanted for whatever reason. I wondered whether I should do what I had done before and force them to give me a new job but didn't want to bother my friends. They were fighting a real war and I didn't want to burden them with my "issues." I talked to my mom, and she told me she felt that it was time to leave; I had done all I could, and now it was time for someone else to take over. Mentally and physically exhausted, I decided to move forward with my scheduled retirement.

As mentioned, the new Director of Naval Intelligence was an old friend of mine, and he invited me to have my retirement ceremony at naval intelligence headquarters in the Washington, DC, area. I took him up on it, as it would allow many of my relatives from New Jersey, Virginia, and Alabama to be able to attend.

Shortly before my retirement, I had been contacted out of the blue by a speaker's bureau who wanted to sign me up to do motivational speaking. I was scheduled for my first talk in a few weeks, and the money I would make for giving one thirty-minute talk was more than I made in a month in the Navy. The beginning of the end of my Navy career may have started at the CNO conference, but when God closes one door, He opens another. For me this was the start of a new chapter in my life as a writer and motivational speaker.

RETIREMENT

I spent the first nine months of retirement doing speaking engagements for organizations ranging from Starbucks to various defense companies. I also worked on a first draft of this book, which because of my security clearances had to have Pentagon security approval before I could show the manuscript to anyone else.

A year after retiring, Lockheed Martin offered me a job helping them design a follow-on aircraft for both the EP-3 and the P-3C. Two years into working at Lockheed, my work on the EP-3 project was done, and I realized I was not really cut out to work for corporate America. I had also started having problems with severe coughing fits and swollen glands that made me look like I had the mumps all the time. I was diagnosed with asthma. The doctor said my health was in pretty bad shape, and if I continued with my heavy schedule at Lockheed while remaining on the speaking circuit, I was facing potential heart problems as well. He put me on two weeks of total bed rest. Guess I was a physical mess!

I started making plans to really retire from the defense industry and focus on what I believed my new career should be: speaking and writing. I had taken the job at Lockheed because of the war, feeling I could still use the knowledge and training I had received in the Navy to help out and make a difference in the defense industry.

A few months after my diagnosis of asthma I had eye surgery that didn't heal properly. Suddenly I couldn't read, something I'd loved since childhood. It wasn't uncommon for me to read four or five books a week on top of all the reading I had to do for my job. The doctors didn't know why my eye wasn't healing, but I suspected it was another sign that my overall health was still not good. That was the final push for me to leave the defense industry. I moved to Durango and contacted an excellent doctor there, but after treating me unsuccessfully for a few months he sent me to a specialist in Albuquerque, New Mexico. The weekend before my appointment, my mom's church in Alabama had a revival, and she asked them to pray for me. When the eye specialist examined my eye, he said, "There's nothing wrong with your eye. I saw the file on what you had been experiencing. What happened since this last report?" I told him about my mom's church. He smiled and said, "That does work."

I was able to resume work on my book and get back on the speaking circuit, though I took my doctor's advice and am not scheduling as many as I did before. I bought a beautiful condo on the river, and I do a weekly radio show on KDUR, the local college radio station. Now that the book is done, I am looking forward to doing what I believe is my mission: helping and inspiring people to achieve their dreams.

Takeaway: You can accomplish a lot if you don't care who gets the credit.

Key principles I learned during my last few years in the navy:

1. All the lessons of life I had learned were things that you didn't just learn once.
2. I had to stay ever vigilant so that each and every day I made sure I stayed the course.
3. When God closes one day, He opens another.

SUPPLEMENT ON CYBER WARFARE

As we conclude this chapter, I want to make sure you grasp the magnitude of the effect a cyber attack could have on this country. Having worked at the Naval War College's war gaming department, where I learned how to think like the bad guys, I truly realized the potential of such an attack. I am going to put my war gaming hat back on and run through a scenario for you from the enemy's point of view. I no longer work for the government, so this is just my take and in no way represents an official view. That said, here's how I believe a cyber attack might be launched against our country.

On Friday, about seven in the evening, I would begin my attack by taking down the computers in the Pentagon and all the other government agencies by using denial-of-service attacks. My inspiration is a real-world incident. For three weeks in 2007, the Baltic state of Estonia came under cyber attack. "Pro-Russian hackers, some likely associated with the government, attacked numerous websites in neighboring Estonia, one of the world's most-wired countries, to protest the controversial removal of a Soviet war memorial located in the capital, Tallinn. The hackers brought down government and other websites, including the office of the president, the parliament, political parties, banks, news organizations, and communications firms, using denial-of-service attacks in which a sever is bombarded with so many bogus requests for information that it overloads and crashes . . . some of the attacks came from botnets—chains of perhaps thousands of zombie computers that have been hijacked by the malicious code of cyber pirates and linked together to take part in raids . . . with or without their owners knowledge."[14]

Then I would create total chaos in DC, by disrupting traffic patterns by hacking into their computer system. I would simultaneously disrupt air traffic computers and use that as another distraction. By now, emergency vehicles would be running around in circles trying to handle all the crisis situations caused by this chaos. I would have terrorists going around at random shooting people in major U.S. cities. The disruption of the communications system would make it difficult to mount a coordinated respond.

I would also hit places like Omaha and Tampa, which have major military commands with excellent communications facilities, with cyber attacks. Once there was chaos in the communications and computer systems in strategic locations around the country, I could begin any type of follow-on attack, like launching cruise missiles from merchant vessels operating in U.S. waters.

Then I would cease while the United States scrambled to respond, trying to figure out where the attack was coming from. "The mazelike architecture of the Internet offers cyber attackers a high degree of anonymity. Smart hackers can route attacks through countries with which the victim's government has poor diplomatic relations and no law enforcement cooperation."[15]

That's how I see it could go down. Lest you think I've gone off the deep end, here's an excerpt from the director of national intelligence's statement for the record of February 2008: "Our information infrastructure, including the Internet, telecommunications networks, computer systems, and embedded processors and controllers in critical industries, is increasingly being targeted for exploitation, and potentially for disruption or destruction, by a growing array of state and nonstate adversaries. Over the past year, cyber exploitation activity has grown more sophisticated, more targeted, and more serious."[16] Many people in government are working very hard to prevent something like this from happening.

NOTES

1. Joel Osteen, *Become a Better You.* (New York: Free Press, 2007), 238.

2. Peter Brookes, "Flashpoint: The Cyber Challenge." *Armed Forces Journal*, March 2008. Available at www.armedforcesjournal.com/2008/03/3463904, p. 1.

3. "Chinese Hackers Prompt Navy College Site Closure." *Washington Times*, November 30, 2006. Available at www.washingtontimes.com/news/2006/nov/30/20061130-103049-5042r/print/.

4. John J. Tkacik, Jr., "Trojan Dragons: China's International Cyber Warriors," 1, WebMemo published by the Heritage Foundation. Available at www.heritage.org/Research/AsianadthePacific/wm1735.cfm.

5. Tkacik, Jr., "Trojan Dragons: China's International Cyber Warriors," 1.

6. "Go the Distance" from Walt Disney Pictures *Hercules.* Music by Alan Menken, lyrics by David Zippel. Copyright 1997 Wonderland Music Company, Inc., and Walt Disney Music Company. All Rights Reserved. Used with written permission, Disney.

7. www.wow4u.com/winston-churchill/index.html.

8. http://en.proverbia.net/citasautor.asp?autor=13773.

9. Earl Shoaf. Available at powerpositivethinking.org/Positive_Quotes.html.

10. Dennis Kimbro and Napoleon Hill, *Think and Grow Rich: A Black Choice.* (New York: Fawcett Crest, 1991), 167.

11. Joel Osteen, *Your Best Life Now.* (New York: Warner Faith Publishers, 2004), p. 211.

12. "Go the Distance" from Walt Disney Pictures': *Hercules.* Music by Alan Menken, lyrics by David Zippel. Copyright 1997 Wonderland Music Company, Inc., and Walt Disney Music Company. All Rights Reserved Used with written permission, Disney.

13. Jack Canfield and Mark Victor Hansen, *Chicken Soup for the Soul: 101 Stories to Open the Heart and Rekinkle the Spirit.* (Deerfield Beach, FL: Health Communications, Inc., 1993), 372–374.

14. Peter Brookes, "Flashpoint: The Cyber Challenge," p.1.

15. Kenneth Geers, "Cyber Warfare: Strategy and Tactics." Available at www .internetevolution.com/author.asp?section_id=628. Page 1.

16. *U.S. Air Force Fact Sheet, Cyberspace 101: Understanding the Cyberspace Domain,* page 2. Available at www.afcyber.af.mil/library/factsheets/factsheet_print.asp? fsID-10784&page=1.

15

Conclusion: Reflections of a Retired Black Woman

One of the most difficult things everyone has to learn is that for your entire life you must keep fighting and adjusting if you hope to survive. No matter who you are or what your position you must keep fighting for whatever it is you desire to achieve.

—*George Allen*[1]

There are many stereotypes about growing old. We are not useless, toothless, and sexless. In fact, old people have a special place in society. My generation has been part of more changes than any other. We have to share that knowledge.

—*Maggie Kuhn*[2]

Like a professional athlete, a professional warrior's career is limited, and I have learned how important it is to know when it's time to move on. My goal as I approached retirement was to leave the Navy at a time of my choosing under honorable conditions. Considering the challenges I had faced throughout my career, this was no small goal.

In this final chapter, I want to offer you my reflections on intelligence as a profession, in relation to the Iraqi weapons of mass destruction (WMD) issue, and such recurring challenges I faced throughout my career as racism, sexism, and office bullies. These are questions I am most often asked during my speaking engagements. I pray that the insights I share will inspire those of

258

you who feel you have had or are now facing an uphill battle trying to achieve your goals in life.

INTELLIGENCE AS A PROFESSION

In the aftermath of 9/11, there was a lot of criticism of the intelligence community. What concerned me was not that people were criticizing but the fact that the critics were basically clueless concerning how intelligence was organized and how it works. When you say intelligence to most people, they think of the Central Intelligence Agency (CIA). Critics did not seem to know that the CIA was only one of sixteen government intelligence organizations or that 85 percent of these intelligence assets reside within the Department of Defense. My question becomes, how can you fix what you don't understand?

There are problem areas, but not all of intelligence is broken and needs fixing. One of the major reasons I decided to write this book was to give the public a better insight into the challenges of intelligence professionals who specialized in support to military operations. When I do public speaking, people seem to be pretty impressed with my achievements, but I tell them there's nothing special about what I've done. Similar jobs and accomplishments have been done by countless others throughout the intelligence community. The young intelligence professionals currently supporting our conflicts in Afghanistan, Iraq, and the Global War on Terrorism have far more challenges than those I faced. My hope is that by sharing my journey, it will give the public a better insight into an area of intelligence seldom mentioned or covered in movies, books, and TV programs.

My second goal in writing this book is to encourage more young people to enter the intelligence field as a profession. Courses on intelligence are popping up in colleges and universities all over the world. I think this is a good thing, but I offer a word of caution: *make the courses relevant.* I'm reminded of the first time I saw comedian Bill Cosby. He was fresh out of college and was discussing the traits of the various academic majors he'd encountered in school. He said the philosophy majors were always wandering around campus asking, "Why is there air?" Cosby, a physical education major, said, "Any phys ed major knows why there's air . . . to blow up footballs and basketballs." I think it's okay to have discussions like, "What is intelligence," but we also need the equivalent of some phys ed majors to balance it out and make it relevant.

I believe that the goal of intelligence college education programs should be to prepare students for entry-level positions in the intelligence community. One way to do that is with a variety of courses but also to encourage summer internships in the various intelligence agencies. There are many career fields within the intelligence community, and students should be exposed to all of them through course work and by bringing intelligence professionals, both active and retired, to talk with them while they are still in school. As I'm writing this, there is a big argument going on among intelligence educators about whether intelligence is an art or science. Here are my thoughts on that.

INTELLIGENCE AS ART WORKING WITH SCIENCE

I believe intelligence is an art that involves the use and understanding of a multitude of sources, tools, and methodologies. To help clarify where I'm coming from, here are the definitions I'm using, which are found in the Merriam-Webster Collegiate Dictionary, 10th edition. Art is defined as the conscious use of skill and creative imagination in the production of aesthetic objects. In this case, I believe the "aesthetic object" is an intelligence product of value to a decision maker. Science is defined as knowledge or a system of knowledge covering general truths or the operation of general laws, especially as obtained and tested through scientific method. In my thinking, if intelligence was strictly a science, given identical situations, if I always did things the same way according to accepted methods, then the results would always be the same.

In real life, I have not found this to be the case. I have provided intelligence support in two wars and many crises. There was much in place I could use, and many of the analytical techniques used for analysis still worked, but there was nothing in place that worked for 100 percent of the requirements of each situation. Without exception, I've found it necessary to approach each situation with as many new methods, techniques, and technologies as possible, which is where I believe the "art" aspect of intelligence comes in.

In today's environment, I believe intelligence analysis is much more far-reaching than simply sifting through the available information and coming up with theories and conclusions. I believe that to do the best intelligence analysis possible, you have to make sure you're receiving data from all of the available sources. What this means is you never assume you're receiving all the data available on a particular issue or category, because the way the classification system works, you may not know what you don't know.

This highlights the importance of collaborating with other agencies and analysts. I found there was always more information to be had and usually could obtain it by simply explaining why I needed it. Once you have obtained all of the available information, you have to get it to the decision makers before it is no longer relevant. Technology is changing at the speed of thought and has helped narrow the time-lapse between receiving and disseminating information considerably.

Warfighters have a saying that on the first day of war, the original plan is already outdated. I've found that on the first day of a war or crisis, the intelligence plan and intelligence architecture is out-of-date as well. Usually not all of the data is outdated but just enough that if you can't change or fix what is, it will seriously hamper your ability to effectively provide intelligence analysis to your particular organization. The first problem I usually ran into was that the available communication circuits were overloaded by the amount of information needing to be transmitted. Part of my job was to find new ways to get analysis out quickly and efficiently to the appropriate decision makers.

To be a really effective and efficient intelligence professional, you have to be able to visualize the desired end state of the intelligence architecture, even if it's something that doesn't currently exist. Then you have to figure out what you need to do to make it happen. Of course the basic technology involved in sending intelligence reports over various communications circuits uses science and technology. The "art" comes in when you have to figure out how to tailor or create a new and/or better communications path to serve the people you're supporting. By visualizing the desired end state, you can then go find the technology to support it. If there's no existing technology in place to accomplish that then you have to create it.

The problem I faced during the first Gulf War, while the senior intelligence officer (N2) for VQ-2, is a good example of what I'm talking about. As discussed earlier, when the detachments first arrived, my intelligence staff had no way of obtaining needed intelligence reports to update and support the air crews before they flew their missions or a way to send out post flight reports after the completed mission. By researching the problem and working with the Office of Naval Intelligence (ONI), we created a system that worked so well it was put into widespread use both during and after the war. I just told them what end results I needed and let them work out the technology. I did this over and over, especially during the last part of my career, most notably while at NAVCENT and overseeing intelligence architecture upgrades.

As an analyst, you have to also understand all the sources available to support your analysis. I have never known an intelligence collection system that did not have a flaw of some sort associated with it. When doing intelligence analysis you have to be aware of that and factor it into your analysis. Before I retired, I always emphasized to new analysts that just because something pops up on your computer screen does not mean it's accurate, true, or relevant. Putting together all of the information you receive, factoring in potential inaccuracies, and developing the best analysis possible, in my mind, falls into the category of "art." I am not aware of any mathematical formula or scientific methodology that can be used to accomplish this process.

IRAQI AND WMD

There's still intense discussion going on about the Iraqi WMD issue. To refresh your memory, in December 1998, United States Central Command (CENTCOM), under orders from the Clinton administration, launched Operation Desert Fox, a four-day operation, "aimed at installations associated with development of weapons of mass destruction, units providing security to such programs, and Iraq's national command and control network."[3] On just the first day of operations, 280 cruise missiles were launched and, as stated in a December 28, 1998, *Time* magazine article, that total was almost as many as was used during the entire first Gulf War.[4] Desert Fox was only one of a series of intense military operations conducted during a period referred to as the "Forgotten War," the time period between when the first Gulf War ended in March of 1991 and the second began in March 2003.

A December 17, 1998, article in the *New York Times* quotes senior U.S. officials discussing Desert Fox as stating, "the air strikes would significantly hamper Iraq's programs to make poison gas and nuclear weapons . . . they readily acknowledged that the weapons programs would continue. . . . Without the U.N. inspection program . . . the Clinton administration would have only a limited ability to determine whether Iraq is manufacturing and stockpiling weapons of massed destruction."[5] The same article quotes Pentagon officials as saying, "It's a very unpalatable scenario. . . . We can keep track of some of what's going on the ground with satellites and surveillance planes. But that's not the same as having inspectors on the ground, poking around or at least trying to poke around Iraqi installation."[6]

My involvement with the Iraqi problem as an intelligence professional ended after my support to the Desert Fox operations, but based on my experience and observations, I believe if Iraq was not hiding WMDs, they were trying to maintain the capability to rebuild them once UN sanctions ended. Just before the start of the current Iraq war, I was interviewed on a radio program and asked if I thought Saddam would use WMDs on British and U.S. forces. I replied that depended on whether Saddam wanted to win the battle or the war. When asked to elaborate, I put on my old war gaming hat and said, "If I was Saddam, I would not use WMDs. If I still had some, I'd either destroy or hide them, possibly by sending them to another country." I explained that my reasoning was due to the fact that during the first Gulf War, when it became apparent Iraq could not maintain air superiority against the coalition forces, Saddam sent most of his remaining aircraft to Iran. Considering he had recently fought a long war against that nation, it was an interesting choice, but he obviously felt he had no place else to send them to preserve them at the time. "If Saddam got rid of the WMDs," I explained, "the United States and Britain would never find them, and we would come out looking like idiots."

We might never know what actually happened, but during the time I was involved with the Iraqi situation, Saddam was acting awfully guilty. The nature of intelligence is that you will seldom have the luxury of enough information to present a case that will stand up in court. Case in point, the Iraq crisis.

RACISM AND SEXISM

People seem amazed that I maintain a positive frame of mind considering I came into the service in the 1970s, when there were a lot of equal-opportunity problems, to include race riots on aircraft carriers. One of the questions I'm asked is if I have experienced discrimination in the military because of my race and/or sex. The short answer is, yes, but the question is actually more complex than most people realize. Most of the time when people think of discrimination, they're thinking of a situation where a person or an organization is deliberately keeping an individual or a group from advancing because of race or gender. This was not the case for most of the problems I faced as a woman in a traditionally male profession.

I've mentioned several times that Navy women were restricted from many jobs until 1994, because of a federal law prohibiting women from serving on ships designated as combatants. There's no doubt in my mind that there were many people that were happy about that law and hoped it would never be changed. Even after the law changed, many wrote letters describing all the reasons women still should not be allowed into combat or even military service and had them published in national publications. My solution was simple: I stopped reading and subscribing to those publications. I wasn't sticking my head in the sand, I just didn't want to get to the point where I started looking at my male coworkers as enemies instead of members of the same team.

I've talked in earlier chapters about having to prove over and over that I was not an equal opportunity statement by someone in government trying to force unwanted changes in the Navy. In fact, the naval intelligence community was very forward-leaning and went out of their way to assign women to jobs that kept us as competitive as possible with our male counterparts. Although I frequently had to deal with initial skepticism upon arrival at a new assignment, once I proved I was capable of doing the job, the amount of problems I had to deal with diminished significantly.

The race thing was a bit more problematic. Just before the start of the first Gulf War, the head of the Navy's Personnel Bureau hosted a "Black Women in the Navy" conference. The conference attendees were the cream of the crop. The senior Navy person in each geographic region selected his area's representative from a group of nominees submitted by the organizations under their command. I was chosen as the representative from the Navy's European command (EUCOM).

The admiral hosting the conference told us we were there for two reasons. He said on an equal-opportunity survey the Navy had recently conducted, black women came out on the bottom in job satisfaction. He asked his people to screen performance reports for all black women, both officer and enlisted, going back twenty-five years, and what they found shocked him. Without exception, black women were ranked in the bottom in the portions of the reports that compared them with their peers. He found it hard to believe that in twenty-five years there had not been one superior performing black woman in the Navy. Because promotions and job opportunities are based on how well you do compared to your peers, this was not a good thing. He said one of our tasks during this conference was to tell him why this was happening and make recommendations to correct the situation.

This conference was one of the worst experiences I had in the Navy. The participants shared many of the unjust situations they had faced, and every woman there had a tale of horror to tell. What made the situation especially depressing was that these were the top black female performers in the Navy, so we all wondered what horrors the average performers were dealing with. The stories many of the female attendees told about the discrimination they had faced bought tears to the eyes of many present, including me.

I tried to lighten things up in my usual style by joking around, which in this case went over like a lead balloon. I think they felt I wasn't taking the situation seriously, while the fact of the matter was my whole attitude was toward finding solutions. I didn't want to spend the whole week listening to tales of woe and crying, I wanted to come up with some real solutions so that effective changes could be made. I agreed there were problems; we clearly established that on day one. My question was, When do we start talking about solutions? To say I was unpopular among most of the other attendees would be an understatement.

Actually, I started out the conference on a bad foot. As I was getting dressed the first day, I realized I had forgotten my hairpins. When hanging down, my hair was longer than Navy standards. I had two choices, go to the first day of the conference in blue jeans, the only civilian clothes I had, or go with my hair down and risk someone seeing my hair was too long before I had a chance to buy some hairpins. I caused a major controversy among the other officers when I walked into the room with my hair about an inch longer than Navy regulations. An African American male captain stood at the door welcoming us as we entered the room. Apparently noticing the length of my hair, he immediately went to the senior black female present and told her to tell me to get my act together. I was furious, stormed right up to him, and cursed him out. To his credit, he apologized instead of writing me up for being insubordinate to a senior officer.

Before coming to the conference, I talked to a number of young Navy women in Europe and asked what concerns they wanted me to bring up for them. They gave me a couple of key points they wanted addressed, but because of my lack of popularity, some of the senior women at the conference didn't want to address or include any of my concerns in the final report. I threw down the gauntlet and told them if my points weren't included I would refuse to sign the final report and would write a separate report for the record. My points were included, and at the end of the conference, the senior black woman present took me aside and said, "I like you. I feel if you get your act together you can go far in the Navy." I was devastated by her comments and returned to my post in Europe with my tail between my legs.

My spirits were lifted immediately when I found that my group in Spain thought the reaction of the conference attendees to me was funny and teased me about being perceived as an "uncouth sailor" by that refined Washington, DC, crowd. On a more serious note, they felt the real problem had been I was coming at the problem from a warfighting perspective, while most of the attendees were bureaucrats, clueless as to what the operational side of the Navy was all about. They couldn't relate to me because they weren't familiar with the environment I was coming from. The senior Navy folks I dealt with felt I had represented the concerns of the warfighting commands very well. They slapped me on the back and told me to shrug it off and get back to the matter at hand, namely preparing for the upcoming hostilities with Iraq.

Personally, I think there is a simple fix to the discrimination problem: Just keep track of how minorities are being graded in performance reports. If someone consistently ranks women and minorities at the bottom, that should be a red flag and a reason for an investigation. If you have a system such as the one I'm recommending in place, it takes the pressure off the individual and puts it on the system, where it belongs. The existing system already monitors the percentage of women and minorities that are promoted each year to ensure fairness. My recommendation is taking the system one level lower to ensure that every individual gets graded fairly for job performances.

What the experience of that conference did for me was reinforce my methods of dealing with discrimination: focus on the mission, keep my sense of humor, and don't go around expecting to be dumped on all the time because of my sex and race. The mental attitude I projected throughout my career was, I am an outstanding intelligence officer. My job is to provide the best information possible so that the warfighter can do his job. My sex or race has no bearing on the work situation. For many years I had a sign posted on my desk that paraphrased a Thomas Paine quote that said, " Lead, follow, or get the hell out of my way."

The key for me was to focus on what I wanted to accomplish, not on what I couldn't or the obstacles I'd have to overcome to get there. By maintaining the right attitude, there is always a solution to any problem. To the next generations of intelligence professionals, I would say persevere. Even when the odds appear to be against you, move forward with honor, courage, and commitment to achieve your goals. In the words of Winston Churchill, "Never, never, never, give up."

Takeaway: Know when it's time to move on.

Key principles I learned throughout my Navy career:

1. Never assume you're receiving all the data available on a particular issue or category, because the way the classification system works, you may not know what you don't know.
2. Focus on what I want to accomplish, not on what I can't or the obstacles I have to overcome to get there.
3. If I maintain the right attitude there is always a solution to any problem.
4. To the next generations of intelligence professionals, I would say persevere. Even when the odds appear to be against you, move forward with honor, courage, and commitment.
5. In the words of Winston Churchill, "Never, never, never, give up."

NOTES

1. Glenn Van Ekeren, *Speaker's Sourcebook II: Quotes, Stories, and Anecdotes for Every Occasion.* (Englewood Cliffs, NJ: Prentice Hall, 1994), p. 9.

2. Van Ekeren, *Speaker's Sourcebook II*, p. 33.

3. Jay E. Hines, "History of the Persian Gulf War, and Subsequent Actions of the U.S. Central Command." Available at www.daveross.com/centcom.html, p. 13.

4. Johanna McGeary, Jaime FlorCruz, Scott MacLeod, Barry Hillenbrand, Paul Quinn-Judge, William Dowell, J. F. O. McAllister, and Mark Thompson, "What Good Did It Do?" *Time* 152, no. 26 (December 28, 1998), p. 2. Available at www.time.com/time/printout/0,8816,989920,00.html.

5. www.nytimes.com/1998/12/17/world/attack-on-iraq-the-strategy-strikes-aimed
-at-crippling-factories-for-weapons.html

6. www.nytimes.com/1998/12/17/world/attack-on-iraq-the-strategy-strikes-aimed
-at-crippling-factories-for-weapons.html

About the Authors

Gail Harris was raised in the ghettos of Newark, New Jersey. At the age of five, she saw a World War II–themed movie called *Wing and a Prayer* starring Don Ameche. Mesmerized by a scene of the actor briefing Navy pilots before the climatic Battle of Midway, she decided that was what she'd do when she grew up. Unaware of the existence of a federal law prohibiting women from going into combat—one that would not be changed until 1994—she forged ahead with her dream. In 1973, she became the first woman in U.S. naval history to serve as an intelligence officer in a Navy aviation squadron, and upon her retirement in December 2001, she was the highest-ranking African American female in the Navy. Her career included hands-on leadership during every major conflict from the Cold War to El Salvador to Desert Storm to Kosovo and at the forefront of one of the Department of Defense's newest challenges, cyber warfare.

Harris was the first female or first African American for every job assignment and was frequently handpicked for challenging jobs based on her outstanding performance. In August 1988, she was pulled from her Hawaiian assignment eighteen months early and sent to South Korea to head up the Defense Department intelligence support for the 1988 Olympics, a task that involved extensive coordination with U.S. and South Korean military, intelligence, and civil agencies.

A Gulf War veteran, Harris spent extensive time in the Middle East and Persian Gulf. Since her retirement, she has worked in the defense industry as an intelligence subject matter expert. She was a contributing author to *Wake Up and Live Your Life with Passion*, which reached number four on the Barnes and Noble bestseller list. Her essay "Reflections of a Retired Black Woman" was published in *Lies and Limericks: Inspirations from Ireland* in October 2006. A frequent guest on radio shows as a defense expert, she hosts her own weekly R&B show, is writing two Broadway musicals, and writes a weekly blog. Three years ago, she moved to Durango, Colorado, where she's living happily ever after.

Address: Second star to the right, then straight on 'til morning.

Pamela J. McLaughlin was born and raised in Utica, New York. She is married and has three grown children and five grandchildren and lives with her husband in Orlando, Florida. She is a retired teacher and has been working since retirement with YMCS as a ghostwriter and copyeditor. She and her husband, Jack, also worked for ten years with University of the Family as national training directors. She has written curriculum for several authors to accompany their books both nationally and internationally, including *Overcoming Abuse and Addiction*, by Pastor Carl Richeal, and *Until I Come*, by Pastor Jim Hockaday. McLaughlin worked with noted author Dr. Larry Keefauver on curriculum for *Good TV*, which has been translated into Mandarin and is being used all throughout Asia. She is currently working on curriculum for Dr. W. Paul "Buddy" Crum to accompany his Marketplace Alliance course "Much More than a JOB," and she writes the "School of Life" courses for IMPaX WORLD founders Greg and Brenda Im. McLaughlin has written five CD-Message books with Dr, Ronald Cottle, founder and president of Beacon University in Columbia, Georgia. She also worked with Gwen David on her autobiography, *Forced Into Greatness*. Other books include *The Anatomy of Success*, by Patrick Ondrey; *Second in Command*, by Jerry Robinson; *Achieving Your Divine Potential*, by Bishop Jim Lowe; and The Power of . . . , a six-book series for Bishop Dr. Abraham Bediako in Hamburg, Germany. She also works with Dr. Keefauver as copyeditor of the *IMPaX WORLD Magazine*.